W9-BTH-189

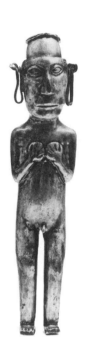

LATIN AMERICAN ART

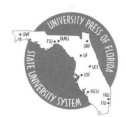

Florida A&M University, Tallahassee
Florida Atlantic University, Boca Raton
Florida Gulf Coast University, Ft. Myers
Florida International University, Miami
Florida State University, Tallahassee
University of Central Florida, Orlando
University of Florida, Gainesville
University of North Florida, Jacksonville
University of South Florida, Tampa
University of West Florida, Pensacola

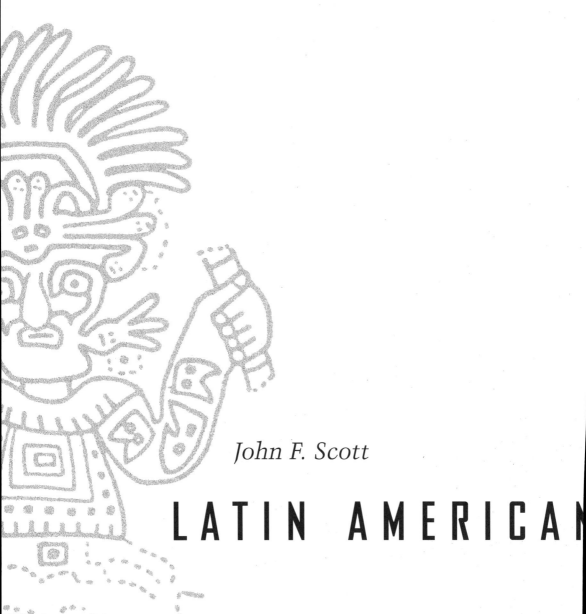

John F. Scott

LATIN AMERICA

University Press of Florida

Gainesville · Tallahassee · Tampa · Boca Raton · Pensacola · Orlando · Miami · Jacksonville · Ft. Mye

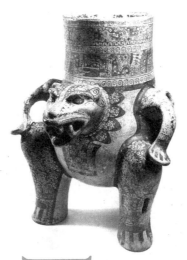

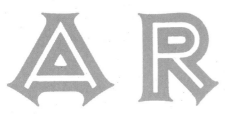

ART

Ancient to Modern

04 03 02 01 00 99 C 6 5 4 3

05 04 03 02 01 00 P 6 5 4 3 2 1

LIBRARY OF CONGRESS CATALOGING-IN-PUBLICATION DATA

Scott, John F. (John Fredrik), 1936–
Latin American art : ancient to modern / John F. Scott.
p. cm.
Includes bibliographical references and index.
ISBN 0-8130-1645-2 (alk. paper)—cloth
ISBN 0-8130-1826-9 (alk. paper)—paperback
1. Art, Latin American. I. Title.
N6502.L367   1999
709'.8—dc21   98-46535

The University Press of Florida is the scholarly publishing
agency for the State University System of Florida, comprising
Florida A&M University, Florida Atlantic University, Florida
Gulf Coast University, Florida International University, Florida
State University, University of Central Florida, University of
Florida, University of North Florida, University of South
Florida, and University of West Florida.

University Press of Florida
15 Northwest 15th Street
Gainesville, FL 32611–2079
http://www.upf.com

Front cover. *Top:* Sicán ceremonial knife, Lambayeque
Department, Peru. Integration, Middle Horizon, A.D. 850–1050.
Photo by Christopher Gallagher, copyright 1996, Art Institute
of Chicago. *Bottom:* Tarsila do Amaral, *EFCB* (Central Railroad
of Brazil), oil on canvas. 1924. Courtesy of Museu de Arte
Contemporánea da Universidade de São Paulo, Brazil.

Back cover. *Top:* Aztec mural, Malinalco, Mexico. A.D.
1440–1521. Courtesy of Instituto Nacional de Antropología e
Historia, Mexico. *Bottom:* Effigy jar, Recuay, Ancash, Peru.
Classic, Early Intermediate Period, A.D. 300–600. Photo
courtesy of Orlando Museum of Art, Orlando, Fla.

To my wife, Lynn, for sharing many adventures in search of this art.

CONTENTS

ILLUSTRATIONS

ACKNOWLEDGMENTS

I would like to thank the Department of Art at the University of Florida for its assistance in funding the illustrations in this volume. The Center for Latin American Studies at the University of Florida has been generous in funding my travel in Latin America, specifically to Santo Domingo and Quito, and to study collections in the United States. They also granted me permission to copy some of the handsome photographs donated to them by my colleague Roy C. Craven, Jr., shortly before his untimely death. Cornell University's Latin American Program funded two unforgettable opportunities for me to travel widely in Bolivia, Peru, Ecuador, Colombia, and Panama to photograph that region's architectural and artistic works. I am grateful to the many curators and directors of museums and private collections for allowing me to photograph works in their collections, some of which appear here.

Additional and much-appreciated support for reproducing the illustrations came from Jane Backstrom, Lakeland, Florida; Jorge Chiappo, St. Petersburg, Florida; and Frederick Thompson of Gainesville, Florida. Camilo Munar of the graphic design area of the Art Department of the University of Florida employed his wizardry with the computer to make the maps for the beginning of each chapter and adapt some line drawings. I appreciate his willingness to work with me under time constraints and wish him well in his future career as a designer.

For assistance in obtaining illustrations of works in their respective institutions, I wish to thank Cecilia Gutiérrez, head of the Photo Archive, Instituto de Investigaciones Estéticas, Mexico City; Paz Cabello, director, Museo de América, Madrid; Eduardo Londoño, sub-director, Museo del Oro, Bogota; Felipe Solís, head of archaeology, National Museum of Anthropology, Mexico City; Alex Faruk Salomón, conservator, Art Gallery of the City of Lima; and Lisbeth Rebollo Gonçalves, director, Museu de Arte Contemporánea, São Paulo, Brazil, who sent a transparency without even being asked.

In this country, I appreciate the help and encouragement of Tom Larose, curator, Appleton Museum of Art, Ocala, Florida; Michael Whittington, curator of Pre-Columbian and African Art, Mint Art Museum in Charlotte, North Carolina; Andrea Kalis, curator, Orlando Museum of Art; Susan Lucke, registrar, and Brian Dursam, director, Lowe Art Museum, Coral Gables, Florida; Eden Wilson, Polk Museum of Art, Lakeland, Florida; Caroline Risman, Latin American Art, Sotheby's, New York; Joyce Marcus and Kent Flannery, Museum of Anthropology, Ann Arbor, Michigan; Gary Libby, director, Museum of Arts and Sciences, Daytona Beach, Florida; Dr. Richard Townsend, curator, Art Institute of Chicago; Elise LeCompte, anthropology division, Florida Museum of Natural History, Gainesville; and Merle Greene Robertson and David Greene, Pre-Columbian Research Institute, San Francisco.

Also very helpful in providing assistance were Sumri Aricanli, Department of Anthropology, American Museum of Natural History, New York; Warren Church, Pre-Columbian Collections, Dumbarton Oaks, Washington, D.C.; Janice Klein, registrar of anthropology, Field Museum, Chicago; Bridget Evans, photography, Guggenheim Museum, New York; Roberto Prcela, photography, Cleveland Museum of Art; Zara Anishanslin, photo archives manager, Textile Museum, Washington, D.C.; Martha Labell, photo archives, Peabody Museum of Archaeology and Ethnology, Harvard University; Warren Bonn, Johnson Museum of Art, Cornell University, Ithaca, New York; Chris Calamine, collections manager, anthropology section, Natural History Museum of Los Angeles County, California; Patrick Sweeney, Davenport Museum of Art, Iowa; and Melody Aeons, Museum of Art, Rhode Island School of Design, Providence.

Finally, I appreciate the suggestions of Susan Milbrath, curator, Florida Museum of Natural History; Barbara Purdy, emerita professor of anthropology; David Bushnell and David Geggus, history department; Michael Moseley, anthropology department—all at the University of Florida; and Prudence Rice, formerly here but now at the University of Southern Illinois. My wife, Lynn Thomson Scott, has been supportive during the many stops and starts it has taken to bring this work to completion. Jack Hopkins, professor emeritus at Indiana University, unwittingly got this project started by asking me to write a chapter on Latin American art. Although it did appear in reduced form, the undertaking made me aware of the need for such coverage and the impossibility of doing it adequately within one chapter.

		Mesoamerica	Lower Central America	North Andes	Central & South Andes	Eastern South America
	PERIOD					
ca. 20,000 B.C.	**PALEOINDIAN**	*Entry of humans into America by land bridge from Siberia*				
		Valsequillo Tequixquiac	[Turrialba]	Tequendama [El Inga]	Nochaco Monte Verde	[Lagoa Santa] El Jobo
ca. 8000 B.C.	**ARCHAIC**	Chilac Zohapilco Puerto Marqués	[Cerro Mangote] [Monagrillo]	Monsú Puerto Chacho Valdivia	Chuquichaca Chilca Chinchorro Cotton Prece-ramic	Pedra Furada Río Pinturas
ca. 1800 B.C.	**FORMATIVE: Early**	S. José Mogote Capacha Tehuacán	None mentioned	Machalilla Cerro Narrío	Initial Period: Sechín Alto Curayacu	[Ciboney]
1000 B.C.	**Middle**	Olmec (1200-500 B.C.): La Venta Las Bocas	[La Montaña]	Chorrera Ilama	Early Horizon: Chavín Paracas: Cavernas	[Tutishcainyo] [Barrancas]
500 B.C.	**Late**	Monte Albán I Izapa Mezcala	Costa Rican jade begins			[Saladero]
100 B.C.	**CLASSIC**	Teotihuacán Monte Albán III Cerro de las Mesas El Tajín Central Maya	Barriles Coclé Goldworking begins	Malagana La Tolita San Agustín Quimbaya Carchi	Necropolis Early Intermedi-ate Period: Nazca, Moche, Recuay, Tiwanaku	[Saladoid] Marajó begins
A.D. 800	**INTEGRATION**	Uxmal Toltec Mixteca-Puebla Aztec	Chorotega Línea Vieja Nicarao	Tairona Chibcha Manteño Milagro Inca	Middle Horizon: Wari, Sicán Late Intermedi-ate: Chimú Late Horizon: Inca	[Aguada] Marajó ends Taíno [Carib] [Tupí]
A.D. 1500	**COLONIAL**	Plateresque Mannerist Baroque Rococo Neoclassic	Purist archit. Golden Altar Antigua	Becerra Father Pedro Legarda Caspicara Samaniego	Bitti St. Jerome M. Santa Ana M. Mestizo Baroque Cuzco School	Late Gothic Plateresque Plain Style Brazilian Baroque French Mission
A.D. 1820	**INDEPENDENT REPUBLICS**	Romanticism Realism *Modernismo* Mural Renaissance Surrealism	Carlos Mérida Morales	Guayasamín Obregón	Rugendas Laso Castillo Sabogal Szyszlo	Pallière Amoêdo Modern Art Week Torres-García Berni, Gamarra
A.D. 1998		Recent	Popular	Viteri		Leirner

Note: Names in brackets do not appear in the text; space prohibits inclusion of additional names.

INTRODUCTION

This brief overview of the art produced within the area of what is now
Latin America attempts to provide an introduction to the artistic heritage of the region south of the United States of America. It is intended
to be appropriate in length and reading level to college humanities
courses. Newcomers to this area of study are presented to the main
cultures and periods without being immersed in any particular one.
Books already exist for specific countries of Latin America; for specific
time periods, such as the Pre-Columbian, the Colonial, and the Modern; and for specific media, such as architecture or painting. This hand-
book gives a broad look at the southern two-thirds of the Western
Hemisphere without exhaustively covering all areas and art forms.
Although the text is not written in a scholarly manner, it provides some
references through interlineal notes, giving author and date of publica-
tion, and a bibliography keyed to those references and including some
general readings within the topics covered in this overview.

I have arranged the material by time periods in order to present parallel developments in the cultures within Latin America. The time
periods correspond to the dominant cultural stages reached in the more
advanced regions of the Americas during that period. The different
cultural stages and corresponding time periods are: hunter-gatherer
(Paleoindian), semipermanent settlements (early Archaic), agricultural
villages (Late Archaic—Formative), chiefdoms (later Formative and
the Intermediate Area), mature kingdoms (Classic), and empires, first
those of the native peoples (Integration) and then of the Iberian conquerors (Colonial). Finally, with the coming of independence and the
creation of modern nation-states, the republics of Latin America inter-
face with the industrialized Western world. Chronologies in the captions will use both the general period terms adopted in this text and the
more specific terminologies appropriate only for each region; see also
the Chronological Chart for overview. Emphasis throughout is on simi-

larities the cultures share with each other during the Pre-Columbian period and with Europe after the Conquest. The surprising correspondences in the art which can be found at parallel stages of social organization depend, I believe, not necessarily on direct diffusion from one early civilization to another, although this no doubt happened on occasions, but rather on what Adolf Bastian called "the psychic unity of mankind" (Lowie 1937: 35–36). This I understand to mean that humans in similar circumstances tend to arrive independently at similar solutions—in this case, of artistic expression. At Cornell, Rice, and the University of Florida, I have used such a synchronic approach in a course comparing early civilizations in the Americas and the Near East, including Egypt, and have included some of my observations in this text although the Near East is not our topic. Naturally each cultural region also has its own continuities of style and subject matter which can be traced by a student reading together those sections dealing with each geographic area. However, these regional traditions are discussed in greater detail in other, readily available books which focus on the specific characteristics of each region's ethnic identity and culture.

The southern two-thirds of the Western Hemisphere is traditionally called Latin America, although the region did not become Latinized until after the Spanish Conquest beginning in 1492 and the Portuguese claiming of Brazil in 1500. French, English, and Dutch colonies were established in the seventeenth century and later by nibbling away at minimally Iberian possessions. The colonial art history of these non-Iberian territories that only gained their independence recently will generally not be covered here. Haiti is an exception since it won its independence from France so early (1804) and has preserved much more of its African heritage. The Spaniards settled those areas of civilization which loom largest in the cultures described here. For this reason, most proper nouns used in the text are pronounced with Spanish conventions even for indigenous names. The text refers to modern political units such as republics and Mexican states to help the reader locate the areas and sites of Pre-Columbian America. The illustration captions place works into modern political departments and provinces not mentioned in the main text. Naturally, such political units are usually anachronisms, since the indigenous cultures preceded the period when these came into being. In many cases the modern political entities still reflect pre-Hispanic cultural units more so than in Anglo-America and Africa, where colonial divisions were made without recognizing ethnic and even geographic boundaries. Maps in the beginning of each chapter will locate the sites and regions referred to in the text for that period.

Other, broad geographic terms are used to refer specifically to Pre-Columbian cultural areas: (1) Mesoamerica: the area of high culture that includes the southern two-thirds of modern Mexico and the Maya area of Guatemala, Belize, El Salvador, and western Honduras; (2) the Central Andes: the coast and highlands of modern Peru and northwestern Bolivia; (3) between these first two, the Intermediate Area: lower Central America (Nicaragua, Costa Rica, Panama) and the northern Andes (Colombia, Ecuador, and westernmost Venezuela); and (4) Nuclear America: all of the above, taken together, are where the major Pre-Columbian cultures flowered. This book will concentrate on this region between Mexico and Bolivia until the nineteenth century, at which time leading art centers developed away from the old Nuclear America.

Dating of much of this material is very approximate. Even in the Iberian colonial period, the anonymity of much of the artistic production and the scarcity of archival research prevents a secure date for a work of art. Attributions can only be precise to a century. Archaeological material can only be dated to within two or three centuries except for a few well-researched areas. In certain areas, only a thousand-year range is possible. Beginning around A.D. 1950, radiocarbon testing provided the first chronometric dates for archaeological material, although even those should be cited with a standard deviation (not done here) indicating that two times out of three the date falls within the bracketed range. Recent observations that the radioactive accumulation in carbon was not uniform throughout the centuries have resulted in further correction to arrive at real solar-year dates. Since firm correlations to correct radiocarbon dates have ambiguous overlapping which allow 200–300 year deviations, I consider it premature to cite corrected dates in this text, and I hope none have slipped in inadvertently. About 3,000 years before present the discrepancy between radiocarbon measurements and true solar years begins to be pronounced and the solar year falls at least 200 years earlier than the radiocarbon measurement—even more the further back you go (observable in Striver and Kra 1986: charts, 919–925). This discrepancy is not a serious problem for most of the period covered after 1000 B.C.

Not surprisingly, an immense variety of artistic forms are found within that large area presently called Latin America, a result of the wide range of cultures and enormous time covered. Compare it to the art of Europe, eastern and western, northern and southern, from the cave paintings through the post-Modern art movements. Even then, the geographical extent of the Americas far exceeds that of Europe, as do the climatic variations, from driest desert to thickest rain forest, from eternally snow-covered mountain peaks to swampy grassland as far as the eye can see. Most of the cultures covered in this survey developed in the highlands and immediately adjoining coast and very few in the grasslands and tropical forests. Until modern times, the Southern Cone (Chile, Argentina, Paraguay, and Uruguay) and the eastern lowlands of South America (Brazil and the Guianas) have not played a major role in artistic production. The text will therefore focus more on the area covered by modern Mexico and Peru, less on Central America, Colombia, and Ecuador, and very little on the islands and eastern South America. Occasional mention for comparative purposes will be made of America north of Mexico—now the United States and Canada—but the focus will be on the development "south of the border." I regret the many omissions necessary to retain a readable overview of art of the major cultures and periods, and I hope the reader will understand the necessity of seeing the forest and not get lost with the special features of each tree. To remedy these omissions, I strongly encourage further reading, looking, and visiting in one's specific areas of interest.

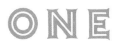

ONE

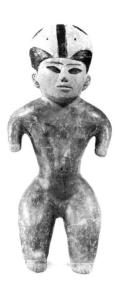

EARLIEST NATIVE AMERICAN ART

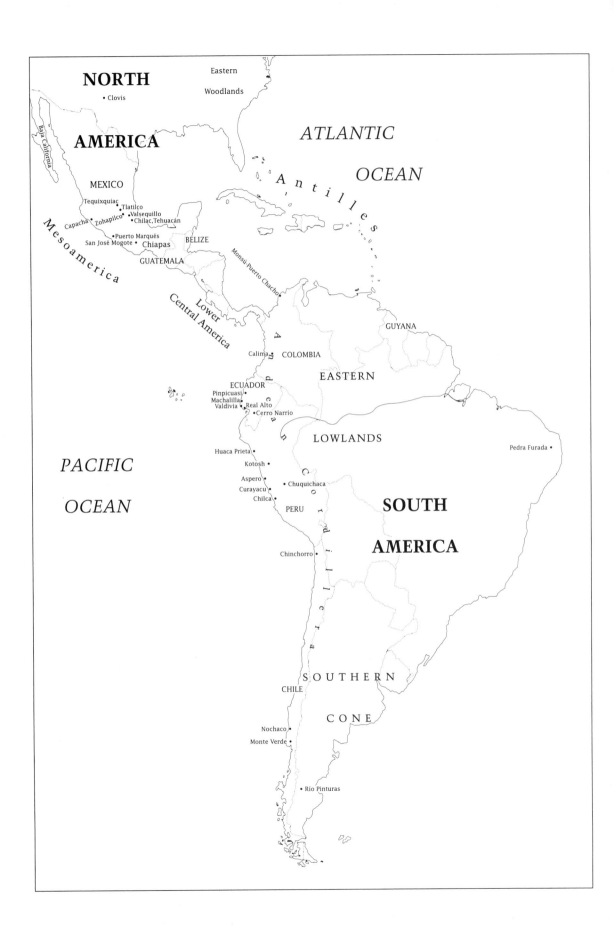

THE AMERICAS ARE truly the "new world," not in the sense that the European explorers of the fifteenth and sixteenth centuries used the term, but for the humans who came to the Western Hemisphere from Eurasia. In contrast to the "old world," the Eastern Hemisphere where they had evolved for millions of years into modern *Homo sapiens sapiens*, the vast lands of the Americas seemed new indeed and rich in animal, plant, and other resources. The time of their arrival is still hotly debated, but, fortunately, it need not overly concern us here, since their early artistic production was very limited. Once in the Western Hemisphere, however, they spread throughout the American mainland in bands, settling in promising areas and finally building permanent villages and organizing a tribal society, basically egalitarian but with leaders qualified primarily by their abilities. For some groups whose population did not grow too rapidly, usually those in deserts or cold climes, this organization remained satisfactory until their contact with Europeans, who devastated their way of life at the same time they recorded what it was like. Analogies with these more recently documented groups provide a basis for reconstructing how prehistoric societies worked, even if their material remains are few.

PALEOINDIAN: VERY APPROXIMATELY 20,000–8,000 B.C.

Native Americans, whom Columbus mistakenly labeled "Indians," descended from wandering bands of Asian hunters who, over the course of many millennia, crossed into the American continent via the land bridge now submerged under the Bering Strait separating Russian Siberia from Alaska. The variety of the language families which existed among indigenous Americans in the most recent half-millennium—ten major stocks with hundreds of languages—emphasizes the recurrent waves of Asian people who then spread throughout the two continents, became separated, and adapted to many different environmental situations. Eight of these major stocks, however, have been tentatively grouped into the Amerind superfamily, suggesting these all date around 12,000 B.C., before the end of the Ice Age, a conclusion supported by genetic and dental evidence (Meltzer 1993: 84). With them they brought crafts—and, even more importantly, ideas—common in the Upper Paleolithic cultures of Eurasia. Important survivals of their ideas probably included intense study of the solar and lunar cycles, reflected in an accurate time count, and a shamanistic approach to intervention in the spirit world, by which one person through experience granted in a personal vision quest becomes transformed spiritually and leaves his or her body to travel under the protection of an animal guardian to the spirit world. Powers granted to the shaman by the spirits there can be used once back in this world to, among other things, combat evil forces, such as those which cause illness. Shamanic societies view the cosmos as having three layers which exist simultaneously: the upperworld, the earth's surface, and the underworld. The upperworld is of the great celestial spirits and flying creatures, and the underworld is of the dead and demonic spirits and creatures of the watery and subterranean realms, but it is not necessarily an unpleasant place. Communication between these realms can be done by shamans via the world tree, the roots of which are in the underworld and the crown of which is in the sky; sometimes the tree is in the center and sometimes at each of the four cardinal directions into which they believed the cosmos was divided.

Like Paleolithic bands, the people who moved in bands across North America were following the large herds of Ice Age mammals which the men hunted for food, clothing, and tools. Thus, the human bands were nomadic, moving as the herds moved. The women followed the men and were primarily responsible for collecting plant materials for food or as raw materials for crafts. Crafts involve human manipulation of naturally available materials to change their shape for functional purposes. Art develops on the basis of the ability to make things (craft) but adds aesthetic communication through visual means.

The best preserved of the crafts are tools made of stone, bone, and horn. These are rarely works of art, however, because they do not communicate something about human experience through handmade forms. Nevertheless, the ability to control the shapes of tools provided the means through which art could be made. As the craftsmen succeeded in controlling the shapes by which tools would function most successfully, they presumably derived pleasure from the act of creation and visually enjoyed the efficient shape which the objects took. We can assume that they began consciously to create forms which pleased them.

The dominant and most handsomely formed man-made objects preserved from the earliest human occupation of America are chipped stone blades. These were hafted (attached) to the ends of wooden shafts and used primarily for hunting. Other tools for preparing animal carcasses for human use are known but are less finely shaped. This stage is known in the New World as the Paleoindian Age or the Lithic Stage, to avoid implying too close association with Old World developments during the contemporary Upper Paleolithic Age. The finest artifacts of the Paleoindian Age are made in a technique refined in the New

World, in contrast to the more common Old World percussion-flaked stone points. This New World specialty is called pressure flaking: the edge of the stone core is chipped off by pressing with another tool. The most widely found point is the fluted type first described from and most closely identified with the site of Clovis, New Mexico, and dating from 9500 to 9000 B.C. Closely related shapes are found not only in the Eastern United States but in Mexico, Lower Central America, and the Andean cordillera of South America. Slightly later and smaller, fish-tail points associated with the Folsom site (also in New Mexico) are related to pointed blades distributed down to the southern tip of South America (Fiedel 1987: 80).

The Clovis-like point from Nochaco, Chile (fig. 1.1), has a sizable concave surface at the lower end of both faces where it could be attached to a large wooden spear handle. The convex swelling of both sides of the point is balanced toward this lower end by the concavities to receive the shaft. The pressure flaking is controlled enough, especially along the cutting outline, to create a consistently rhythmic line, swelling upward to the upper third of the body and then tapering smoothly into a point, similar to a Gothic pointed arch. The entire shape is more biomorphic than the Gothic arch, which was based on regular geometric designs. The graceful Clovis form, in fact, does suggest the shape of a leaf. Therefore, the form of the object, the chief function of which was to end the life of a great mammal, has in itself a reference to life through its biomorphic shape. The makers frequently chose beautiful stones to chip for aesthetic as well as for functional reasons. Given the overriding importance of hunting as the main source of food and the prestige undoubtedly associated with the large spears of great hunters, we certainly would not be surprised to learn that the large tapered points had an importance far beyond that of mere function.

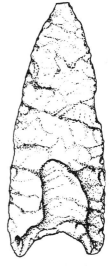

Representational art in the Paleoindian Age is not as plentiful as it is in Upper Paleolithic Europe during the parallel culture of Ice Age hunters there (35,000–10,000 B.C.). Dated around 20,000 B.C., from an area of the central Mexican highlands now submerged under the Valsequillo Dam, is an incised drawing on mastodon bone depicting some of the great animals hunted by the Paleoindians (fig. 1.2). One image, perhaps a deer, is superimposed over the other of a mastodon and of prior cut marks. Such superposition suggests that the act of creating the image

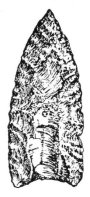

FIG. 1.1. Nochaco, Osorno, Chile. Clovis-like points, pressure-flaked basalt, 2¼" high, and obsidian, 1½" high. Paleoindian, ca. 9500–8500 B.C. Whereabouts unknown. Drawings after Zulema Seguel and Orlando Campana.

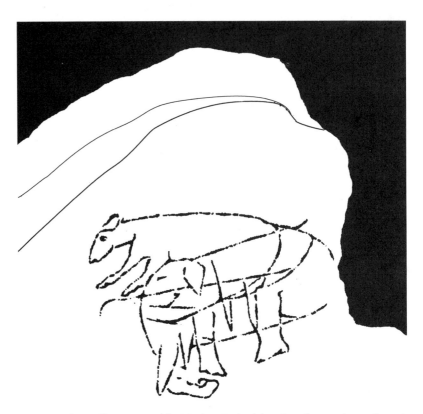

FIG. 1.2. Valsequillo Dam, Puebla, Mexico. Incised drawing of mastodon and rumi-
nant on mastodon bone. Paleoindian, ca. 20,000 B.C. Mexico: Instituto Nacional de
Antropología e Historia. Line drawing after David Hiser.

of a living creature was itself important; it was not just a means for
making a finished product of aesthetic value. Like Paleolithic renderings, these images were probably made by the hunter shaman to capture the animals' spirits prior to the hunt. Nevertheless, the completed
image has the biomorphic fluidity already mentioned in regard to the
abstract form of the Clovis-like point. Also from the same general area
of Mexico, at the Paleoindian site of Tequixquiac, is a camelid pelvic
bone carved to accentuate its resemblance to the head of a canine,
providing us with a rare example of sculpture in the round (fig. 1.3).

Remains of buildings dating to as early as 11,500 B.C. have been found
in the cool woodlands at the southern Chilean site of Monte Verde.
They formed a small hamlet clustered along one side of a stream and
included what is apparently a ritual building with a wishbone plan on
a raised platform. The remaining residential structures were rectangular, built of large logs and vertical planks with animal skins probably
tied between them. Plentiful large timber encouraged heavy wooden
building not typical of Paleolithic Old World structures, which were
mainly constructed of found materials. In all areas at this time, people
also inhabited natural caves and rock shelters.

Smooth implements used for grinding (called handstones or *manos*) on concave mortars (called *metates* after an Aztec term referring to stones for grinding maize) are the most commonly found items from the more intensive gathering lifeway of the Archaic. They are related to the smooth stone utensils from the Old World Neolithic and are analogous to the "new stone" forms for which that period was named. For the finest polished stone art associated with the Archaic we must look to the eastern woodlands of the United States, where sleekly stylized objects known as birdstones and beautifully abstract shapes called bannerstones were probably used as counterweights or stabilizers for spearthrowers. Elements of spearthrowers from the Archaic have been found in the Americas, but none from Latin America possess the visual communication required to be art works until much later, during the Period of Integration.

Documented examples of rock painting and incising cannot be assigned with any security to the Paleoindian Age in America, although some paintings most likely were executed for the same reason as the incised images of animals on the Valsequillo hand-held bone: to capture the spirit of the animal to be hunted. Claims for great antiquity (30,000 B.C.) for a painted rock shelter at Pedra Furada in northeast Brazil have not been substantiated by independent observers, although flakes of stripe-painted rock appeared there in a context more securely dated

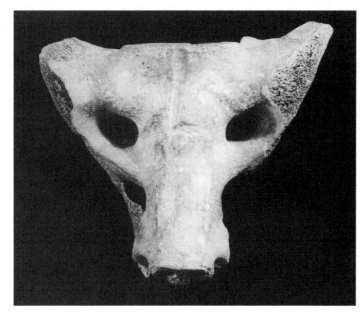

FIG. 1.3. Tequixquiac, State of México, Mexico. Camelid pelvis bone worked in shape of canine head, 6" high. Paleoindian, ca. 10,000 B.C. Mexico City: Museo Nacional de Antropología. Photo courtesy of Instituto Nacional de Antropología e Historia.

15,000 B.C. (Meltzer 1993: 75–76). The best surviving rock paintings, in the central mountains of Baja California, have been dated to as recently as five hundred years before the Conquest (Meighan 1978: 11); however, they were made by a culture which only hunted and gathered, like the peoples of the early Archaic, and had no agriculture. Similar to cave paintings of the Upper Paleolithic in France and Spain, these works re-create the impression of the living animals through large-scale representations, executed in several colors, of the creatures in fluid movement. Unlike European paintings in deep caves, however, the American works are placed under shallow overhangs, visible therefore under natural light and not seen in the otherworldly context of a deep cave. They also include representations of human beings, which are almost totally absent from European Paleolithic paintings. In this regard, they parallel the location and subject matter of the Spanish Mesolithic rock-shelter paintings, where elaborate hunt scenes and even human ritual are rendered. Like them, they exhibit a balance between reverence for the power of nature as exemplified by the great mammals and an acknowledgment of the active energy of humans, especially when cooperating in a group.

FIG. 1.4. Río Pinturas, Santa Cruz, Argentina. Painting of hunters with large camelids, yellow paint on rock, 53" wide. Archaic, 8000–4000 B.C. Line drawing after Alberto Rex González.

Spiritual forces were illustrated by frontal figures, basically human in proportions but with some animal attributes such as horns. Their details are obscured by painted patterns or an unmodified silhouette. The blend of human and animal suggests shamanic transformation and the spirits seen in the shaman's visions. Such images are included in the paintings of Pedra Furada, Brazil.

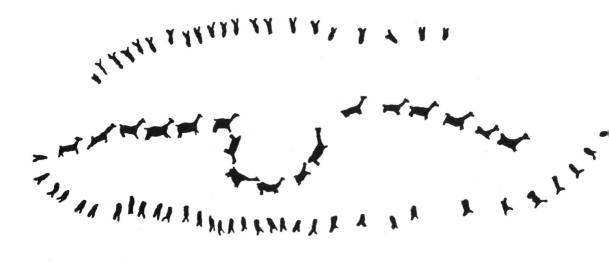

LATIN AMERICAN ART

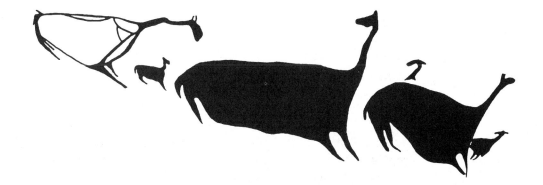

Rock paintings from the southern flanks of the Andes are contemporary with the American equivalent of the Mesolithic, when hunting was no longer so important after the extinction of the great Ice Age mammals about 8000 B.C. Plant foods became far more intensively collected, with the seeds and other coarse materials prepared first by grinding on the distinctive mortar with a handstone or pestle, all of which were made of smoothed stone.

In America this stage is called the Archaic, beginning before the introduction of agriculture and continuing even after some plants were domesticated but had not yet become a dominant part of the diet. Artistically the American Archaic still focuses on animal representations, usually within the context of tools. Paintings from the central Andes south to the dry plains of Patagonia, Argentina, depict camelids, the wild ancestors of llamas and alpacas which were domesticated beginning around 5000 B.C. The animals are often shown pursued by hunters in active poses but without much detail (fig. 1.4). Similar paintings from the Central Andes are primarily executed in red pigment (Rick 1988: 23) and parallel the style and technique of Spanish Mesolithic hunt scenes, which were also executed in shallow rock shelters. Depicted animals range in size from about 4 inches long, the size of Spanish Mesolithic figures, to more than 1 yard long, on the scale of Franco-Spanish Paleolithic paintings of animals. The larger ones, such as those from Chuquichaca, Peru (fig. 1.5), have greater fluidity and movement, with heads turned looking over their shoulders in wary tension and enormous undulating torsos, as if emphasizing both their meatiness and their pregnancy, both associated with survival in a hunting culture. These features parallel the famous Paleolithic cave paintings of southern France and northern Spain. Unusual in this painting is the rendering of overlapping animals, which creates a sense of depth usually expressed through the convention of vertical perspective. In this widespread technique, the farther back a figure is, the farther away it is to be read in space.

EARLIEST POTTERY: COLOMBIA AND ECUADOR, ABOUT 3350–1200 B.C.

Toward the end of the Archaic, villages in northwestern South America, in the modern countries of Colombia and Ecuador, began to produce pottery. Normally pottery can only be used by a fully sedentary population, since it breaks easily and would be impractical for people who moved seasonally. These people could stay in one place because they had predictable sources of food, including access to rich waterborne resources, some domesticated crops such as manioc, and, after 4000 B.C., maize, which had first been cultivated in Mesoamerica. Pottery-making involves a complex technology which not only requires clay of a certain consistency but also demands the introduction of a binding material called temper which strengthens the clay during shaping, drying, and heating at a high enough temperature to chemically convert it into an almost stone-like material. As such, it marks an important change from human dependence on natural materials to making an artificial material, much as domestication requires creating an "artificial" animal dependent on humans. Pottery is important to archaeologists because, although the containers break, the sherds into which they shatter are nearly indestructible. The variations in their shapes and decoration provide a sensitive indication of changes in time and place.

The earliest pottery dates to around 3350 B.C. and was found at the site of Monsú on the Caribbean coast of Colombia (Reichel-Dolmatoff 1985: 176). The artists took advantage of the plastic nature of the clay, which permits the material to be shaped with just light finger pressure—so different from the manipulation of hard materials like flint and bone, the primary earlier sculptural media—to create patterns of circular and angular grooves which sometimes suggest highly abstracted faces. The subsequent style in the area is even more plastic, as seen in the oldest complete vessel in the New World (3100 B.C.), found at the neighboring site of Puerto Chacho (fig. 1.6). Here the potter manipulated the rims and lugs into animal heads and other parts. The later Taino of the Caribbean, who were making similar pottery when Columbus arrived, considered the little figures on the rims and side lugs to be spirits which animated all aspects of the world. A like intention probably motivated the early pottery makers of the Caribbean coast of South America, whom we can assume were women, the traditional pottery makers in the Americas.

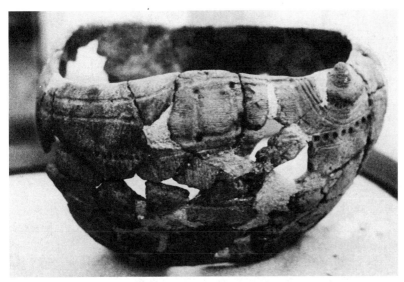

FIG. 1.6. Puerto Chacho, Bolívar, Colombia. Repaired complete vessel with *adornos* on rim, pottery, 8¾" high x 13" diam. Archaic, ca. 3100 B.C. Santafé de Bogotá: National Museum. Photo by John F. Scott.

Farther south, the villagers of Ecuador's Valdivia culture also made pottery. The Valdivian site of Real Alto was quite large during this period (3000–2000 B.C.), with about two thousand inhabitants. Each of its oval dwellings with mud-covered log walls and gabled thatched roof housed about twenty people. No doubt these structures were much like those built by tropical forest natives such as the Arawak of Guyana in historic times, after European contact. The Real Alto houses lacked well-defined corners which would have organized and articulated the space more emphatically. The basically circular plan reflects the fluid nature of their thinking and the egalitarian form of their society, where everyone of a certain sex and age group was theoretically equal. Similar round houses made of reeds were found on the south-central coast of Peru, at the site of Chilca, dating to the latter fourth millennium B.C. In Mexico around 3000 B.C., semi-subterranean oval houses have been defined at Chilac in the Tehuacán Valley. In Ecuador the village of Real Alto as a whole had a more clearly defined order than its individual oval houses; they were grouped in regular rows around a sunken plaza, which served as a meeting place for the entire village (fig. 1.7). Adjoining this plaza were two community structures raised on low mounds: one, about the same size and structure as a dwelling, was used for ritual banquet ceremonies; the other, a smaller charnel house of quatrefoil plan, served as the repository for the remains of an honored dead woman, with whom several men had been buried (Lathrap et al. 1977: 9).

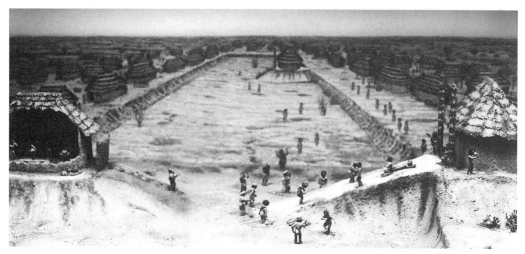

FIG. 1.7. Real Alto, Guayas, Ecuador. Village reconstruction, 900' long. Archaic, ca. 3000–2200 B.C. In Museo del Banco Central, Quito. Photo by John F. Scott.

Elaborate burials of members of egalitarian societies in family groups generated another art form in the Chinchorro culture of the northern desert area of Chile from about 3000 to 1500 B.C. After the soft tissue of their dead decomposed, the bones were reassembled on wooden armatures stuffed with straw, and the faces were re-created with very simplified features in clay modeled over the skull. Such veneration of the bones of ancestors is typical of early village cultures of the Neolithic level; similar clay modeling of the faces of the dead was also practiced in ancient Jericho and historic Melanesia.

The Valdivia culture created the earliest known figurines of humans as independent sculptures in the Americas. Shortly after 3000 B.C., when Valdivia potters were producing incised monochrome wares, as did the potters of northern Colombia, Valdivia craftsmen made small stone images from local water-smoothed pebbles which probably suggested human proportions to their collectors (fig. 1.8). Some pebble figurines have nothing more than vertical striations suggesting the long hair of later female figurines. Highly abstracted facial features, notably large squared oval eyes (right), make their appearance, as do string-sawed divisions of the lower part of the stone to suggest the separation of the legs. Until about 2300 B.C., the artists apparently attempted to render more features, until someone had the idea of making the figurines from the same plastic medium already used by village potters for many centuries. The makers of the earliest pottery figurines, while retaining the general rectangular proportions of the stone predecessors, could now render round breasts, buttocks, and gloriously full heads of hair (fig. 1.9). Later Valdivia clay figurines exhibit more perfunctory body features and proportions but show more facial expres-

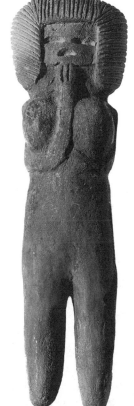
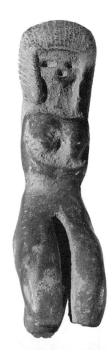

Below: FIG. 1.8. Valdivia, Guayas, Ecuador. Figurines, stone, largest 3½" high. Archaic, ca. 3000–2400 B.C. Guayaquil: Museo del Banco del Pacífico. Photo by John F. Scott.

Right: FIG. 1.9. Valdivia, Guayas, Ecuador. Female figurines, ceramic, 3¾" and 2⅞" high. Archaic, 2400–2000 B.C. Coral Gables, Fla.: Lowe Art Museum, University of Miami, 84.241.6 and 84.241.7, gift of Mr. and Mrs. Robert M. Bischoff. Photo courtesy of museum.

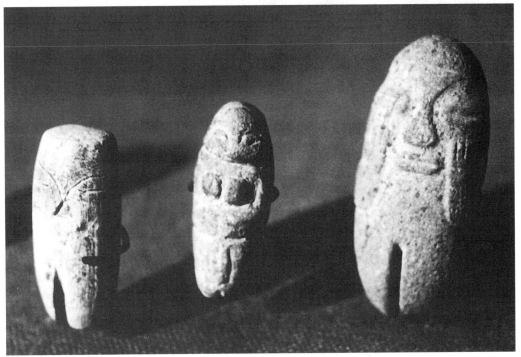

sion by means of curved eyebrows and mouth, resulting in smiling faces in the latest Valdivia stage.

About 1600 B.C. a new style named Machalilla appeared in Ecuador, possibly brought by people from the lowland tropical forest of the upper Amazon River (Lathrap 1975: 33–34). They introduced new decorative motifs into the ceramics: sharp incisions in more regular geometric forms, highlighted by white pigment rubbed into grooves; red paint applied to a buff-colored field; and a new spout type in the shape of a stirrup, which appears not only on the Ecuadorian coast during the Machalilla period but also in the southern Ecuadorian highlands at Cerro Narrío. Far to the northwest on the Mexican coast, a style called Capacha, documented about 1450 B.C., includes incised monochrome bottles with stirrup spouts formed by two separate tubes joining at the top to make one spout (like fig. 3.4). Machalilla figurines continue the emphasis on facial features shown in the latest Valdivia phase, but they deviate more strongly from human naturalistic proportions; the head becomes flattened and the features spread across the entire face (fig. 1.10). Sloppily painted geometric red lines decorate the surface. Eyes made with oval pellets of clay divided horizontally by an indented line make their first appearance in Machalilla. These often are called "coffee-bean eyes," an anachronistic term because coffee was not introduced into America until after the Spanish Conquest.

Other areas of Nuclear America have evidence of figurines which might well have been inspired by Ecuador's precocious Valdivia culture. In highland central Mexico, the mainly nonceramic Zohapilco culture (2500–2000 B.C.) produced baked-clay figurines having the general proportions of Valdivia types but with a poorly defined upper torso and head (fig. 1.11). The lower torso and fragmentary legs, however, are far more naturalistic, with biomorphic swelling of the torso and fluid curves from torso to legs. Crude pottery contemporary with this figurine has been found in Mexico at Puerto Marqués on the Pacific coast of Guerrero and in the central highlands of Puebla, around Tehuacán. Its rough temper, poor polish, and low firing resulted in a pitted surface, which led an excavator to dub it "pox pottery" because it looked like skin scarred by chicken pox.

COTTON PRECERAMIC: PERU, 2800–1800 B.C.

The final preceramic culture found in the wide central coastal area of modern Peru has been named the Cotton Preceramic after its main agricultural product, domesticated cotton. Although other plants were domesticated, including gourds used as containers, the egalitarian

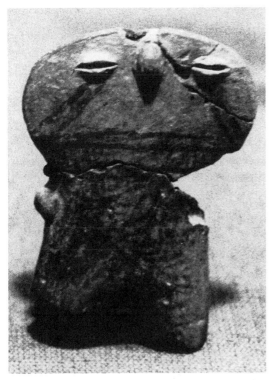

Left: FIG. 1.10. Machalilla, Manabí, Ecuador. Fragmentary solid figurine with coffee-bean eyes, red paint on buff ceramic, 5¾" high. Formative, ca. 1500 B.C. Guayaquil: Museo del Banco del Pacífico. Photo by John F. Scott.

Below: FIG. 1.11. Zohapilco, State of México, Mexico. Female figurine, baked clay, 2¼" high. Archaic, 2500–2000 B.C. Mexico City: Museo Nacional de Antropología. Line drawing after Christine Niederberger.

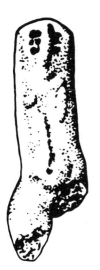 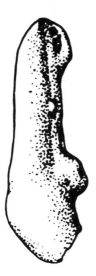 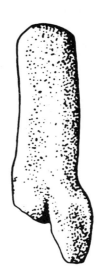

people relied on the rich products of the sea for their food. However, from the highlands the coastal people did obtain domesticated plants, primarily root crops such as the many species of potato, and domesticated animals such as the llama and the guinea pig. Here we will apply the term Cotton Preceramic to both the coastal and the highland cultures.

Baked-clay figurines from the Cotton Preceramic level of Peru during the third millennium B.C. may derive from the Valdivia style, which they resemble in their slit features, modeled hair, and a swelling on the torso suggesting an arm held under the breast (fig. 1.12). Their large heads and squat proportions suggest the somewhat later Machalilla style. A stone figurine (not illustrated), dated to 1900 B.C. or earlier, from the highland site of Kotosh, also resembles the earliest type of stone figurine from Valdivia levels of a half-millennium earlier. The figure has been abstracted to a vertical shaft with grooved neck and drilled pits for facial features. None of these figurines is as common or as well made as the Valdivia types (see fig. 1.10) from which we assume they derived.

The absence of ceramics in the Peruvian Cotton Preceramic period is doubly surprising because the coastal Peruvians were obviously familiar with Ecuadorian ceramic art. A similar stylization of a human face featuring squared eyes and long oval mouth is found on a Valdivia ceramic bowl and burned into the surface of a gourd (fig. 1.13) from the north-coastal Peruvian site of Huaca Prieta. We can only assume that the Peruvians did not create ceramics at this time because the domesticated gourds apparently served the same function and were easier to adapt as containers and to transport during seasonal migrations.

Textiles are undoubtedly the most impressive and informative representational art from the Cotton Preceramic in Peru. They already foreshadow the immense significance textiles would have in the Central Andes throughout that civilization's Pre-Columbian history. Hand-

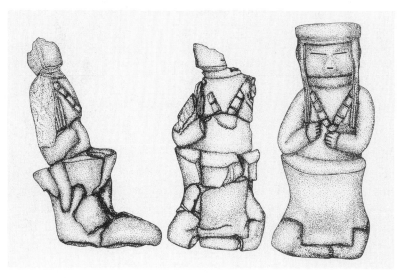

FIG. 1.12. Áspero, Lima, Peru. Figurine with slit features, modeled hair, baked-clay, 6⅛" high. Archaic, Cotton Preceramic, 2800-2000 B.C. (Figure at right is a reconstruction.) Line drawing after Robert Feldman, courtesy of Michael Moseley.

LATIN AMERICAN ART

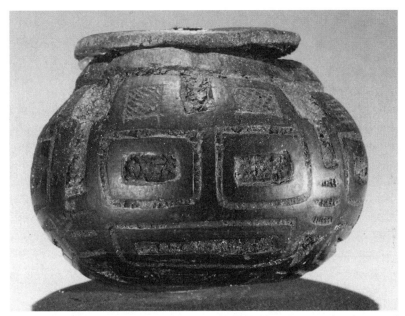

FIG. 1.13. Huaca Prieta, La Libertad, Peru. Lidded gourd pyroengraved with squared faces, 2⅜" high. Archaic, Cotton Preceramic, 2000–1900 B.C. New York: American Museum of Natural History, 41.2/2554. Photo by Rota, neg. no. 125750, courtesy of Department of Library Services, American Museum of Natural History.

twined without the use of a loom, these Preceramic cotton cloths are small and their use difficult to guess. Their weavers formed the designs by the addition of a warp float, originally of a different color visible on one side but with age now only traceable under microscopic analysis. These weavers probably were women, based on historic roles of Andean peoples. The designs represent creatures with religious significance, such as a condor with a coiled serpent inside its belly as if seen with an X ray (fig. 1.14). Double-headed serpents and back-to-back birds provide the first examples of other long-enduring Andean mythical motifs. Depictions of frontal human figures, of which none from this period have survived complete above the torso, exhibit the characteristically Andean artistic convention of splayed feet with all toes rendered as if seen from above. All these designs are paralleled in textiles from the central coast of Peru some three millennia later, although by then the medium had advanced tremendously to include a multitude of techniques and colors on large loom-made cloths (see fig. 4.30).

Ritual architecture is the most advanced feature of the Cotton Preceramic in central Peru. Enormous rectangular enclosures define ceremonial spaces which ascend natural hills to create terraces of increasingly restricted access. The uppermost level is often a warren of small rooms presumably for the use of religious specialists. In spite of these large constructions, no class distinction appears in the burials, suggesting a tribal level of culture in which capable individuals organized neighboring villages speaking the same language to contribute the necessary labor (Moseley 1992: 107). The mainly rectangular structures are occasionally softened by curved or circular corners, which suggest biomorphic shapes. In fact, the Andean architects traditionally conceived of buildings and even whole cities as living creatures, as shown in the Inca plans of Cuzco (see fig. 4.34) and Huánuco Pampa, shaped like a puma and an eagle, respectively. Trapezoidal niches mark the main room of a temple at the highland site of Kotosh. On the wall directly beneath the central niche is modeled a pair of crossed hands, suggesting that the whole building is animated (fig. 1.15). The longitudinal plan of coastal temples also may refer to a long anthropomorphic body, with a sunken circular central court looking like a navel and the intricate small rooms of the top suggesting the head, alluding to the administrative function it presumably had. The coastal temples are primarily built of roughly cut stone set in adobe mortar, a technique similar to that used for highland temples. The dichotomy between coastal and highland building materials typical of later times had not yet developed.

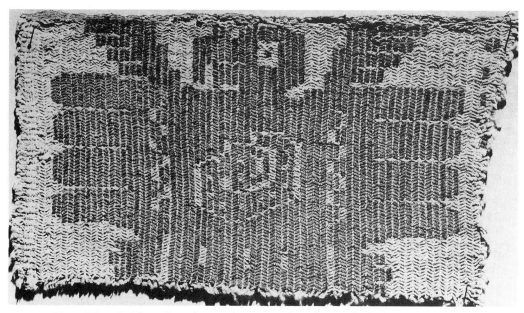

FIG. 1.14. Huaca Prieta, La Libertad, north coastal Peru. Textile with retouched color on yarns, revealing image of condor with coiled serpent in belly, twined cotton, 4⅛" high x 8¼" wide. Archaic, Cotton Preceramic, ca. 2000–1900 B.C. New York: American Museum of Natural History, 41.2/1501. Photo by Rota, neg. no. 328612, courtesy of Department of Library Services, American Museum of Natural History.

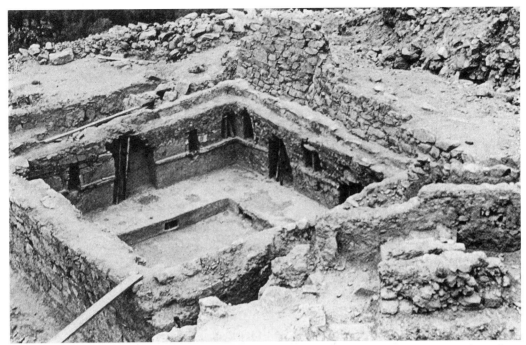

FIG. 1.15. Kotosh, Ancash, Peru. Temple of the Crossed Hands, stone with mud mortar, ca. 15' wide. Archaic, Cotton Preceramic, 2000–1600 B.C. Photo by Roy C. Craven, Jr., courtesy of Visual Resources Center, University of Florida.

EARLY FORMATIVE: 1800–900 B.C.

Eventually villages became larger and more permanent, since they were settled year-round and not subject to the seasonal abandonment of part of their population. Houses were typically no longer circular, as during the Archaic, but rectangular, allowing more dense settlement, since rectangles fit together better than circles, and suggest greater articulation of function, including a hierarchy of importance of locations. Small public buildings with an almost square plan can also be identified, as in San José Mogote, Oaxaca, in south-central Mesoamerica (fig. 1.16). Dated about 1350 B.C., it is 17¾ by 14½ feet and was smoothly surfaced with white stucco plaster. In the middle of the plastered floor is a pit that would have been filled with powdered lime, which was probably taken during ritual ceremonies to enhance the effect of a narcotic plant leaf, such as tobacco. The building was placed on a low platform from which one crossed over a threshold to step down into the room. Lack of household debris and its ritual magnetic-north orientation suggest it was an initiates' Men's House (Marcus and Flannery 1996: 87).

Figurines became far more popular after Mesoamericans settled into permanent villages and pottery was established as a standard craft, two features which mark the transition from the Archaic to the Formative

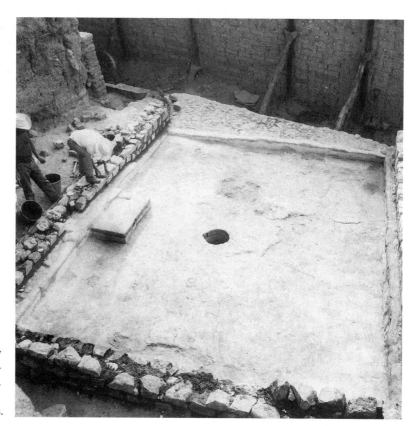

FIG. 1.16. San José Mogote, Oaxaca, Mexico. Small public building, pine posts, wattle-and-daub and lime plaster, 17¾' x 14½' plan. Early Formative, Tierras Largas phase, ca. 1350 B.C. Photo courtesy of K. V. Flannery and J. Marcus.

Age. A wide range of styles characterize Mexican figurines. The earliest ones are solid and thus small, since larger solid forms would explode when fired. Features and clothing are often indicated by applied pellets and fillets of clay, with poking and grooving used to create the small details (fig. 1.17). Their makers rendered a wide range of costumes and postures, including dancers. Most of the figurines represent females, but some are males. The latter may wear heavy belts later associated with players in a ball game; others have small masks tied to the lower half of their faces. Actual small pottery masks from this period geometrically simplify the facial features, and bold facial paint is applied to the flattened surfaces. The presence in burials of groups of figurines placed to form a scene suggests that a primary purpose for making these figurines was to represent for eternity ritual performances such as dances (Scott 1987: 8). Their gracefulness and liveliness make them one of the most approachable art forms in the Pre-Columbian world.

Around the thirteenth century B.C., ceramic figurines throughout Nuclear America were made larger to become far more impressive as representations of humans. Large hollow ceramic figures were created in both the Central Andes during the Initial Period of ceramic creativity in the Formative (1600–900 B.C.) and in southern Mesoamerica during the Early Formative there, which begins about 1800 B.C. with the introduction of fine ceramics in the coastal Maya peripheral area in Belize, southern Guatemala, and adjoining Chiapas state on the Pacific Coast of Mexico. The earliest ceramics from this area are already very finely made, not at all like the crude "pox" pottery abortively introduced nearly a millennium earlier further north in Mexico. Their design suggests the gourds which preceded them as containers. The best dated hollow figure (fig. 1.18), from the central highlands valley of Tehuacán, has a large smoothly curved helmet with contrasting zoned patterns painted on it, swelling thighs and shoulders, short "flipper" arms and thick, stubby legs, and a broad face. From the Central Coast of Peru during the Initial Ceramic Period, a large hollow pottery figure from Curayacu reflects its aesthetic of polished surfaces and geometric stylization. From the same region, another Initial Period ceramic art work, a fine globular jar from nearby Ancón, creates bold patterns made by its large incised zones separating two different colors.

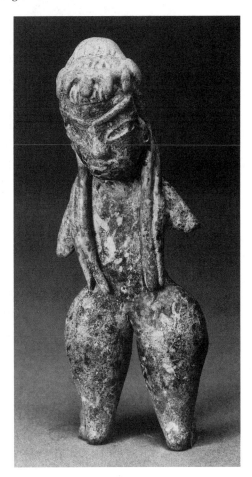

FIG. 1.17. Tlatilco style, central Mexico. Standing female figurine, solid ceramic, 4¼" high. Early Formative, 1200–900 B.C. Coral Gables, Fla.: Lowe Museum of Art, University of Miami, 86.181, gift of Dr. and Mrs. Allan Kaplan. Photo courtesy of museum.

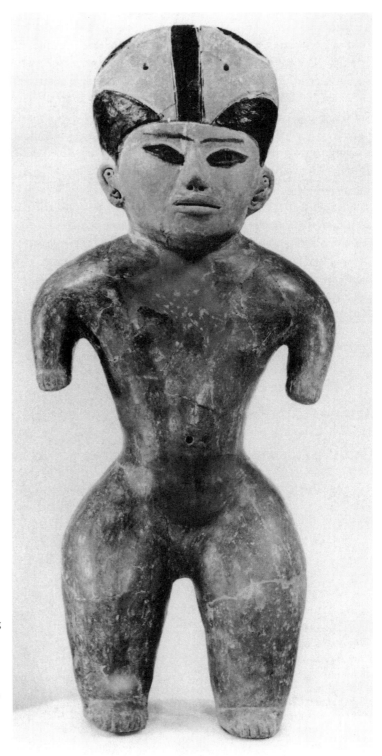

FIG. 1.18. Tehuacán, Puebla, Mexico. Standing figure with helmet, hollow painted ceramic, 17" high. Early Formative, 1200–900 B.C. Andover, Mass.: Robert S. Peabody Museum of Anthropology, Phillips Academy. Photo courtesy of museum.

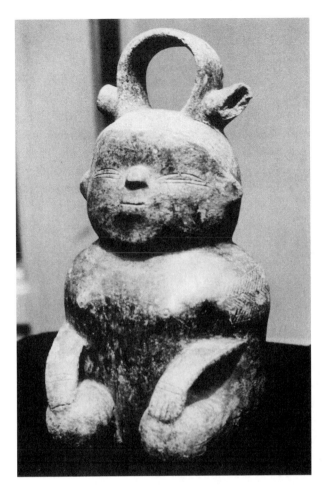

FIG. 1.19. Calima region, Valle de Cauca, Colombia. Looped double-spouted human effigy bottle, pottery, 9½" high. Formative, Ilama phase, 800–100 B.C. Houston, Tex.: Alice Tillett collection. Photo courtesy of Mrs. Tillett.

In Ecuador, hollow figurines with red-painted geometric patterns had already appeared during the Machalilla period. The subsequent phase in coastal Ecuador, called Chorrera (1000–300 B.C.), produced masterpieces of great control and power: large standing hollow figures with serenely closed eyes, smooth helmets sometimes with asymmetrical designs, and bulbous forms seen not only in the helmet but also in hips, shoulders, and facial features (pl. 1). Color is applied in zones bordered by cleanly incised lines, unlike the sloppily painted lines of Machalilla. The smoothly colored slip of diluted clay was left matte or was polished with a stone, creating an attractive play between the two surface textures. Color range is greatly increased over that of Machalilla with the use of white, black, reds sometimes approaching maroon, and buffs approaching yellow. Potters also adopted these innovations to vessels and created a wide variety of natural forms, all carefully observed for their shapes yet stylized to reveal the geometric order behind the vagaries of realistic nature. They form effigy bottles, many of which have a tapering vertical spout and an attached loop handle.

Chorrera's later date indicates that it was the recipient of ideas from Mesoamerica and Peru, thanks to its central location, but its artists synthesized these new concepts with a strong aesthetic control unequaled in quality by other areas. Ecuador's historic tradition of long-distance trading voyages on large balsa sailing rafts, by which they traded such goods as the valuable orange-colored bivalve shell (*Spondylus*), brought it into contact during the later Formative with both areas of Nuclear America destined to be centers of civilization.

In what is now Colombia, a strong reflection of the Chorrera style appears in the large hollow effigy figures often modeled on the front of vessels of the Ilama phase in the Calima area, just north of the modern city of Cali, during the first millennium B.C. (fig. 1.19). Although these figures are monochrome, they have the bulbous forms and serene facial expressions, including the large closed eyes, which reflect Chorrera features. A distinctive double spout with a bridge handle arching between identifies this style as Colombian, although spouts on ceramics from the Late Formative south coast of Peru are similar (pl. 3). At the end of the Formative, a related culture in Colombia called Malagana introduces the full range of color found in Chorrera, although it, too, has the distinctive Colombian spout. Often buried with these pottery pieces are relatively thick gold objects, crafted by hammering, a technique which came from Peru during the Late Formative and is associated with the Chavín style presented in chapter 2.

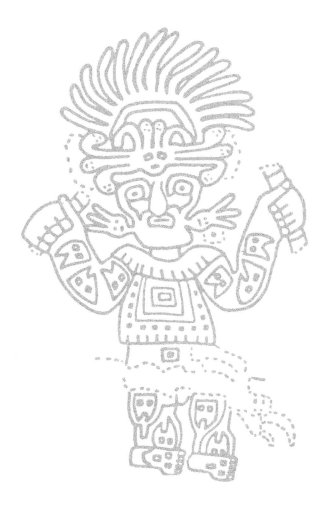

TWO

FIRST HIGH CULTURES

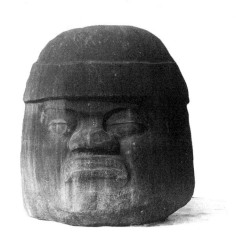

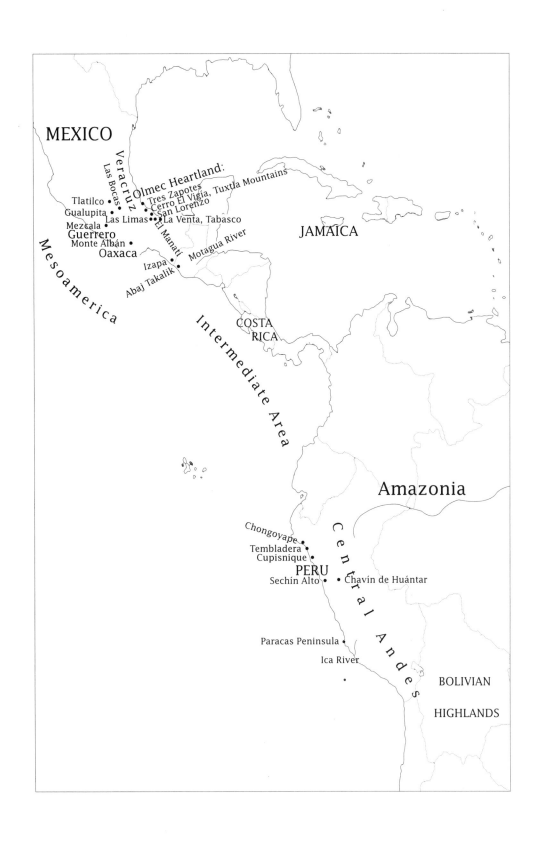

MEXICO

Veracruz

Olmec Heartland:

Tlatilco
Gualupita
Las Bocas
Las Limas
Mezcala
Guerrero
Monte Albán
Oaxaca

Tres Zapotes
Cerro El Vigía, Tuxtla Mountains
San Lorenzo
La Venta, Tabasco
El Manatí
Motagua River

Izapa
Abaj Takalik

JAMAICA

Mesoamerica

Intermediate Area

COSTA
RICA

Amazonia

Chongoyape
Tembladera
Cupisnique
PERU
Sechín Alto   Chavín de Huántar

Central Andes

Paracas Peninsula
Ica River

BOLIVIAN

HIGHLANDS

SOCIETIES DISPLAYED evidence of ranking at the beginning of the Formative in Peru and Ecuador with differences in burials and the co-ordination of labor for public works. By the Middle Formative in Peru and Mesoamerica, elite groups established ranked cultures that unified those areas, becoming the respective "mother cultures" of their regions. While there may have been a military component to this unification, and trade certainly brought the areas together, the strong similarity of art styles and motifs within each major region suggests that religion was the most important unifying force. The more utilitarian objects remained distinct among the various groups, yet the finest arts show considerable similarity. It was once believed that the two high cultures of Mesoamerica and Peru were contemporary and influenced each other, but recent research has shown that the Olmec of Meso-america flowered considerably earlier than the site of Chavín de Huán- ✳ tar in Peru.

OLMEC OF MESOAMERICA: 1200–600 B.C.

In Mesoamerica, the earliest of the high cultures is known today as the Olmec, after the historic Aztec name for the inhabitants of the "rubber land," the Gulf Coast region of southern Veracruz and Tabasco states of Mexico. This area was a center for natural rubber used for the resilient balls in the Mesoamerican ball game. Several such rubber balls have been found in excavations at the tropical lowland site of El Manatí in the southern part of Veracruz state, Mexico. Massive public works and colossal stonework characterize Olmec society and imply the presence of a powerful ruler who could command the labor necessary to produce such works. The culture first appears, in a fully mature state, around 1200 B.C. at the site of San Lorenzo, a partially artificial formation created by building giant symmetrical ridges of earth extending from a natural plateau which rose above the alluvial plain leading to the Gulf of Mexico (Coe and Diehl 1980: 28). The form of the plateau, although hard to reconstruct after three millennia of erosion in this area of heavy rainfall, suggests an image, perhaps of a bird or the more abstracted winged paw, which can be read as a bird wing and a clawed foot simultaneously. Olmec ceramics often have such designs incised on their surfaces. Draining the top of the site, beautifully cut basalt channels serve as a water control system which empties into basins carved in the form of giant ducks or the toothless baby jaguar associated with the later rain god of Mesoamerica.

Early interpretations stated that the jaguar was the sole Olmec deity, depicted in many forms from zoomorphic crouching feline to anthropo-

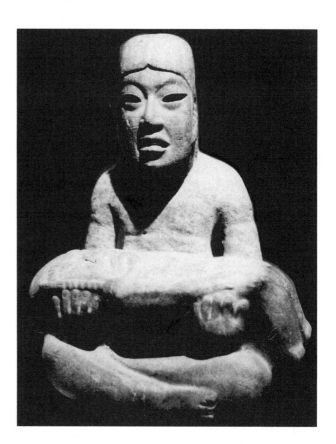

FIG. 2.1. Las Limas, Veracruz, Mexico. Olmec. Seated male figure holding cleft-headed were-jaguar baby, greenstone, 21¾" high. Middle Formative, 1000–600 B.C. Jalapa: Museo de Antropología de la Universidad Veracruzana. Photo by John F. Scott.

morphic face, with only the downturned fleshy mouth recalling the feline muzzle. A large greenstone sculpture of a person cradling a part human-part jaguar baby (traditionally referred to as a were-jaguar baby) in its arms was discovered at Las Limas and immediately but errone-ously dubbed a "Madonna" (fig. 2.1). The seated adult figure is actually a male of the type represented on the "altars" discussed below. Incised on his shoulders and knees are four profile heads, each of which has a cleft on top and a fanged mouth. Differences among the four heads suggested they prefigured some of the historic gods of Mesoamerica: the death god, a crocodilian earth monster, a fire god, and the god of spring vegetation. From this observation a more elaborate pantheon has been reconstructed (Joralemon 1996: 54), whose most important god was the dragon, opposed by a bird monster (here with eyebrows shaped like flickering flames). A maize god incised on the chin of the Las Limas figure opposed the rain god represented by the toothless baby on his lap. Finally a fish god (originally identified as a death god) op-poses a banded-eye god, perhaps associated with the god of spring veg-etation, who symbolizes renewal of life. Many of the deities have jaguar features. Elsewhere in Olmec iconography is the feathered serpent, an important benevolent god in later Mexico. These gods, embodied in great creatures like the harpy eagle and the crocodile or cayman, are also found in the pantheon of Pre-Columbian South America.

Images of these deities, especially the rain god and fire dragon, were incised and/or carved on axe heads made of jade or other similar greenstone, considered by the Mesoamericans at the time of the Spanish Conquest to be their most valuable material, far exceeding gold in esteem (gold was introduced to the area during the late first millennium A.D.). Jade was believed to contain life itself, and a jade bead was often placed in the mouths of the dead to revive them in the afterworld. Jade—or more properly jadeite, not the nephrite of China—is one of the hardest stones and required countless hours of abrasion with diamond-bearing sand to be shaped. For this reason, and because its color was its most important trait, softer greenstones were often used which we now call "cultural jade." Procurement of the rare greenstone (as well as obsidian, a volcanic glass prized for its ability to hold a sharp edge or a sharp reflection) motivated the Olmecs' wide-ranging trading expeditions, by which they united many village societies. The resulting cultural link and the elite art style which it passed along explain why the Olmec are often credited with being the "mother culture" of Meso- ✗ 19 america.

The slightly later site of La Venta, the chief city of the Olmec polity from 1000 to 600 B.C., had around 18,000 inhabitants (Ciudad 1989: 61). Recent excavations have led Rebecca González Lauck to consider it an urban capital and the Olmec culture a true civilization (1996: 75). Abundant burial of greenstone, often in vast deposits, like gold at Fort ⟶ Edificio + obligion del mundo Knox, was sealed by abstract stone mosaic masks of a deity. A carved jade axe head excavated at La Venta has the everted mouth of a jaguar and a cleft in the head where the soft spot of a baby's skull is (pl. 2). In other works, the cleft seems to symbolize a furrow in the earth from which sprouts vegetation such as maize. The density of the blue-green jade makes the axe head heavy and cool to the touch, suggesting cool water locked inside the stone. The figure's prominent flame eyebrows, however, identify it as the fire dragon, a meaning accentuated by the redness of the mineral cinnabar rubbed into the grooves. Thus, the figure brings together the opposites of fire and water, two basic states of matter. It also embodies what will become a characteristic Mesoamerican tendency toward duality, in which apparent opposites are aspects of a multifaceted unity.

As depicted in their art, the Olmec rulers clearly had close associations with the gods. Large basalt "altars" (probably really throne bases) at both San Lorenzo and La Venta reveal powerful men holding ram-

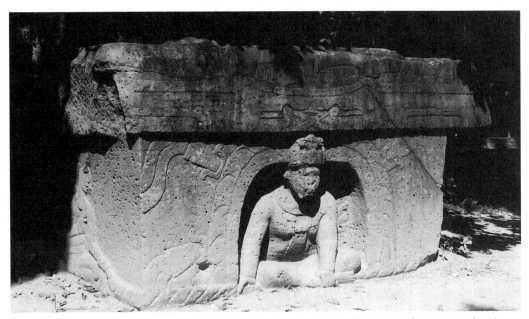

FIG. 2.2. La Venta, Tabasco, Mexico. Olmec. Altar 4 with niche figure holding rope tied to prisoner, basalt, 55" high. Middle Formative, 1000–600 b.c. Villahermosa: Parque Olmeca. Photo by John F. Scott.

bunctious part-jaguar children. The elaborate headdresses on the men carved on Altar 5 from La Venta suggest they might be rulers. More specifically rulerlike is the vigorous figure rendered in high relief from the niche on La Venta Altar 4, who grasps a rope asymmetrically (thus increasing the twist of his torso and the bulging of his muscles); he controls a tied human figure rendered in low relief on the side of the altar (fig. 2.2). The niche in which this powerful figure sits has flames carved inside it, suggesting that it is the mouth of the molten interior of the earth, so well known to Mesoamericans via the numerous active volcanoes which wrack their land. Surrounding the niche are depictions of maize cobs with silky tassels, implying the fertility of the land under this leader's rule. Above the figure is an abstracted jaguar motif, not a mask but a pelt, characteristic of thrones of later Maya rulers.

To date, seventeen colossal basalt heads have been unearthed. Their heights range from over 5 to over 9 feet, and all weigh several tons. These are very likely portraits of the Olmec rulers, identifiable by their distinctive helmetlike headdresses, one of which has a representation of a jaguar pelt paw draped over it (fig. 2.3). Each head has different features and proportions and each has a different expression. All have very alert eyes, wide open with iris and pupil rendered, and all exhibit an appropriate air of command. Like later Maya stelae (cut stone commemorative slabs set vertically into the ground), these heads were probably erected during the reign of each ruler and memorialize not only the individuals but also the deities under whose patronage they ruled. These gods are symbolized by the designs on the helmets, which are literally above the rulers like the sky gods on Maya stelae. Basalt must have had great significance in these colossal monuments because the rulers had to order quarried pieces to be transported at least fifty miles from the nearest source in the Tuxtla Mountains, probably by raft along the coast and up the slow-moving rivers. Basalt is a volcanic stone, created by molten lava, symbolizing the volcano's fiery power the way that jade symbolized water locked in stone. Natural columns of basalt break off from the Tuxtlas directly into the Gulf of Mexico and were transported to La Venta, where they surround the sacred enclosure under which the greenstone hoard was buried and create tomb enclosures in which the members of the chiefly families were buried. Built on the axis opposite the sacred enclosure at La Venta is a large mound, precursor of later Mesoamerican pyramids, which is a naturalistic replica of a volcano, with fluted sides and rounded cone (fig. 2.4).

Ceramics, which played a minor role in the artistic production of the Olmec heartland, reflected in abstracted form the motifs most fully presented in the monumental sculpture. In the distant provinces of the

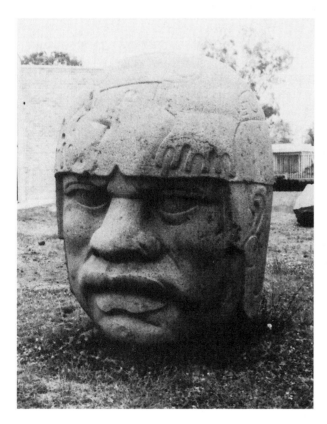

FIG. 2.3. San Lorenzo, Veracruz, Mexico. Olmec. Monument 5, colossal head, basalt, 72¾" high. Early Formative, 1200–900 B.C. Jalapa: Museo de Antropología de la Universidad Veracruzana. Photo by John F. Scott.

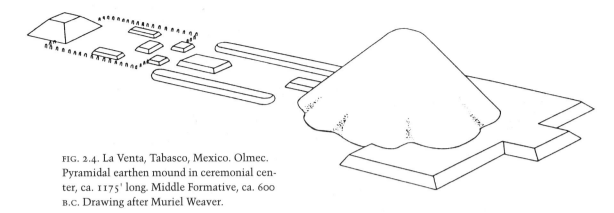

FIG. 2.4. La Venta, Tabasco, Mexico. Olmec. Pyramidal earthen mound in ceremonial center, ca. 1175' long. Middle Formative, ca. 600 B.C. Drawing after Muriel Weaver.

Olmec culture, particularly the Central Mexican highlands, ceramics became much more important in their arts, which they derived from the Olmec. In the Olmec heartland, hollow ceramic sculptures of babies with slight jaguar-like facial features were modeled in the smooth, fine, white clay available on the alluvial plain of the Gulf; it is often called kaolin because of its similarity to the white clay of the same name used in Chinese porcelain. In the central highlands, such fine white clay apparently was not available, so their potters simulated it by painting a white slip over a coarser buff clay. Central Mexican sites such as Las Bocas (Puebla), Tlatilco (Valley of Mexico), and Gualupita (Morelos) all produced large, very naturalistic babies modeled with dramatic sophistication (fig. 2.5), unlike the continuing local village tradition of small solid ceramic figurines such as figure 1.17.

POST-OLMEC MESOAMERICA: ABOUT 500–100 B.C.

After the abandonment of La Venta, for reasons not understood but probably involving a breakdown of the Olmec trade network which sustained it, many areas of Mesoamerica which had trade associations with the Gulf Coast Olmec continued independently to acquire and roughly block out the shape of material which the Olmec had obtained from them through trade. Basalt from the Tuxtla Mountains was still quarried by the local group and turned into monumental sculptures but of a very simplified form. From this I have suggested (Scott 1980: 236) that this group had previously done the rough cutting for Olmec traders but had shipped the stones to the Olmec centers to be finished. When the Olmec no longer acquired this good in trade, the local people made the forms as they had before but erected them in a condition the Olmec would have considered unfinished. The major work of this Tuxtla group is the colossal stone head found on the slopes of Cerro el Vigía, where the basalt stone may have been quarried (fig. 2.6). Its features are

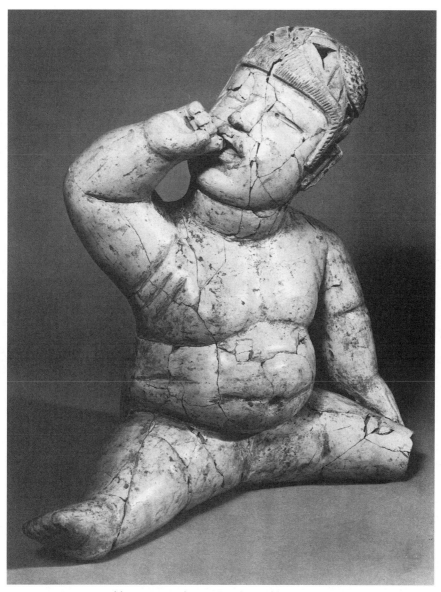

FIG. 2.5. Las Bocas, Puebla, Mexico. Olmec. Were-jaguar baby figure, hollow white ceramic, 13⅜" high. Early Formative, ca. 1000 B.C. New York: The Metropolitan Museum of Art, 1979.206.1134, bequest of Nelson A. Rockefeller. Photo courtesy of museum.

rendered on the surface like strips, and its closed eyes suggest that the ruler represented was already dead and was being treated like an ancestor. A similar conception is found on the Pacific Slope of Guatemala, where the colossal sandstone sculptures at Monte Alto also have closed eyes. They, however, are much more roughly shaped, making it unlikely that the leaders directing these carvings had ever studied real Olmec colossal heads or knew of them directly. Although we don't know how much contact this region had with the Olmec, the area was the major source of cacao in post-Classic times and thus may well have attracted Olmec traders. Cacao, the beans of which were used to make

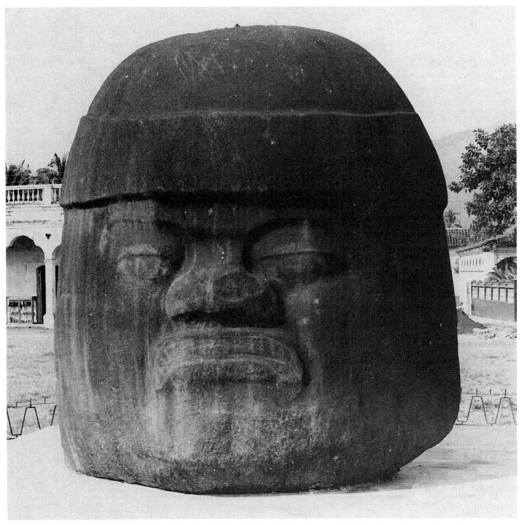

FIG. 2.6. Cerro el Vigía, Veracruz, Mexico. Colossal head, basalt, 134" high. Late Formative, 600–300 B.C. Santiago Tuxtla: Plaza. Photo by John F. Scott.

LATIN AMERICAN ART

a stimulating drink like bitter chocolate, was also used as a medium of exchange at least during the Integration Period. The main source of jade, on the northern slopes of the Guatemalan mountains, may have funneled through this region on its way to the Olmec.

In Oaxaca during the Late Formative, Post-Olmec potters revived Olmec traditions of whiteware ceramic effigies. However, they created a new vessel form by modeling the slightly feline infantile features to a cylindrical stand which was probably used as a brazier. Burning incense placed on an interior platform about two-thirds of the distance from the bottom would be seen through the two perforated eyes of the face, identifiable as that of a deity by the symbols on its headband. Monumental stone construction at the hilltop site of Monte Albán, which became the capital city of the Zapotec kingdom in Oaxaca during this time, commemorated its conquests on the walls of buildings by stacking tiers of low-relief figures of mutilated and slain enemies, many of whom have the thick lips associated with the Olmec. Glyphic writing, which had begun in Olmec times as small groups of pictorial symbols on portable objects, appears in longer and more prominent texts during this Post-Olmec period on large paired stone stelae with a double row of symbols possibly referring to the date and the people involved in a conquest (Marcus and Flannery 1996: 161).

The Olmec composition of a figure seated in a niche under the mask of the jaguar deity is converted in the Late Formative (500–100 B.C.) into a human figure in the mouth of a giant reptilian monster. This composition is found at three sites. The closest to the Olmec in style is at Abaj Takalik, on the Pacific Slope of Guatemala, where the face of a colossal head may have been removed and a figure seated in a serpent's mouth substituted for its nose (Scott 1988: 29). On the Pacific littoral of Chiapas state, at the sculpturally important site of Izapa, Monument 2 renders a much more naturalistic man in the jaws of a serpent (fig. 2.7). And at the site of Tres Zapotes, at the foot of the Tuxtla Mountains, which also has late Olmec sculpture such as colossal heads, Stela A presents flanking figures in low relief centered on a high-relief figure in towering headdress contained in the abstracted jaws of a monster. Both Tres Zapotes and Izapa go on to develop rich scenes of numerous figures in ritual and/or mythological settings carved in low relief on stelae, which become a dominant art form in southern Mesoamerica during the Classic era, as discussed in chapter 3.

To date, the Motagua River Valley of the northern Guatemala piedmont is the only known Mesoamerican source of jade used by the Olmec lapidaries. Other areas which may have supplied the precious

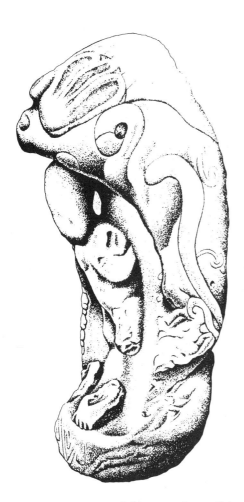

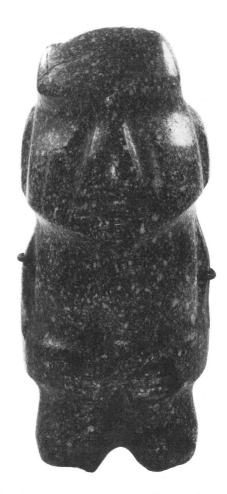

Left: FIG. 2.7. Izapa, Chiapas, Mexico. Monument 2, man in jaws of serpent, basalt, 92½" high. In situ. Late Formative, ca. 300 B.C. Line drawing after Ramiro Jiménez Pozo.

Right: FIG. 2.8. Mezcala region, Guerrero, Mexico. Axe god, greenstone, 11" high. Late Formative, 300–100 B.C. Gainesville, Fla.: Harn Museum of Art, S–81–12, gift of Mrs. A. H. Spivack in memory of Dr. A. H. Spivack. Photo courtesy of museum.

jade and other greenstones have not been positively identified yet. The western Mexican state of Guerrero has mineral-rich mountains and produced abstracted versions of Olmec jade forms, notably the anthropomorphic axe heads. A style named for the village of Mezcala features a highly simplified human shape apparently derived from the Olmec axe heads (fig. 2.8). Unlike them, though, Mezcala figures were defined by string-sawing to create the legs and the sharp planes of the face and body. Abrasive sand containing hard particles was stuck to wet cordage to abrade the stone in long straight grooves. Technically its grooves resemble the rough cutting seen in the colossal stone sculpture elsewhere, implying that the Guerrero natives were accustomed to conveying the partially finished jade to their former Olmec contacts to be finished in the Olmec heartland. This tradition may have lasted long in this isolated area of Mesoamerica, for Aztec offerings made about A.D. 1500 included numerous coarsened versions of these figures, plus masks and temple models, some of which were possibly heirlooms or buried treasure wrested from Guerrero natives by the Aztecs as tribute.

The presence of frequently reworked Olmec-style jade objects in Costa Rica originally led to speculation that this Central American country was the source of the distinctive Olmec bluish jade. Technical analysis of Costa Rican jade reveals, however, that much of it was imported from Guatemala's Motagua River Valley (Lange et al. 1981: 171); thus, this area must have been a common source of the stone for both Costa Rican and Olmec lapidaries. The most characteristic Costa Rican jade sculpture of the early period (300 B.C.–A.D. 300) is the axe god, conceptually similar to Olmec effigy axe heads but usually more birdlike in features and angular in style, with obvious drill pits and string-saw marks (fig. 2.9). Depending on the hardness of the stone

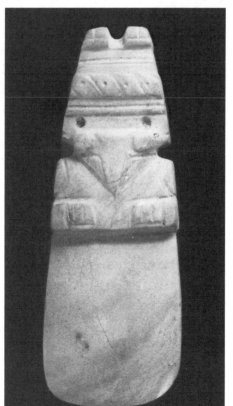

FIG. 2.9. Northern Costa Rica. Axe god with bird features, jade, 5¼" high. Late Formative-Early Classic, 300 B.C.–A.D. 300. Ocala, Fla.: Appleton Museum of Art, G12737. Photo courtesy of museum.

used, hundreds of hours of abrasion with sand under cords or hollow canes were needed to wear down these features; polishing the stone also required weeks of work. Perhaps with the demise of their Olmec clients shortly before 300 B.C., the Motagua lapidaries sent partially worked effigy axes to new clients in Costa Rica, who finished them according to new aesthetic canons and represented different tropical forest animals like the toucan and the crested harpy eagle. Spectacular creatures of the tropical forest provided early models for art even outside their natural habitat, as the art of Chavín demonstrates.

CHAVÍN, PERU: ABOUT 900–200 B.C.

In the Central Andes, a wide range of sculpture has been found at the ceremonial center at Chavín de Huántar, a site which has long been considered the fountainhead of high civilization in Peru. Recent research in the development of ceremonial centers during the preceding Initial Period (1800–900 B.C.) suggests that Chavín was a summation of the architecture and iconography of temples in the large area around it, both in the north highlands and the north-central coast. Nevertheless, by the fifth century B.C. the prestige and religious importance of Chavín de Huántar undoubtedly served to integrate and disseminate these images to a much wider area (Burger 1985: 283), from the far north to the south coast of Peru, with later echoes in the south highlands of Peru and Bolivia. The Chavín presence identifies the Early Horizon, dated 900–200 B.C., the first major evidence of the integration of previously separate regional cultures of the Central Andes into a unified elite culture widely spread horizontally across the geography (hence the term Horizon style for this and the subsequent periods of stylistic integration in the central Andes).

The architecture of Chavín de Huántar is derived from earlier monumental architecture of the Cotton Preceramic, which continued to develop on the coast during the Initial Ceramic period. The colossal and only slightly excavated site of Sechín Alto (fig. 2.10) was built on a natural hill, where the temple structures overlooked the valley landscape toward the east. Stretching out below are parallel adobe mounds with large plazas descending the slope on axis, most containing sunken circular forecourts. The later plan of Chavín de Huántar is based on this type of architecture, although its ritual structures are not very large in comparison to this earlier coastal construction. The main plan of Chavín is U-shaped, with its tallest structure flanked by two wings reaching out to embrace a plaza space, in the center of which is a sunken circular court. Like much earlier Cotton Preceramic structures, this

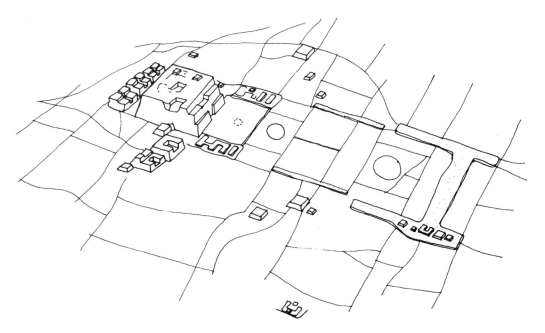

FIG. 2.10. Sechín Alto, Ancash, Peru. Reconstruction of architecture, 3700' long with sunken circular court, main platform 115' high. Formative, Initial Period, 1600–900 B.C. Line drawing by Carlos Williams, courtesy of Michael Moseley.

arrangement must symbolize the earth in its tiered variety, from the sunken navel suggesting the entrance to the underworld to the terraced levels culminating in a stylized mountain, a landscape very familiar to the inhabitants of the Andes. Like tunnels into the core of the main structure, passageways hidden from the exterior may represent stylized caves penetrating the heart of the mountain. At the central crossing of these passageways stands the original major idol of the complex, a fanged composite creature pecked in low relief on a huge dagger-shaped stone, called the Great Image (fig. 2.11). The worship of extraordinary natural shapes as sacred features called *huacas* (originally the Quechua Indian word *waqa*) was practiced among the Inca at the time of the Conquest, and can be applied retroactively to the Great Image at Chavín de Huántar.

The face of the Great Image has the characteristic upturned lips, large fang, and snub nose of the jaguar, a creature already abundantly represented in Olmec art at this time. Multiple stacked images of this same face are carved on the top extension of the Great Image, implying that the jaguar spirits continue forever as the stone penetrates into the heart of the temple/mountain. Similar continuous feline faces wrap around the middle of the body, forming a belt beneath which are represented the human legs of the composite creature. The hair of the feline terminates in small serpent heads, an expression of the abundant natural life

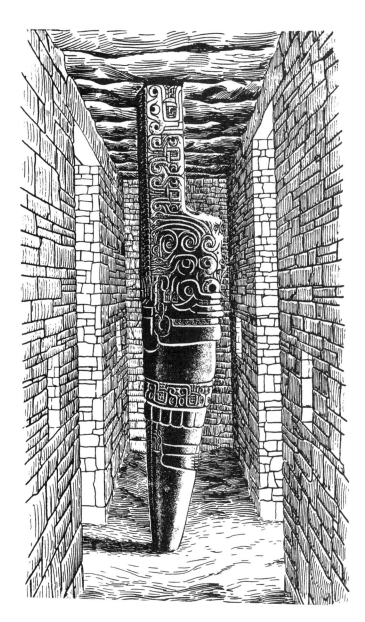

FIG. 2.11. Chavín de Huántar, Ancash, Peru. Great Image, stone, 178" high. In situ. Formative, Early Horizon, 900–500 B.C. Line drawing after Pablo Carrera.

bursting forth from this deity. Heads of similar creatures are carved in the round on the projecting ends of tenon stones which are inserted into the exterior walls of the temple, staring down at the visitor (fig. 2.12). Only their heads emerge from the 40-foot-high cut stone wall, implying that their bodies have merged with the temple and their life force remains partially contained in it. The faces on these heads vary from quite human to very animal. Their style is bulbous, again suggesting the outward swelling of the life force, implied also by the ubiquitous serpents in lieu of hair. Cornice stones cut in low relief with sharp

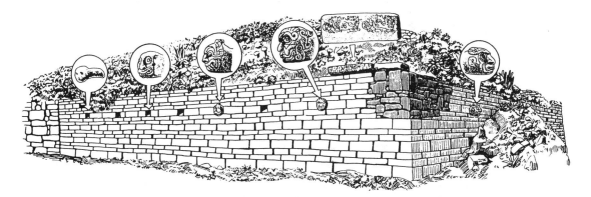

FIG. 2.12. Chavín de Huántar, Ancash, Peru. Western wall of temple, cut stone, 386½' long x 13⅛' high. Formative, Early Horizon, 700–500 B.C. Line drawing by Pablo Carrera.

precision on the temple represent the complete jaguar (fig. 2.13), this time with its spots (thereby distinguishing it from the other large American feline, the *puma*, also a Quechua word). Even the spots are animated, some becoming serpents coiled into a figure eight, others becoming eyes. The entire body of the jaguar becomes the head of a giant jaguar which spits the tail out of its jawless mouth; the tail has scales like a serpent and terminates in another head. The legs become jaguar heads, which spew taloned bird feet. This art abundantly stated the swelling proliferation of life.

Tropical forest creatures other than the jaguar are also rendered in Chavín art. Serpents always appear in subsidiary roles (see the thin edge of fig. 2.12), but the taloned feet identified in figure 2.13 belong to the harpy eagle, America's largest eagle and a resident of the nearby tropical forest. Also resident there is the cayman, one of the crocodilians which

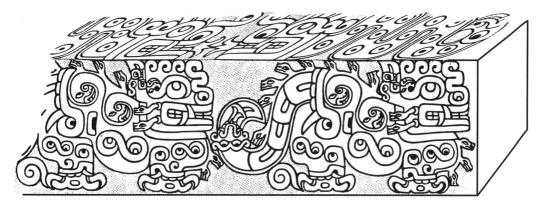

FIG. 2.13. Chavín de Huántar, Ancash, Peru. Cornice stone. Planar relief on underside shows feline with figure-8 spots, 18¼" x 39" wide; confronting serpents on horizontal face, 9½" high. Formative, Early Horizon, ca. 500 B.C. Line drawing after John Rowe.

inhabit the lowland rivers on the Amazonian side of the Andes. The presence of these large tropical forest animals in the art of the Andean highlands and arid desert Pacific coast led to the hypothesis that much of Chavín religion derived from the jungles east of the Andes (Lathrap 1971). But the mythical importance of these creatures was also widespread in the Intermediate Area, that zone between the Central Andes and Mesoamerica which had been so influential in the period before the twin high cultures of the Olmec and Chavín arose.

Human representations at Chavín are much rarer than animal images but become more common later in the evolution of Chavín art. John Rowe (1967: 84) noted that the Great Image was converted into a Smiling God by the addition of a lower jaw and human teeth. This god is normally much more human in appearance, although he retains the feline mouth (as do important Olmec human figures), serpent hair, and clawed feet. Also anthropomorphic, the Staff God, with down-turned mouth, a quadruple-headed snake belt, and vertical staffs in his laterally extended hands, confronts the viewer. On the 10-foot-tall, crisply carved Raimondi Stela (fig. 2.14), the finest and most authoritative presentation of this deity holds out twin staffs which appear like maize stalks in the upper section and like animals, perhaps caymans, in the lower. A towering headdress composed of animal muzzles emerging from other muzzles reinforces the theme of natural fecundity stated earlier in the Great Image. This image of the Staff God is, however, one that is far more widespread because of its later date, when it was transported to various parts of Peru. It appears in gold at the far northern site of Chongoyape and on painted cotton textiles in the Ica Valley of the south coast of Peru. In fact, textiles, gold, and other portable objects may well have been the means by which the images of Chavín were so widely spread. This would certainly account for the very different media onto which they were copied after they were out of the Chavín area, where they are only known in stone and ceramic.

As with Olmec ceramics from the Gulf Coast heartland, pottery from the site of Chavín de Huántar abstracts a few themes developed more fully in the monumental art. The finest pottery was found as offerings in the passageways of the temple and comprised beautifully polished blackware subtly incised and carved with low-relief images of animal motifs, often virtually unrecognizable when taken out of context. Pottery bowls and bottles, the major early media, render zoomorphic forms in polished black with the reserve spaces textured with rocker stamping achieved by rocking the edges of scallop shells back and forth across the surface of the vessel before firing. Some representations, surpris-

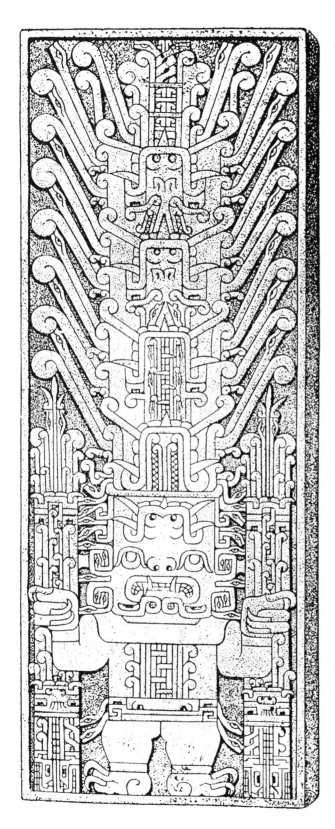

FIG. 2.14. Chavín de Huántar, Ancash, Peru. Raimondi Stela of Staff God, incised granite, 76¾" high x 6¾" thick. Formative, Early Horizon, 500–200 B.C. Lima: National Museum of Archaeology and Ethnology. Line drawing after Pablo Carrera.

ingly similar to the winged-paw motif of the Olmec, seem to synthesize reptilian scales, bird wings, and feline claws.

On Peru's north coast, the use of stone was rare during the Initial Period and into the Early Horizon; instead, modeled and stuccoed earth created monumental architectural decoration. In this north coast tradition, commonly called Cupisnique after a site where many such pieces were uncovered, high quality ceramics assume a very important role in presenting the Chavín religious images. Their ceramists often created stirrup-spout vessels, with heavy proportions and a flare or lip at the top, and color, both dull prefired earth tones and brighter post-fired pigments applied to the matte zones of the decoration. A beautiful bottle shows multiple views of the Chavín jaguar reassembled like a collage (fig. 2.15). Modeling on effigy pots is frequently very plastic, with vigorous bulbous shapes contrasting with concave details. Monochrome or a limited use of color on the stirrup-spout jars establishes a north coast preference which will endure until the Spanish Conquest.

PARACAS, PERU: ABOUT 600–100 B.C.

The southern Peruvian coast, which had not participated in the high development of ceremonial constructions during the Cotton Precera-mic and Initial periods, must have enthusiastically received the cult expressed by the art of Chavín and become much more a part of Central Andean cultural development. Curiously, the peoples of the south coast never did engage in great efforts at building monumental archi-tecture, for they seemed not to have formed as large political units as the north and central regions did. Their efforts seemed more directed toward providing a staggering abundance of grave goods for their elite, although that elite may not have had the power or the desire to order large constructions. The finest art comes from two types of shaft-and-chamber tombs: first in the hollowed "caverns" that give the style its name Paracas *Cavernas*, each reached by a vertical shaft opening di-rectly into the roughly excavated chamber, then in the more finely cut stone rectangular tomb chamber reached by steps, restricted to the Necropolis on the Paracas Peninsula, which juts far out into the Pacific.

The pottery of Paracas Cavernas took the motifs from Chavín tex-tiles and other portable art and converted them into increasingly ab-stracted and two-dimensional designs applied to their bottles, which typically were topped with two vertical spouts spanned by a slightly arched bridge. The breakdown of forms, often a feline face, into more and more fractured geometric segments, especially horizontal bands

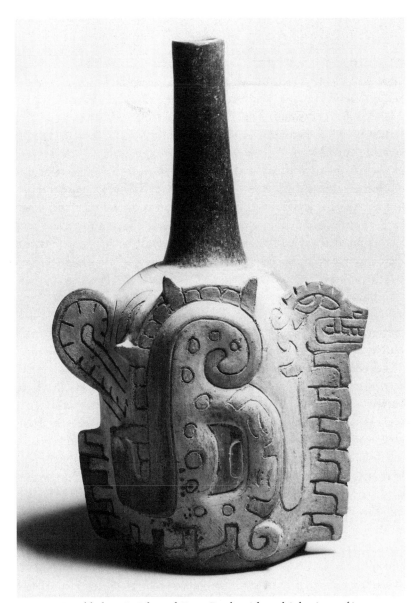

FIG. 2.15. Tembladera, La Libertad, Peru. Bottle with multiple views of jaguar reassembled, pottery with resin paint, 12¾" high. Formative, Early Horizon, 500–200 B.C. New York: The Metropolitan Museum of Art, 1978.412.203, bequest of Nelson A. Rockefeller. Photo courtesy of museum.

(pl. 3), parallels the Analytic Cubist phase of Modern art. As in Analytic Cubism, images were divided into strips and became increasingly unrecognizable, and color played a lesser role in the definition of forms and was much more muted in chroma and limited in hue. Unlike the Cubists, however, the Paracas artists made no attempt to create the illusion of even restricted spatial depth but preferred to render flat ribbons of contrasting color like an appliqué quilt. The concept of form expressed in the ceramics seems to derive from the flattened images and geometric angularity of textiles. Toward the end of the Cavernas phase (and thus the end of the Early Horizon), Paracas pottery painters suddenly switched to a style of bold, simple geometric forms in bright, strongly outlined colors. The technique is reminiscent of the Synthetic phase of Cubism, which also created the impression of a collage of cut-out forms whimsically recalling objects in the world but not attempting to look naturalistically like them. Colors were applied to the vessel surface after firing using a resinous medium, causing them to seem thick and gritty. The dominant creature rendered in this Synthetic Paracas style is called the Oculate Being because of the boldly colored goggles around its prominent eyes.

In the subsequent phase called Paracas Necropolis, around 200 B.C., just at the transition between the Formative and the Classic period, preferred pottery is plain-surfaced and plant-shaped, and so becomes much less important for the expression of religious imagery. Textiles, preserved by the extremely dry climate of the south coast, become the dominant medium. Naturally mummified eviscerated bodies were buried in bundles comprised of as many as two hundred individual pieces of cloth, some plainweave cotton but many elaborately decorated with richly colored wool weft. A new preference for embroidery to render their figural motifs freed the weavers from the limitations of loom weaving and its right angles. Embroidery can follow the inspiration of the moment and need not to be planned on the loom and woven into the warp. For this reason, among others, Necropolis fabrics display an enormous variety of creatures, most of which are probably mythological, repeated in a constantly varied pattern of orientation, contrast, and color, even though the design does not change at all. Birds, often much more angular than other animals, recall the design of the early Huaca Prieta textile condor (see fig. 1.14) and often have two heads sharing the same body. Human forms actively float about the field of the cloth, carrying severed human heads in the time-honored practice among South American natives of capturing the souls of their enemies by possessing their heads. The woven heads repeated in two directions facing the center of a Paracas mantle (fig. 2.16) seem disembodied and skeletal, referring to the spirit world the deceased will inhabit after burial. Knitted in three dimensions on the border of the mantle are more than ninety individual figures, including variations of the so-called Cat God (line drawing in fig. 2.16), a composite creature whose furry body is sometimes based on a Pampas cat; it wears bristling white whiskers around the mouth and a diving bird diadem on its forehead.

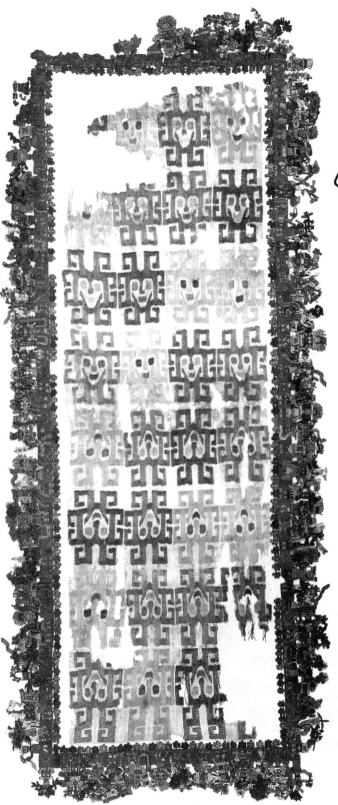

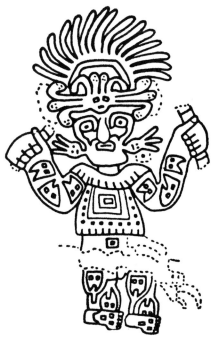

FIG. 2.16. Paracas, Ica, Peru. *Left:* Woven mantle with knitted border of divinities in procession, cotton and wool, 58¾" x 24½." *Above:* Line drawing of the Cat God, one of the figures in the mantle's border. Formative, Early Horizon, ca. 200 B.C. Brooklyn, N.Y.: Brooklyn Museum of Art, 38.121, John T. Underwood Memorial Fund. Photo by Justin Kerr and drawing both courtesy of museum.

This creature also engages in headhunting, like the humans already mentioned. It plays a more dominant role in the art of the Nazca style, which follows Paracas Necropolis in the south coast of Peru.

By the end of the first millennium B.C., then, both Mesoamerica and the Central Andes had witnessed the rise of high cultures which expressed themselves in monumental architecture and fine stone carving. Olmec and Chavín influence had spread throughout their areas, causing both to be labeled "mother cultures" of their respective regions. Their influence seems to have been carried by traders and religious proselytizers rather than by military conquest and did not deeply affect the daily life of the people. They maintained local differences that would surface much more strongly during the next period, characterized throughout Nuclear America by the lack of a dominant, centralizing culture. By this point, however, both areas shared a great many cultural traits, and regional differences in artistic manifestation only masked underlying similarities in basic practices and beliefs.

THREE

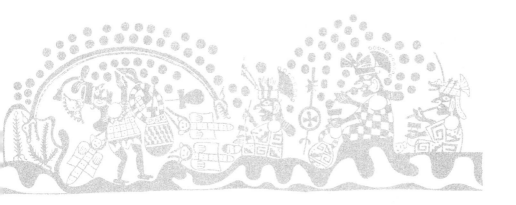

THE CLASSIC CIVILIZATIONS

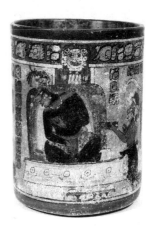

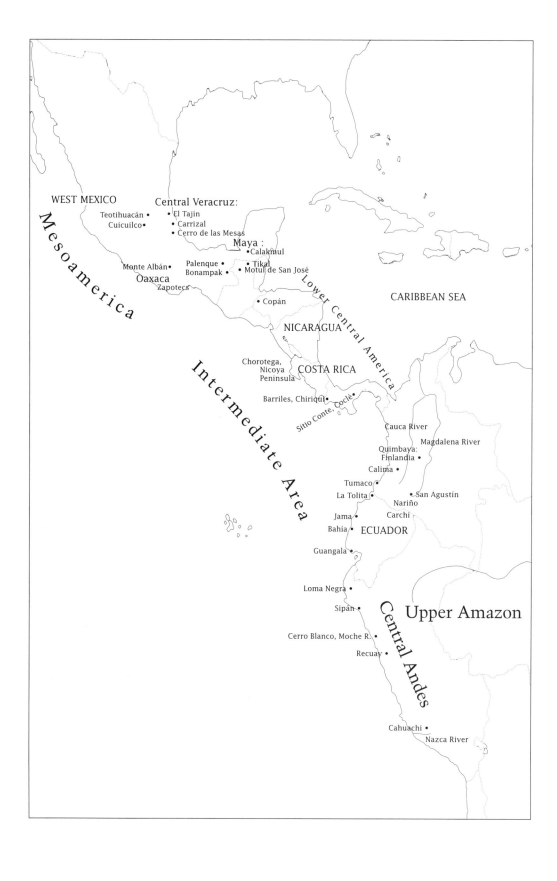

WEST MEXICO

Central Veracruz:
• El Tajín
• Carrizal
• Cerro de las Mesas

Teotihuacán •
Cuicuilco •

Maya :
→ • Calakmul

Monte Albán •

Palenque •
Bonampak •

• Tikal
• Motul de San José

Oaxaca
Zapotecs

• Copán

Mesoamerica

Lower Central America

CARIBBEAN SEA

NICARAGUA

Intermediate Area

Chorotega,
Nicoya
Peninsula

COSTA RICA

Barriles, Chiriquí •

• Coclé

Sitio Conte,

Cauca River

Magdalena River

Quimbaya:
Finlandia •

Calima •

Tumaco •
La Tolita •

• San Agustín

Nariño

Jama •

Carchi

Bahía •

ECUADOR

Guangala •

Loma Negra •

Sipán •

Central Andes

Upper Amazon

Cerro Blanco, Moche R. •

Recuay •

Cahuachi •

Nazca River

THE CLASSIC PERIOD is the chronological term generally used for Mesoamerica from about 100 B.C. to A.D. 800. It includes the Proto-classic (100 B.C.–A.D. 250), now often called the Terminal Preclassic. The Classic period will here be extended to the entire Nuclear Area to denote the period of full flowering of several civilizations, especially in their arts, as it has been applied already to Peru and Colombia. The Terminal Classic (830–1000) will be included under the discussion of the Integration Period.

Throughout Mesoamerica and the Central Andes, states were created on the cultural base of those first high cultures studied in chapter 2. Significant populations concentrated in urban centers and thus merit the title of civilizations. The evidence suggests most were ruled by hereditary kings, although areas of less complex organization persisted in some regions, especially the Intermediate Area. In certain of these cultures, specifically the Moche and the Maya, we can identify the kings in the representational art and in their tombs. In many other contemporary cultures, even when centralized control could only have been exercised by kings, we have no visual or textual evidence of their existence or certainly of their names. In the past this Classic period had been called the period of Theocratic States because it once was believed that the government was run by priests, but now we know that secular rulers assumed many priestly functions. The ruler was often the titular head of the established state religions of these early governments. Because rulers often wore religious paraphernalia, they can easily be mis-identified as priests or gods. In some cultures where we cannot identify the rulers, the identity of deity images remains ambiguous: are they priests dressed with divine attributes, or are they rulers carrying divine images to support their right to rule?

NAZCA, PERU: ABOUT 100 B.C.–A.D. 600

The Nazca culture of the southern coast of Peru, dating to most of the Early Intermediate period of the Central Andes, provides an example in which the nature of the government and identity of its rulers remain enigmatic. The culture of Early Nazca, which evolved directly from the preceding Paracas culture, seems unaffected by the tendency elsewhere toward urban centers. The extensive constructions at Cahuachi, its pyramidal monuments still visible on the desert floor, formed a pilgrimage center spread out along the south bank of the Nazca River. During the Andean summer, this ceremonial center received a temporary influx of worshippers and their rich burials, but at other times was nearly vacant (Silverman 1988: 404). Much of Nazca art found intact in

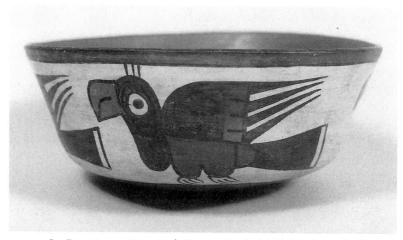

FIG. 3.1. Ica Department, Peru. Early Nazca. Bowl with bird design, polychromed pottery, 3½" high x 8½" diam. Classic, Early Intermediate Period, 100 B.C.–A.D. 200. Coral Gables, Fla.: Lowe Art Museum, University of Miami, 88.0113, gift of Bea Drimmer. Photo courtesy of museum.

burials communicates bright praise for the abundance of nature: fruits and animals looking plump and receptive for human exploitation. The style, whether rendered on textiles, scraped into the desert tableland, or painted on pottery (fig. 3.1), renders these subjects in clear, geometrically simplified forms. They are generically naturalistic without being at all literally realistic. In the painted pottery, the bright colors—as many as six colors on one vessel—are achieved here for the first time in Peru through prefired painting, by which watery clay slips, bordered by black lines, will fire to glowing, brightly burnished earth tones. Because of the rich variety possible in pottery, it became the major artistic medium, supplanting textiles in importance. Although occasionally painted directly onto cloth, the textile designs were more typically woven on the loom, adhering to its geometric constraints, rather than embroidered free-style as on Paracas mantles. The Andean practice of venerating shrines following pilgrimage paths on certain days perhaps explains the so-called Nazca Lines which cross the high desert pampas above the irrigated valleys. Formed by scraping away the top layer of dry, darkened earth to reveal the lighter layer below, some represent the same naturalistic creatures as the pottery, but the majority are straight lines, radiating from different points and crisscrossing.

A mythical being traditionally called the Cat God appears in complex representations which surely have more features than just those of a feline already seen on the knitted Paracas mantle (see fig. 2.16, detail). The Cat God has the same distinguishing features. Its frontal fanged face is surrounded with whiskers, it wears a diving bird headdress, and its long animal body is wrapped around the vessel and ends in a striped, bushy tail suggesting the Pampas cat. The presence in Nazca burials of whiskered masks and diving bird designs (fig. 3.2), made of hammered gold sheets with minimal detail tapped out from behind in the *repoussé* technique, suggests that some individuals wore or carried these easily recognizable features to identify themselves visually with that mythical creature. No representations of Nazca rulers are identified, but they may have taken the guise of their major deity by wearing ornaments of

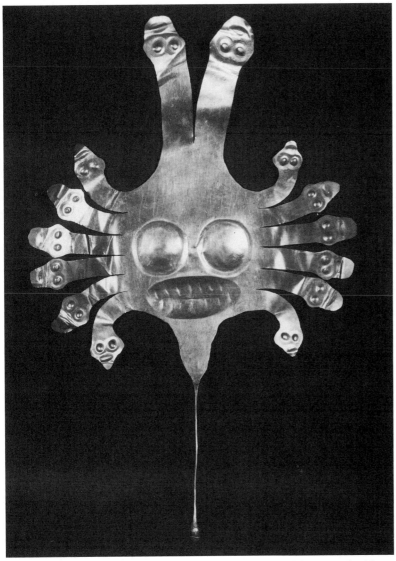

FIG. 3.2. Ica Department, Peru. Early Nazca. Diving bird wand, hammered gold, 11" high. Classic, Early Intermediate Period, A.D. 1–200. Philadelphia: The University Museum of the University of Pennsylvania, 60-4-5. Photo (neg. #S8–85764) courtesy of museum.

precious gold, much rarer in Nazca than in the more northern cultures of South America. The hammered sheets with repoussé detailing of Nazca gold ornaments reveal a more simplified technology than that of the preceding Early Horizon.

Late Nazca art represents human beings far more often than does the Early Nazca style. Human faces are often shown in rows of heads along the base of vessels, either male, with moustaches, or female, with Betty Boop style black hair and bright red cheeks (pl. 4). These lines of identical faces of vigorous young adults suggest mass support for the humans or divinities represented in painting or low relief of the main body of vessels which served as grave gifts to the important deceased. In spite of their idealized style, these heads may be considered portraits. On a minority of vessels, however, disembodied heads represent trophy heads as evidenced by their closed eyes, stitched mouths, and cut necks.

MOCHE, PERU: ABOUT A.D. 1–700

Far more information can be gleaned from the art of the contemporary state on the north coast of Peru. The Moche, the Mochica-speaking people of that area, left extensive descriptions of themselves, their activities, and their mythology in their art. Recent excavations have revealed the burials of some of their rulers in Sipán (Alva and Donnan 1993), one of whom, now called the warrior priest, had a gold mask covering the lower part of his face. A more complete gold mask, the lower part painted black, is said to have come from a burial in the Pyramid of the Moon at Moche. Gold masks of rulers are known from many early kingdoms, such as those from the tomb of King "Tut" in Egypt. In both Egyptian and Moche full-face masks, naturalistic features are best seen in the curvature of the facial planes; in both, however, the outlines of the eyes are exaggerated. Realism—meaning in this case the representation of specific individuals—also characterizes the mature Moche art style. While the early Moche gold mask seems more idealized, later Moche portrait head jars with their characteristic stirrup-spout handles are easily recognized as depicting specific men (pl. 5). Frequently the same face painted in different patterns reappears in different tombs in different valleys (Whittington 1990: 44). These jars are mold-made, insuring a repeated faithful likeness; the mold itself may have been sent by the leader to the provinces to be used there to make vessels. Local artists then improvised facial painted patterns after the figure came out of the mold but before it was fired.

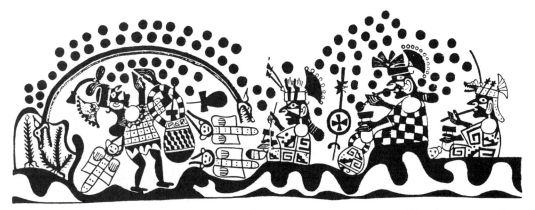

FIG. 3.3. Moche, La Libertad, Peru. Men taking coca in landscape, rollout scene of fine-line painting from pottery stirrup-spout vessel, 9½" high. Classic, Early Intermediate Period, A.D. 300–500. Stuttgart, Germany: Lindenmuseum. Line drawing after Gerdt Kutscher.

Pottery molds in Peru, as well as in Ecuador and Mesoamerica, were widely used during the Classic period in the manufacture of pottery images. Initially molds insured high quality and iconographic control; toward the end of the Classic, however, they resulted in the degeneration of the images through lack of precision, elimination of the back mold, and perfunctory cover of the rear of the piece.

Painting in Moche art is far more descriptive than in Nazca. Fine-line brush drawing on the rounded bodies of jars render a wide range of scenes, some probably realistic, some certainly mythical. Of considerable interest to students of the history of art is the depiction of figures hunting, running, fighting, and engaging in religious rituals in a landscape, often apparently the dry, cactus-strewn desert that surrounds the fertile river valleys of the northern Peruvian coast. Irregular terrain is captured with undulating lines indicating rocks, and supporting plant profiles (fig. 3.3). The three men use long, knobbed sticks to remove lime powder from the small gourds in which it is carried. They chewed the lime with coca leaves stored in loop-handled textile bags. The lime enhances the hallucinatory effect of the coca and causes visions, here represented by spots and an arching double-headed snake symbolic of the sky or, specifically, the Milky Way. Coca chewed alone, as Andean people still do, simply reduces fatigue. More elaborate scenes are arranged in tiered registers, separated by nondescriptive horizontal, heavy black lines. In one jar (fig. 3.4), nude prisoners—probably war captives—run to a leader seated on a pyramid, the tiers of which are indicated by alternating red and white bands. Anthropomorphic animals and death priests float above and below the main scene; they use a crescent-bladed knife to dismember captives. The leader's snarling mouth suggests a key attribute of a deity, which also has fangs. While

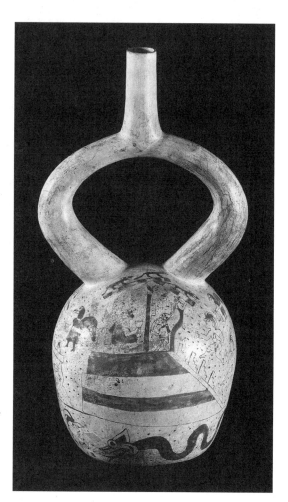

FIG. 3.4. La Libertad, Peru. Moche. Stirrup-spout vessel with fine-line painting of prisoners being brought to ruler, pottery, 12½" high. Classic, Early Intermediate Period, A.D. 300–500. New York: American Museum of Natural History, 1/907. Photo by Coles, neg. No. 121093, courtesy of Department of Library Services, American Museum of Natural History.

we cannot be sure the prisoners are not being sacrificed to a god, early rulers in general assumed priestly roles, dressed as gods, and participated in divine qualities as a sign of their right to rule. The Moche fanged gods themselves are often associated with blood rituals: a gold and turquoise nose ornament from the northern site of Loma Negra shows a decapitator god holding the crescent-bladed knife he used to sever the head he holds aloft (fig. 3.5). This god has been identified as the Active deity, who in pottery depictions also does battle against reptiles and fish in support of mankind's dominion. His father, the Creator God of the Mountains, a more passive deity, sits in a mountaintop cave surrounded by rounded peaks (Benson 1972: 27–28), accepting the mountain sacrifice of humans, a practice known later from actual Inca rituals. On other vessels, the same composition of rounded peaks shows the head of a fanged god emerging from corn cobs, suggesting that he is the lord of fertility, descended from the Smiling God of Chavín (see fig. 2.11).

Terraced pyramids such as that represented in figure 3.4 existed at sites throughout the Moche realm. The capital city below Cerro Blanco in the Moche River Valley, which gives its name to the whole culture, has two major structures: the Pyramid of the Sun (*Huaca del Sol*) (fig. 3.6), a long, stepped terrace of adobe bricks culminating in a 135-foot-high platform with its back to the sea, much like Cotton Preceramic temples; and the Pyramid of the Moon (*Huaca de la Luna*), a smaller complex with mural paintings similar in style and content to the fine-line painting on bottles. The Pyramid of the Moon shows very little evidence of occupation, suggesting it was primarily religious in nature, whereas the Pyramid of the Sun was densely occupied and had numerous burials, indicating it was probably the sacred residence of the ruler and his court, which was enlarged on the death of each king. These two structures face each other across a broad plain once filled with elite residences, some visible in the foreground of figure 3.6, that also con-

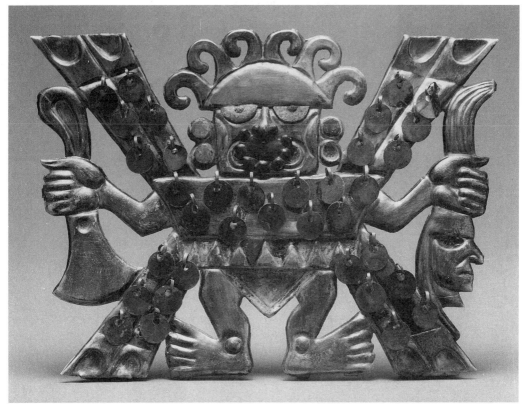

FIG. 3.5. Loma Negra, Piura, Peru. Moche. Decapitator god holding knife and head, turquoise and gold overlay for nose ornament, 2¾" high. Classic, Early Intermediate Period, A.D. 100–300. New York: The Metropolitan Museum of Art, 1979.206.1247, bequest of Nelson A. Rockefeller. Photo courtesy of museum.

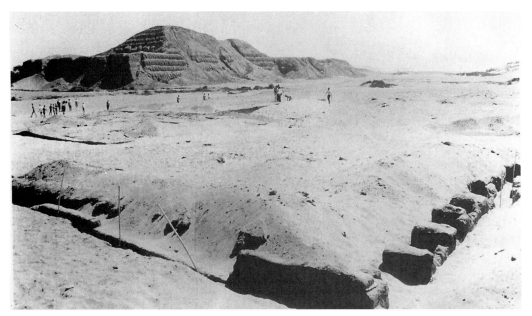

FIG. 3.6. Cerro Blanco, La Libertad, Peru. Moche. Huaca del Sol, adobe brick, 135' high, with remains of houses in foreground. Classic, Early Intermediate Period, A.D. 300–600. Photo courtesy of Michael E. Moseley.

tained numerous burials (Donnan and Mackey 1978: 59). Drift sand left as a result of a climate change has covered these residences, temporarily uncovered recently by archaeologists. The two major structures epitomize the coexistence of royal and divine in the Moche capital.

LA TOLITA-TUMACO, ECUADOR-COLOMBIA: 300 B.C.–A.D. 400

Further north on the Pacific coast, in what is now Ecuador, a group of small polities developed among ethnic groups that spoke languages related to Mochica. Like the Moche and their predecessors, the people constructed large earthen mounds known locally as *tolas*. These do not, however, preserve the clear geometric forms of the Peruvian pyramids. Like them, they had buildings on top constructed of perishable materials. These served as temples and elite residences. Figure 3.7 is a ceramic interpretation of such a mound from a neighboring culture, including a ruler seated at the summit. Inside these mounds were rich burials, much like those found at Sipán, with complexly modeled, specular gray ceramics and intricately hammered and soldered metal objects, notably of gold and platinum, the latter metal unique to Ecuador.

The style of the coastal Ecuadorian figures can be as naturalistic as those of the Moche, and like them are often made in molds. During the Regional Developmental Period (300 B.C.–A.D. 600), as it is known in Ecuador, several coastal styles developed from the previous Chorrera culture: Guangala, Bahía, Jama-Coaque, and La Tolita-Tumaco. This last style stands out because of its inventive and arresting images. In its most elaborate sculpture, the power of the jaguar is asserted in a twisting, rampant figure with a prominent penis and a fierce snarl (fig. 3.8), recalling Moche gods (see fig. 3.5). The influence of this style once reached to the middle of the Colombian coast. Three-dimensional contrapposto—the naturalistic push and pull of the parts of the body against each other—is unusual in early art but is found in the best work of these self-confident kingdoms of the South American coast during the Classic era. They had apparently dominated their environment, which offered a rich supply of food and trade items. They could afford professional artists who conveyed this positive attitude toward mankind and the nature that served their society so well, yet which, like the roaring sound in their much-prized and widely traded conch shells, contained the mysterious voice of the divine.

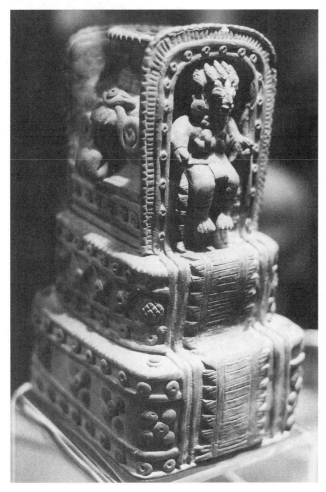

FIG. 3.7. Cojimíes, Manabí, Ecuador. Jama-Coaque. Model of pyramidal mound with perishable structure and ruler on top, blue and yellow painted pottery with appliquéd pieces, 7¾" high. Classic, Regional Developmental Period, A.D. 1–300. Quito: Museo del Banco Central. Photo by John F. Scott.

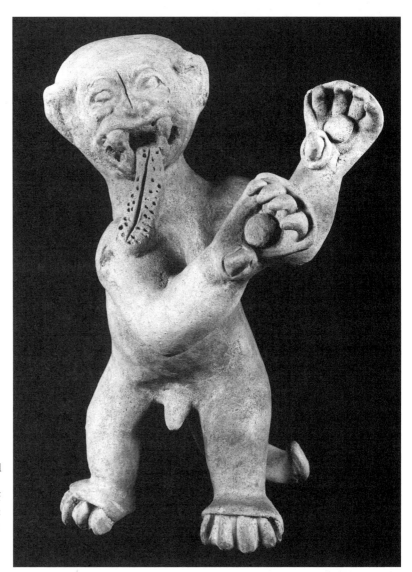

RECUAY, PERU: ABOUT A.D. 300–600

The highland cultures of South America, although they certainly
traded with the coast, did not possess so rich a culture during the Classic. Their architecture is neither spectacular nor large in scale, suggesting a smaller work force and less powerful centralized control. Their
largest surviving constructions are tombs, many of which are similar to
the shaft with expanded chamber seen already in Paracas Cavernas
during the Late Formative.

The Recuay culture, in mountainous river valleys inland from the
southern part of the Moche state, built large cut-stone charnel houses
for their venerated dead. Its most interesting grave offerings are rectan-

gular pottery vessels populated with small three-dimensional scenes, usually focusing on a flat-faced figure, who may represent the honored mummy bundle. This figure may be surrounded and protected by female retainers, whose flat, round faces are reminiscent of the female heads along the bottom of Late Nazca bowls (see pl. 4). Thus, these vessels represent the charnel house, and by extension, the land of the dead.

Typically, Recuay ceramic sculpture is more geometrically abstract than north coast sculpture. Recuay figures have flat faces, sharp noses, large outlined eyes, tubular bodies, and rigid stances (pl. 6). The creamy white semiporcelain contrasts strongly with the bold red paint, upon which a waxy, resist-painted design burns off in a second firing, leaving all unpainted areas blackened. This striking three-color negative decorative technique is echoed along the Andes, not only in the Classic period but until the Spanish Conquest. Resist paint is commonly used to depict the profile of spiky dragonlike creatures known as the Recuay cat, seen facing each other on the man's shirt and to his side in plate 6. Its sharp claws, rendered with concentric arcs, repeat the curve of its arched back. Its head, formed of two concentric circles, has serrated fangs extending at right angles, a parallel tongue, and an arching crest extending backward from the snout, echoed by a similar stepped design representing the tail. This creature is widespread in Andean art, from the Moche kingdom (where it is rendered more naturalistically and is identified as a moon monster), south to northwestern Argentina, where it is incised on Middle Horizon blackware, and north to Coclé, Panama (pl. 7). Throughout its range this creature may represent a protective animal spirit of the night (Scott 1995).

CARCHI-NARIÑO, ECUADOR-COLOMBIA: ABOUT A.D. 1–600

In Ecuador and Colombia many cultures of the Classic period employed elaborate shaft-and-chamber burials. The deepest tombs were found in the Carchi-Nariño culture, named for the northernmost highland province of Ecuador and the adjoining southern highlands of the modern Colombian department of Nariño. During the earliest phase, called Capulí, the shafts can be as deep as 50 feet with radiating chambers opening around the bottom of the central shaft. Buried in these chambers along with the dead are offerings of ceramics and gold as well as seashells. Pottery decoration exhibits two-color negative, with resist black geometric designs applied to an overall red field. Figures modeled in the round include males chewing a wad of coca (fig. 3.9), while seated on benches resembling the stools often used by shamans among recent

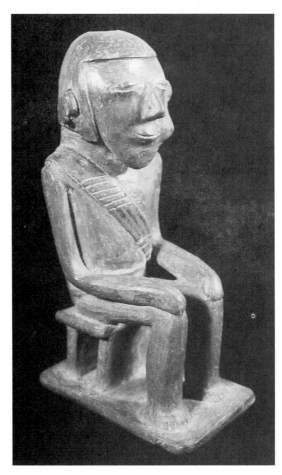

FIG. 3.9. Carchi-Nariño, highland Ecuador-Colombia. Coca-chewer seated on bench, negative-painted pottery, 10½" high. Classic, Regional Developmental Period, A.D. 400–800. Ocala, Fla.: Arthur I. Appleton collection. Photo courtesy of Appleton Museum of Art, AL 686.

tropical forest tribes (Lathrap 1975: 47). Like the Recuay figures, their modeling is angular, with ball-shaped heads and cylindrical limbs placed at right angles to other forms. The imposition of strong geometry onto natural forms seems more characteristic of smaller societies producing only what they need. Gold, however, which usually is restricted to elites because of its scarcity, suggests a more stratified society in Capulí. Their gold was formed into objects of personal adornment: nose pendants and discoidal earrings. Their silhouetted designs, which appear to be cut-outs but actually are cast in molds, integrate small natural forms into intricate geometric patterns of bilateral and biaxial symmetry.

CLASSIC QUIMBAYA, COLOMBIA: ABOUT A.D. 1–500

Only grave robbers have found scarce shaft-and-chamber tombs buried under volcanic ash covering the fertile mountain slopes between the middle courses of Colombia's two major rivers, the Cauca and the Magdalena. No tombs from this area have been scientifically excavated.

The art style here, called Classic Quimbaya, derives from the Chorrera and the Ilama phases (see pl. 1 and fig. 1.19). Like those styles, the Classic Quimbaya style is characterized by simplified natural shapes and idealized, smoothly swelling globular forms. However, it has greater realistic detail. The culture producing these tomb contents has traditionally been known as the Quimbaya after a small warlike tribe inhabiting the middle Cauca Valley at the time of the Spanish Conquest, although they were reported to be latecomers to the area. The actual makers of "Classic Quimbaya" art, whoever they were, modeled large monochrome or three-color pottery vessels, painted in white, red, or just dark brown, in the form of nude women with serene expressions, their eyes closed and their mouths smiling, as if in a trance (fig. 3.10).

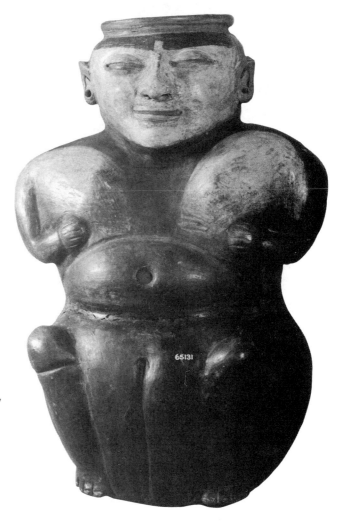

FIG. 3.10. Caldas, Colombia. Classic Quimbaya. Seated figure, tricolor ceramic, 16¼" high. Classic, A.D. 100–500. Chicago: Field Museum of Natural History, 65131. Photo by John F. Scott, with permission of museum.

The Treasure of the Quimbaya, now in Madrid, includes among its cast gold pieces several beautiful containers for holding the powdered lime used to activate the coca leaves while chewing. This practice has already been seen among the Moche of Peru, who carried the lime in hollowed gourds (see fig. 3.3). Among the high chiefs of the Quimbaya, these gold containers often took the form of humans (fig. 3.11), their eyes similarly closed in a trance, seated on stools like the Capulí coca chewers. More realistic in their details than works from the earlier Chorrera and Ilama cultures, they are rendered wearing crescent-shaped gold nose ornaments and beads wrapped around their ankles and arms much like those still worn by the tropical forest Indians.

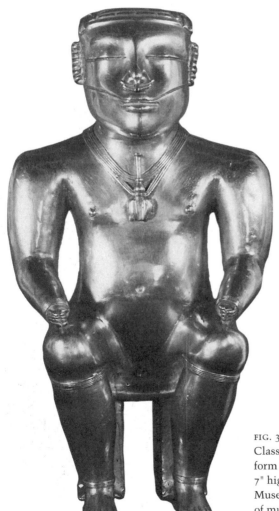

FIG. 3.11. Finlandia, Quindío, Colombia. Classic Quimbaya. Lime container in the form of a nude seated chief, cast gold, 7" high. Classic, A.D. 100–500. Madrid: Museo de América, 17447. Photo courtesy of museum.

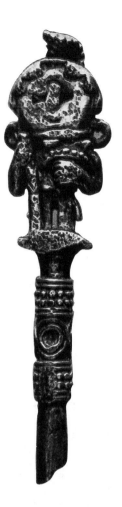

FIG. 3.12. Finlandia, Quindío, Colombia. Quimbaya. Pin top with standing helmeted figure, cast gold, 3½" total length. Classic, A.D. 100–300. Madrid: Museo de America, 17251. Photo courtesy of museum.

Since so few finds have been made of this material and those treasures are so sumptuous, they must represent the burials of important chiefs. No architecture survives that housed these chiefs during their lifetimes. Small platforms of the contemporary Yotoco phase in the Calima region of the Cauca River Valley may indicate locations for structures, but the plans of their superstructures are not yet known (Herrera et al. 1984: 394). Well-defined footpaths along the hilltops have just been identified which reveal continuous communication and link these cultures.

SAN AGUSTÍN, COLOMBIA: ABOUT 100 B.C.–A.D. 300

The designs on the head of gold pins helps to link the cultures of Classic Quimbaya, the Yotoco phase in Calima, and the great mortuary site of San Agustín in the mountainous headwaters of the mighty Magdalena River. In the Treasure of the Quimbaya and in Calima burials, among other subjects represented on the heads of such pins—really pointed dippers for extracting the powdered lime from the containers—is the stubbily modeled body of a man wearing a helmet pierced with horizontal rectangular eye and mouth slits (fig. 3.12). He often carries naturalistic animals in his hands or on his back, perhaps as a sign of his spiritual helper, a concept often found in shamanism. This same figure is carved on two of the large stone sculptures erected on hilltop locations around San Agustín. Recent excavations there have permitted the reconstruction of several earth-enclosed chambers each containing a major tomb and an attached shrine, in this work honoring a massive, fanged figure protected by two club-brandishing warriors, who also have spiritual animal protectors arching over their heads (fig. 3.13). Chiefs buried in these mounds were placed in stone sarcophagi or slab-lined chambers. This style, which reaches its apogee during the first few centuries A.D., marks the most impressive stone carving of its period in South America and rivals contemporary stone sculpture of Teotihuacán in Mesoamerica (see below). Both express the power of the figure through the blocky stoniness of the sculpture; the bulky proportions; the oversized, broad head with forceful features; and the large scale which overawed mortal viewers.

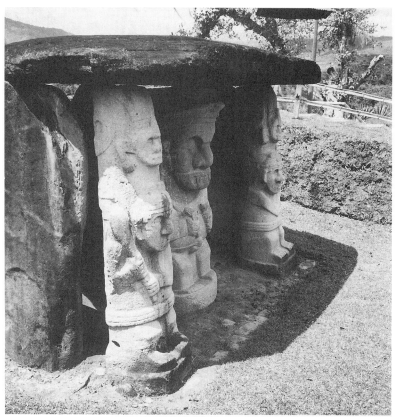

FIG. 3.13. San Agustín, Huila, Colombia. Tumulus with main figure and flanking protectors, stone, largest 90" high. In situ. Classic, 100 B.C.–A.D. 300. Photo by John F. Scott.

COCLÉ, PANAMA: ABOUT A.D. 500–800

Composite creatures alternate with recognizable animals in the charming art of the Coclé province of central Panama, where the main archaeological site, Sitio Conte, must have been the capital of a major chiefdom. Sumptuous burials of the elite not only contain plentiful gold disks and polychrome pottery but also the bodies of numerous people sacrificed to accompany the deceased chiefs. An anthropomorphic creature commonly called the "Alligator God"—although there are no true alligators in Panama, only caymans and crocodiles—dominates the iconography of gold disks apparently worn as pectorals by the chiefs (fig. 3.14). Like the Recuay monster (see pl. 6), it has prominent fangs, an angular scroll projecting from its head, and a belt-like tail with serrated scrolls. When goldwork first appeared in Panama about A.D. 200, it already employed every technique known in South America, including lost-wax casting, which came in from Colombia as part of an international style. During the apogee of the site, A.D. 500–800, the "Alligator God" is also rendered by painted designs using bristly, whiplash black outlines containing red and purple on a white ground (pl. 7). The linear grace of the brush stroke and the upswept shape of the pedestal bowl typify the Coclé style, the most elegant in lower Central America.

LOWER CENTRAL AMERICAN SCULPTURE: A.D. 300–800

Further north, stone carving depicting chiefs characterizes the Barriles style, which dominated the greater Chiriquí area along the western border between modern Panama and Costa Rica. Lining one side of a rectangular raised earthen area (Stirling 1950: 234), postlike stone carvings abstractly represent chiefs who wear conical headdresses and stone relief copies of gold pendants (fig. 3.15); later versions of these gold pendants are illustrated in figure 4.6. In both Costa Rica and Nicaragua these carvings mark the beginning of the tradition of increasingly

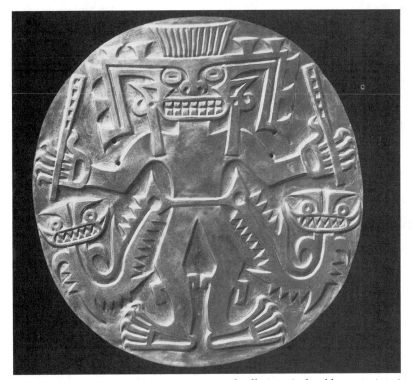

FIG. 3.14. Sitio Conte, Coclé, Panama. Disc with Alligator God, gold *repoussé*, 8⅛" diameter. Classic, A.D. 500–800. Philadelphia: The University Museum, University of Pennsylvania, 40–13–3. Photo (neg. #S8–19696) courtesy of museum.

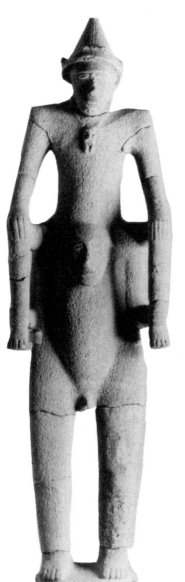

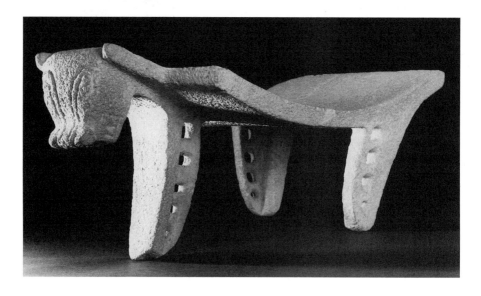

Left: FIG. 3.15. Barriles, Chiriquí, Panama. Man carried on shoulders of another man on column, sandstone, 87" high. Classic, A.D. 300–500. Panama City, Panama: Museo Nacional. Photo courtesy of Visual Resources Center, University of Florida.

Below: FIG. 3.16. Nicoya Peninsula, Guanacaste, Costa Rica. Chorotega. Tripod jaguar metate, volcanic stone, 13" high x 15" wide x 28½" long. Classic, Early Polychrome Period, A.D. 500–800. Gainesville, Fla.: Harn Museum of Art, S–74–34, gift of Irvin Ebaugh. Photo courtesy of museum.

realistic stone monuments honoring noble ancestors, a tradition which lasted until the Spanish Conquest beginning in 1502 on the mainland (see also fig. 4.11). Lower Central American elites sat upon monumental sloped stone *metates* to symbolize their control of food sources and productivity. In Barriles, metate legs represent subservient human figures, but in Costa Rica they include figures of wild animals such as birds, jaguars (fig. 3.16), and monkeys, probably totem animals from which they believed they descended and received their power.

TEOTIHUACÁN, MEXICO: A.D. 1–750

Earthwork constructions bordering plazas built by chiefs in Lower Central America recall the more extensive earthen mounds constructed earlier by the Olmec and their contemporaries during the Early and Middle Formative. In the Late Formative, Mesoamerican people built more permanent constructions first faced with and then made entirely of stone. The earthen reproduction of a volcano already seen dominating the Olmec capital of La Venta (see fig. 2.4) became more abstract during the Late Formative at the central Mexican site of Cuicuilco, where the plan was formalized into a series of concentric circular stages of decreasing sizes made of clay and faced with rough stones.

The final step in the abstraction of the man-made volcano or mountain was taken at Teotihuacán, in the northern part of the Valley of Mexico, at the dawn of the Classic era (around A.D. 1). Here the largest pyramid construction of the entire Classic period, measuring 738 feet square and originally at least 184 feet high, was executed in a relatively short time using earth braced with angled stone buttresses. This massive structure not only was divided into horizontal stages like Cuicuilco, but also was organized in a square plan suggesting the division of the cosmos into four cardinal directions, each of which had symbolic meaning and divine attributes. The original staircase was centered on the west side, angled slightly so that the sun sets directly opposite it the day the sun is at its zenith, thus supporting the traditional name by which the later Aztecs knew this structure: the Pyramid of the Sun (fig. 3.17). According to Aztec mythology, the gods gathered at Teotihuacán after the fourth destruction of the world and sacrificed themselves so that the sun would have blood nourishment to rise for the fifth creation. However, the recent discovery of a cave terminating in a multilobed chamber directly underneath the Pyramid of the Sun suggests that it may also have been revered as the traditional place of origin (Heyden 1975: 135). Caves also were sacred to the rain god Tlaloc in later times, and remains of children sacrificed at the four corners of the Pyramid of the Sun suggest an association with that god also, for it was believed the tears of children called forth the rain from the sky.

The temporary structures built on top of early pyramids permitted the design of the temples to be easily changed according to the religious season. The appearance of temple buildings may be reconstructed through a pair of Early Classic fresco paintings from one of the elite residences at Teotihuacán (one is illustrated in fig. 3.18). This scene includes the façade of a building decorated with feathers which sits on a low platform with a central staircase containing footprints indicating the route taken by the humanized feline at the right. The sloped platform is capped with a long rectangular frame projecting from the top of its wall; this combination is known as the *talud* (slope) and *tablero* (frame) in Spanish. This *talud-tablero* architectural profile is characteristic of a religious building (Kubler 1973: 28) wherever Teotihuacán influence is strong. Façade motifs of this design line the great north-south avenue linking the Plaza of the Pyramid of the Moon with the great market and religious enclosures at Teotihuacán. Within residential courtyards, small temple models serve as platforms for domestic rituals.

With such big constructions suggesting coordination of an enormous labor force, it has been assumed that this city was ruled by a king who could command its population of up to 200,000 to obey him when large public works were needed. Possible locations for the ruler's residential palace have recently been identified. Early on, when the Pyramid of the Sun was the ritual center, the kings may have lived in the Xala Compound near its base. Later, after the construction of the Citadel and its

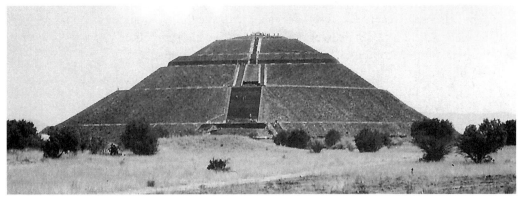

FIG. 3.17. Teotihuacán, State of México, Mexico. Pyramid of the Sun, cut stone surfacing with adobe interior, 738' square x 148' high. Protoclassic, A.D. 1–150. Photo by Carl Feiss, courtesy of Visual Resources Center, University of Florida.

LATIN AMERICAN ART

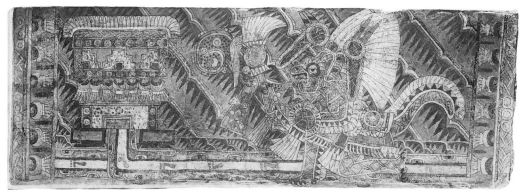

FIG. 3.18. Teotihuacán, State of México, Mexico. Tetitla Palace. Net jaguar and temple, fresco, 83½" long x 28⅝" high. Middle Classic, A.D. 450-650. Washington: Dumbarton Oaks Research Library and Collections, B-62.TF. Photo courtesy of Dumbarton Oaks Research Library and Collections, Washington, D.C.

Temple of Quetzalcoatl, the ceremonial residences were probably on either side of that temple toward the back of the Citadel, although it is doubtful that there was enough space for the administrative functions of kingship, which must have taken place elsewhere (Cowgill 1983: 331–335). The organization and position of the Palace of Quetzalpapalotl, directly adjoining the Plaza of the Pyramid of the Moon, might qualify it as appropriate to receptions required by a political leader such as a king. Its patio (fig. 3.19) is totally enclosed, with carved stone low-

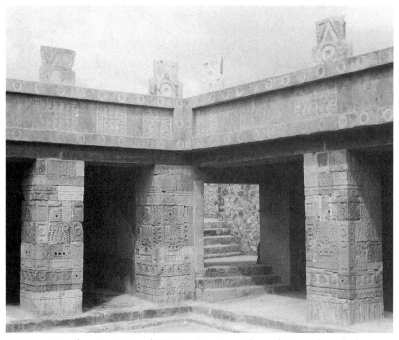

FIG. 3.19. Teotihuacán, State of México, Mexico. Palace of Quetzalpapalotl, courtyard. Painted stone, obsidian eyes in column. Middle Classic, A.D. 450–650. Photo by John F. Scott.

relief images of a bird-butterfly with inlaid obsidian eyes applied to the column surfaces. The rectangular columns and heavy *tablero* cornice crowned by stepped terra-cotta flanges creates a design of right angles typical of the Teotihuacán style, with its standardized architectonic forms.

Behind the central avenue, numerous other residential compounds conform to a basically square format, mainly laid out in a grid 187 feet square (Heyden and Gendrop 1988: 37), which comprised a checkerboard plan throughout the city. Their very restricted and obscured entrances would not serve for public access. These were private residences of various social classes housing people with probably some degree of relationship. Placed in the center of most compounds, bilaterally symmetrical patios centered on a single small, stepped platform serving as a miniature temple. On each side were shallow porches with two columns framed between projecting walls (*distyle in antis* in Greek architecture). The porches were decorated with mythical scenes and religious rituals painted on freshly stuccoed walls (such as fig. 3.18).

The architectonic style typical of Teotihuacán is easily seen in its larger sculptures, from giant idols of water deities to numerous braziers representing the Old Fire God (fig. 3.20). Here the shrivelled body of the latter has been abstracted as a hollow cubical framework supporting a large circular bowl in which offerings were burned. The weight of the brazier bottom absorbs the top of the Old God's deeply wrinkled face; the bottom of the bowl absorbs the old man's neck. The trapezoidal shape of his face frequently appears in masks of a type found wherever Teotihuacán influence reached.

The broad extent of Teotihuacán influence in Mesoamerica during the Middle Classic (especially between A.D. 450 and 650) certainly suggests an expansive state which incorporated other ethnic groups into an empire. Surprising in this context is the absence of overt militaristic imagery at the capital city of that state, Teotihuacán itself, although covert imagery has been identified (Pasztory 1976: 238–240). Also surprising is the lack of representation of kings who must have ruled this state; however, name glyphs on recently discovered murals identify eight historical figures, probably leaders of some kind (Millon 1988: 119). Typically, art of early kingdoms advertised the prowess, both dynastic and religious, of rulers. Possibly Teotihuacán stylistic influence was brought about not through conquest but via the extensive network of traders like those in Aztec times who infiltrated other cultures. The acceptance of the visual style of a strong state by less devel-

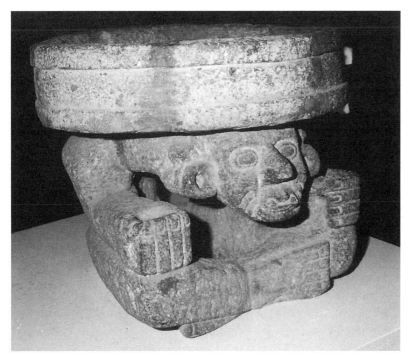

FIG. 3.20. Teotihuacán, State of México, Mexico. Old Fire God brazier, stone, 19¾" high. Middle Classic, A.D. 450–650. Teotihuacán: Site Museum. Photo by John F. Scott.

oped peoples is voluntary, as a way of being associated with its wealth and prestige. Teotihuacán was the largest city in the Americas of its day, with a population of between 125,000 and 200,000. It housed ethnic enclaves from other areas of Mesoamerica: Central Veracruz natives, Zapotecs, and Mayas. Its products were of very high quality: polychrome stuccoed pottery tripods and fine orangeware vessels were widely traded, as was lustrous obsidian, the black or green volcanic glass used to make tools such as knives and mirrors. Through this trade, and by means of small populations from Central Mexico who colonized or resided in other areas, the influence of this first fully urban state spread to western Mexico, Oaxaca, Veracruz, and the Maya area.

MONTE ALBÁN, MEXICO: ABOUT A.D. 300–700

The Zapotec kingdom in Oaxaca had been an independent state long before Teotihuacán gained its prominence in Mesoamerica at the beginning of the Classic era. Its early art style revived Olmec traditions of whiteware ceramic effigies and relief sculpture. Later styles showed the influence of Izapa relief sculpture on stone slabs commemorating conquests on the building façades of its capital at Monte Albán (Scott 1978: I, 62). During the Classic period, however, ceramic urns (fig. 3.21) echoed the rectangular style of architectonic sculptures used as temple furniture at Teotihuacán: a central face, whose proportions are notably broader than high and whose simple trapezoidal shape abstracts human details yet keeps an underlying naturalism. This face was surrounded by twin ear flares, a heavy necklace, and a massive headdress featuring the central face of a god and crowned by multiple sprays of feathers. Seated with legs crossed, the figure recalls the skeletal framework of the stone Old Fire God brazier but is stronger and more vertical. The frontality of the elaborately dressed figures on the Zapotec urns mask the unadorned cylindrical vases behind; they specifically recall incense-burner lids from Teotihuacán, which hide a vertical chimney behind a face framed by mold-made symbolic decorations. Sets of these urns placed in tombs often represented a god flanked by several priestly companions like figure 3.21. Teotihuacán did not have the need for such grave goods because cremation was the preferred way to dispose of the dead; its incense burners were ritually smashed after being used.

In contrast to Teotihuacán's silence about its kings, stone stelae erected around the architecture in Monte Albán commemorate rulers and conquests in heavy sunken relief with glyphs specifying dates and names, like the ruler 8 Deer, who was born on the day of the same name in the ritual calendar (fig. 3.22). His posture is much more animated than the formal, stiff figures in other reliefs and pottery: he leans forward on his staff, set at a diagonal, and lifts up his far leg, which crosses behind his near one to create a sense of more movement and depth than is usual in Pre-Columbian art. Around the corner of the South Platform from this stela is a larger stela representing the enthronement of King 12 Jaguar, also named for his birth date, for whom 8 Deer may have been a royal ancestor (Marcus and Flannery 1996: 218).

The architecture at Monte Albán also recalls Teotihuacán's *talud-tablero* motif, except that the tablero frame only projects beyond the top and the sides of the projecting cornice, rather than surrounding the entire cornice as at Teotihuacán. Strict rectangular geometry pervades each architectural unit (pl. 8) containing a central patio, a pyramid on one side and a low platform on the other. The urban plan of the buildings facing the great central plaza is even more precisely aligned than at Teotihuacán, except for an earlier building that predated the rigid Classic alignment and may have had an astronomical orientation.

The ball game was by now a standard activity in every Mesoamerican city, embodying the belief that men should sacrifice their blood and

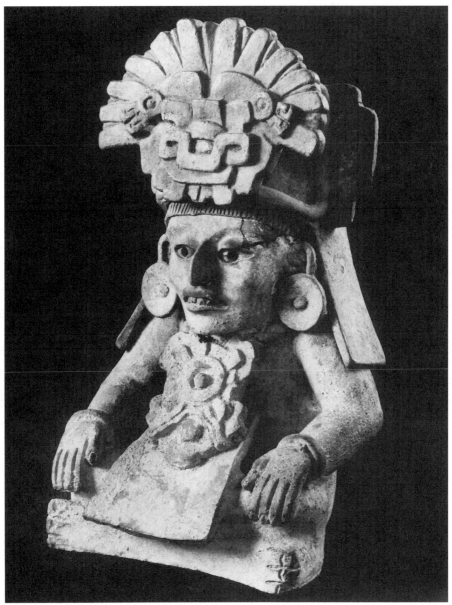

FIG. 3.21. Monte Albán, Oaxaca, Mexico. Zapotec. "Companion" urn of seated male, white-slipped gray pottery, 18⅞" high. Early Classic, A.D. 300–500. Gainesville, Fla.: Harn Museum of Art, C–80–12, gift of Mrs. A. H. Spivack in memory of Dr. A. H. Spivack. Photo courtesy of museum.

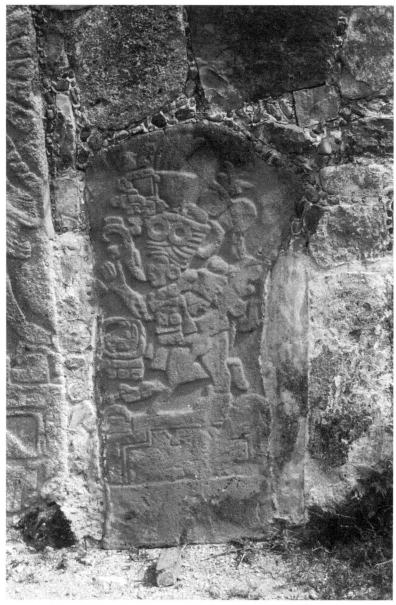

FIG. 3.22. Monte Albán, Oaxaca, Mexico. Stela 4 of man named 8 Deer, carved stone, 73¼" total height (49¼" carved visible portion) x 29½" wide. Early Classic, A.D. 300–500. Concrete cast in situ of original now in Museo Nacional de Antropología, Mexico City. Photo by John F. Scott.

even lives to maintain the rhythm of the cosmos as symbolized by the moving ball. At Monte Albán, in a corner off the main plaza, a rectangular ball court (fig. 3.23) provides the vertical and sloping surfaces against which the rubber ball was deflected after being hit by a player. Where the court widens at the open ends on either side of the parallel sloped sides, the ball would be out of play. Spectators would only incidentally be allowed to watch standing on top of adjoining architecture; the sloped area which looks like bleachers now was originally stuccoed to make a pair of smooth planes inclined toward the central court.

VERACRUZ, MEXICO: ABOUT A.D. 500–1000

More is known about the ball game in the Gulf Coast of Mesoamerica, probably its place of origin. On one of the numerous ball courts at the capital city of El Tajín, a series of reliefs clarifies the events connected with the game. One late rendering from Tajín's South Ball Court depicts the two adversaries facing each other within the court (fig. 3.24). They both wear thick belts to deflect the hard rubber ball and a projecting protector for the abdomen, although this apparatus is too tall to be functional. This latter feature is traditionally called a *palma* or palmate stone because of its upward flaring palm-leaf shape, whereas stone belts have been dubbed yokes because of their shape. Many early versions of these belts (fig. 3.25) show high-relief carving in the image of a great toad, a manifestation of the earth monster. This mythical Mesoamerican creature captured the sun when it sank into the underworld (set in the west), the place of the dead. Men played the ball game to revive the sun from the underworld through their blood sacrifice, as the gods

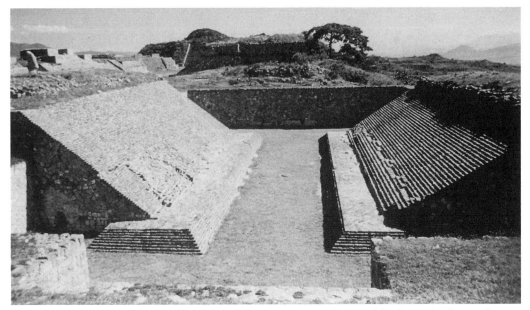

FIG. 3.23. Monte Albán, Oaxaca, Mexico. Ball court, cut stone originally smoothly plastered and painted, 134½' long. Middle Classic, A.D. 500–700. Photo by Carl Feiss, courtesy of Visual Resources Center, University of Florida.

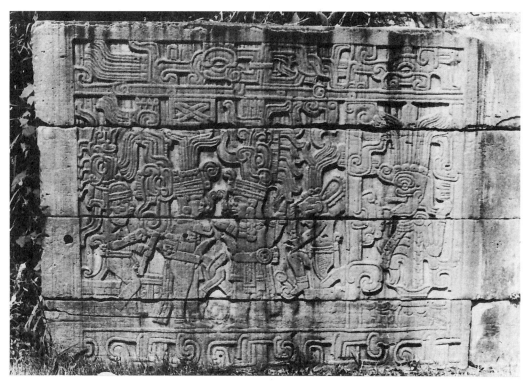

FIG. 3.24. El Tajín, Veracruz, Mexico. South Ball Court scene, low relief on cut stone blocks, 61½" high x 78" long. In situ. Late Classic, A.D. 750–900. Photo by John F. Scott.

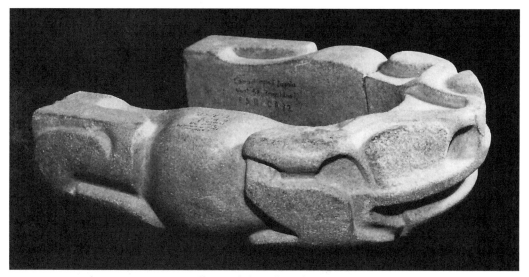

FIG. 3.25. Carrizal, Veracruz, Mexico. Ball game belt with toad motif in high relief, stone with red cinnabar pigment, 16" long x 15⅜" wide. Protoclassic, 100 B.C.-A.D. 200. Jalapa: Museo de Antropología de la Universidad Veracruzana. Photo by John F. Scott.

themselves had done at Teotihuacán to revive the cosmos in its present creation. In the ball game, the blood was shed by the sacrificed player, who is shown with his heart extracted in another panel of the South Ball Court relief.

The design of the Pyramid of the Niches in El Tajín reveals another aspect of the meaning of the pyramid structure so prevalent in Mesoamerica. There are 365 niches recessed into four façades of this central pyramid (fig. 3.26), including those underneath a staircase added later. Such numbers suggest that the pyramid correlates the solar year with the four cardinal directions of the world. Later Mesoamerican ritual books sometimes include a drawing showing the cosmos divided into four quadrants, with a continuous outline around the quadrants which could fold into a truncated pyramid if it were cut out. This outline is marked with 260 dots, correlating with the number of days in a complete cycle of the ritual calendar. Therefore the organization of both time and space is contained in the symbolism of the pyramid. Thus, it is not surprising that versions of this shape were built throughout Mesoamerica.

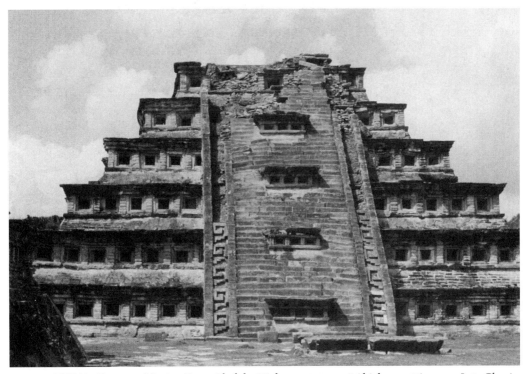

FIG. 3.26. El Tajín, Veracruz, Mexico. Pyramid of the Niches, cut stone, 62' high x 115¾' square. Late Classic, A.D. 600–900. Photo by John F. Scott.

Farther south, the Gulf Coast produced a wide variety of ceramic sculptures during the Classic period, including some of nearly life-size human figures, recalling similar finds in ancient China of the third century B.C.. An important example of this "monumental ware" (fig. 3.27), excavated at Cerro de las Mesas, represents the Old Fire God we have already seen at Teotihuacán, although braziers from the latter site are larger and of stone. Unlike the hollow, geometric abstraction of the

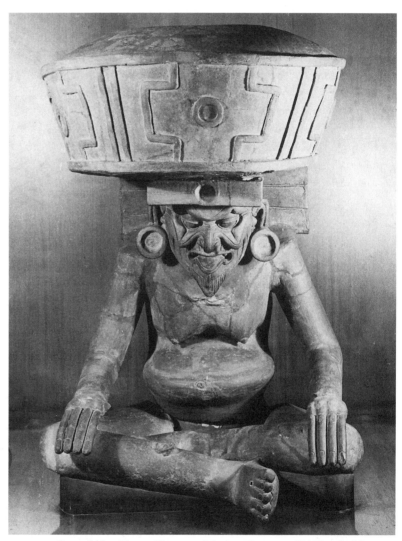

FIG. 3.27. Cerro de las Mesas, Veracruz, Mexico. Two-part Old Fire God brazier, ceramic with pink paint, 33" high. Early Classic, A.D. 300–600. Mexico City: Museo Nacional de Antropología, 4–1887. Photo courtesy of Instituto Nacional de Antropología e Historia.

Teotihuacán brazier, the figure from Cerro de las Mesas is much more naturalistic, with a fully rounded head and torso. His head supports the brazier, rather than merging with it. Buildings at Cerro de las Mesas, although made of clay and not well preserved, have a *talud-tablero* profile similar to those at Teotihuacán.

MAYA, GUATEMALA-BELIZE AND NEIGHBORING MEXICO AND HONDURAS: ABOUT A.D. 250–830

An additional insight into the meaning of the pyramid comes from the Late Classic Maya culture. The most important city-states during the height of the Classic were correlated with the cardinal cosmic directions (Marcus 1976: 19): Tikal (now in Guatemala), Copán (Honduras), and Palenque and Calakmul (both now part of Mexico). At least two pyramids—the Temple of Inscriptions at Palenque and the Temple of the Giant Jaguar at Tikal—were constructed to house the tomb of a major king. The pyramid supporting the Temple of the Giant Jaguar at Tikal (fig. 3.28), erected over the tomb of King Ah Cacau, has nine levels, appropriate to its function as a burial monument since Mesoamericans believed the underworld had nine levels. Therefore the pyramid not only represents the four directions of this world but also the continuity between this earthly world and the next. The king clearly was considered more than an ordinary mortal; in life he was watched over by the gods, and in death he became one of them. His permanent stone temple on top of the pyramid therefore housed the cult of the now divine king. A sapote wood lintel spanning the doorway into the inner chamber of the temple (fig. 3.29) shows a profile view of the ruler seated on a throne. He wears a headdress of overlapping feathers surrounding the face of the sun god (with its distinctive large "god eye" with a pupil placed cross-eyed). The throne itself has a jaguar pelt behind the intertwined mat and a pendant human head which faces us. Behind the seated king rears a giant jaguar, fanged mouth agape and claws outstretched, acting as the protector of the royal personage. Since Olmec times, the jaguar has been the totem of royal lineages; only royalty may wear its pelt. On the right, a more simply dressed man with dwarf proportions stands in service in front of his lord. Stylistically the figures display the fluid naturalism of Late Classic Maya art: a true profile view with correct proportions and lifelike curvature of the arms and legs (the only body parts not obscured by the heavy layers of jade ornament). Glyphs place this event on the day corresponding to 4 February 704 in the Christian calendar.

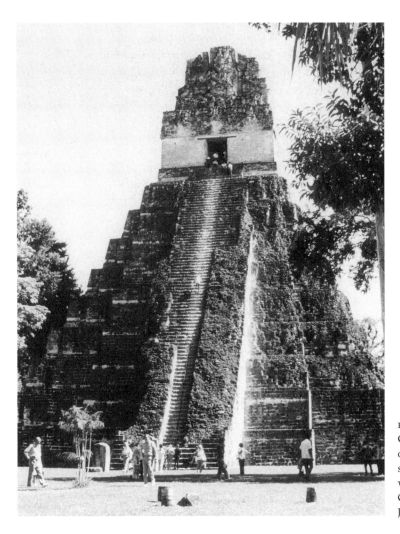

FIG. 3.28. Tikal, Petén, Guatemala. Maya. Temple of the Giant Jaguar (#I), cut stone originally covered with painted stucco. Late Classic, A.D. 731. Photo by John F. Scott.

The Maya obviously placed great emphasis on their rulers, although none of these rulers reigned over a state as large as that of Teotihuacán. This emphasis found expression not only in architectural monuments related to the king, but also in carved portrayals of the royal family. Following a tradition begun during the Olmec expansion and continuing in the Late Formative, the Maya erected vertical stone monuments called stelae that depicted the ruler with his protective deities, often represented in animal form. An Early Classic example from Tikal represents the frontal portrait of a king known as Curl Nose (fig. 3.30) at the time of his succession to the throne on 13 September 379. In unmodulated low relief with little detailing, his squarish proportions, shell necklace, headdress with stiff parallel rows of feathers, and frontal

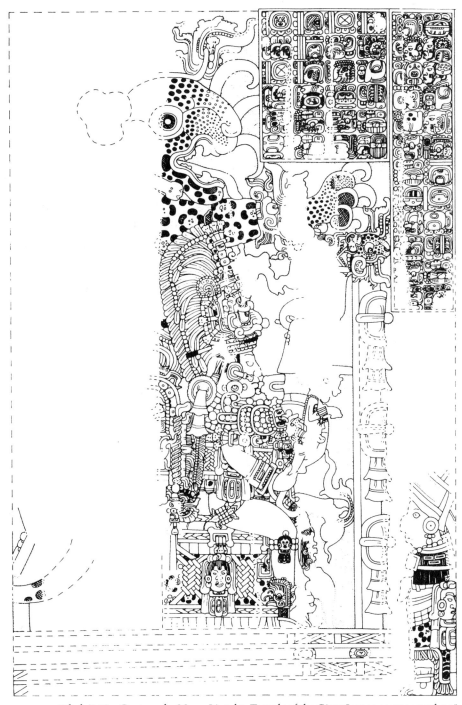

FIG. 3.29. Tikal, Petén, Guatemala. Maya. Lintel 3, Temple of the Giant Jaguar, sapote wood, 72″ long. Late Classic, A.D. 704. Drawing after Christopher Jones, University Museum, Philadelphia, Pa.

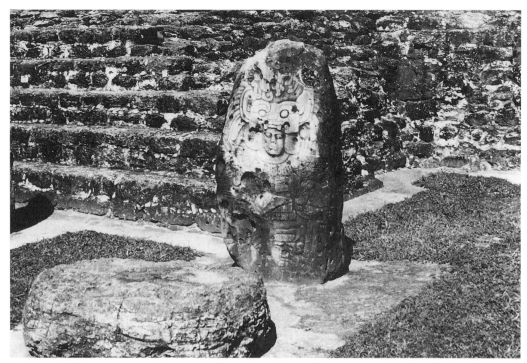

FIG. 3.30. Tikal, Petén, Guatemala. Maya. Stela 4, King Curl Nose, limestone, 61¾" high, with stone altar. Early Classic, A.D. 379. In situ. Photo by John F. Scott.

position recall the Teotihuacán style, especially as rendered in stuccoed vases that were traded into the Maya area. Dating to the Middle Classic period, a small platform behind the Temple of the Giant Jaguar has the *talud-tablero* profile and doughnut-shaped circles symbolizing greenstone (fig. 3.31), indicating the direct Teotihuacán influence in Tikal during this Middle Classic period.

Yet the Maya continued their own style, even while copying some Mexican designs. In the Late Classic, this style develops into the most elegantly naturalistic in all Pre-Columbian art. Its fluidity can be seen in the few remaining frescoes in palaces and on polychrome painted vases placed in tombs of the elite. A vase, in such fine condition that it must be from a tomb, shows the son of the ruler of the city of Ik' (modern Motul de San José, Guatemala) seated on a throne addressing two visitors (not fully visible in this photograph) sitting on the floor in front of him (fig. 3.32). Food was offered in pottery dishes such as this one, inscribed and ultimately placed in tombs. The scene takes place inside a palace supported with broad piers with masks hung from their tops. Painted around the top border of the cylinder vase, in a fluid form of the syllabic script unique to the Classic Maya, is the Primary Standard Sequence, a series of phrases that describe the making and dedication of the vessel. The artist's name, unfortunately illegible, appears behind the ruler. No other Pre-Columbian culture developed a complete writing system: the contemporary Mexican cultures could write proper names and dates but did not express complete thoughts, and no South American culture presents unambiguous evidence for any writing.

The only complete cycle of frescoes in Classic Maya comes from the three-room reception palace at Bonampak, a small city in southern Mexico. In the first room, one first sees the royal males dancing in the lower register, just above the raised platform where the actual nobles were entertained. In the middle register, an assemblage of standing

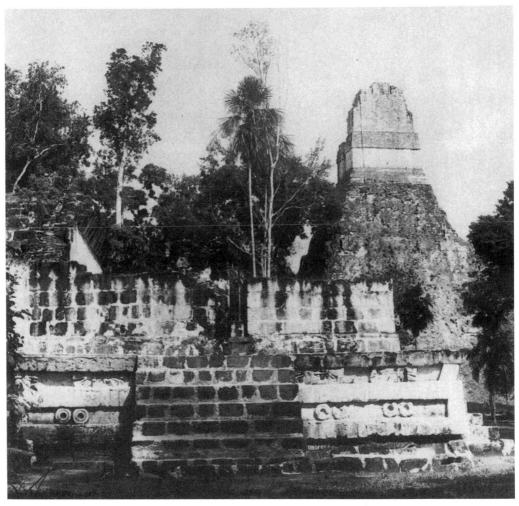

FIG. 3.31. Tikal, Petén, Guatemala. Maya. Structure 5D-43 with Teotihuacanoid *talud-tablero* profile, Middle Classic, A.D. 450-700. Photo by Roy C. Craven, Jr., courtesy of Center for Latin American Studies, University of Florida.

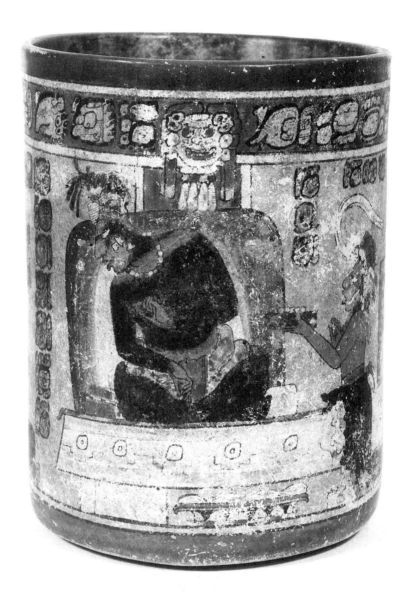

FIG. 3.32. Motul de San José region, Petén, Guatemala. Maya. Vase, poly-chromed pottery, 8" high x 6½" diam. Late Classic, A.D. eighth century. Washington: Dumbarton Oaks Research Library and Collections, B-564.68.MAP. Photo courtesy of Dumbarton Oaks Research Library and Collections, Washington, D.C.

nobles discuss the small heir to the throne being presented to them on the right by a servant, who turns back to look at his lord (pl. 9). The adjoining wall, triangular in shape because of the corbeled vaulting framing it, contains the royal family on a large, four-legged throne. In the center of the throne, the lord Chaan-Muan sits cross-legged and leans commandingly forward, his intense gaze riveting the servant across the angle of the interior wall corner. Behind him, a matronly woman of his family is rendered in a true profile with a beautiful fluid line, as is a more slender and probably junior royal woman standing on the ground to her left rear. Her body overlaps the throne, creating some illusion of depth in space. No indication of modeling of the bodies is shown, although fluid, sometimes transparent draperies suggest their roundedness. The shallow illusion of this family scene is far exceeded by the crowded battle scene in the second room and the rituals performed on tiered pyramids rendered both in the judgment scene in Room 2, dated 2 August 792, and the ritual dance in Room 3 (Miller 1996: 160–161).

At the western Maya site of Palenque, the Pyramid of the Inscriptions was named for its extensive hieroglyphic texts which refer to the exploits of the lord buried below. His tomb is reached by a hidden staircase encased in a tunnel with thirteen corbeled arches forming the passageway. Thirteen in Mesoamerica refers to the number of layers in the heavenly upperworld, suggesting that the king would ascend to the uppermost heaven after his burial. On the piers surrounding the entrances to the temple on top of the nine-level pyramid, fine low-relief sculptures executed in stucco render figures such as King Pacal II, the occupant of the tomb, presenting his royal child (fig. 3.33), who will succeed him according to the laws of dynastic primogeniture (Greene 1983: 38). Originally painted in light reddish flesh tones that contrast with the divine blue tone used for serpents, jade, and feathers, and the underworld yellow of jaguars, the figures show realistic detail which permits the individuals to be identified: the six-toed human foot of the child identifies him as Chan-Bahlum; his other leg turns into a serpent, indicating his supernatural attributes (Schele and Freidel 1990: 236).

Below, carved in relief on the sarcophagus lid in Pacal's mortuary crypt, the dead king falls into the jaws of the underworld monster (fig. 3.34), the same creature who devours the ball symbolizing the sinking sun in Veracruz art (see fig. 3.25). Life grows from the body of the dead king in the form of a mythic world tree whose blooms are celestial serpent heads. The carvings on the sides of the sarcophagus testify to the ancestors of Pacal, now immortals themselves. Underneath the

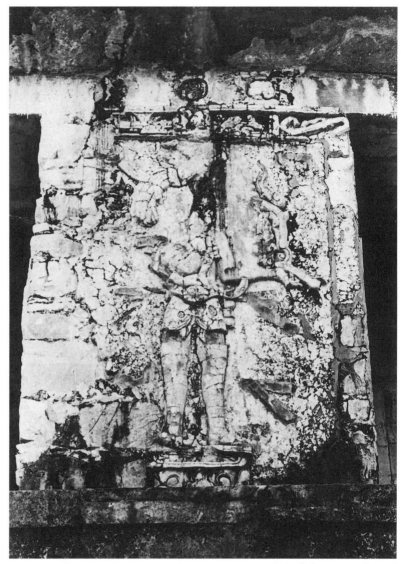

FIG. 3.33. Palenque, Chiapas, Mexico. Maya. Remains of relief of King Pacal II and Prince Chan-Bahlum, Pier B, Temple of Inscriptions, stucco pier, life-size figure on 105¼" high x 65¾" wide frame. In situ. Late Classic, A.D. 683. Photo by Roy C. Craven, Jr., courtesy of Center for Latin American Studies, University of Florida.

sarcophagus lay two plaster heads, once thought to represent gods but now considered portraits, perhaps removed from architectural settings prior to sealing the tomb, like the reserve, or extra, heads in ancient Egypt. The one believed to represent the young Pacal (fig. 3.35) realistically portrays his facial structure, recognizable not only from his actual skull but also from many relief depictions of him. Western Maya

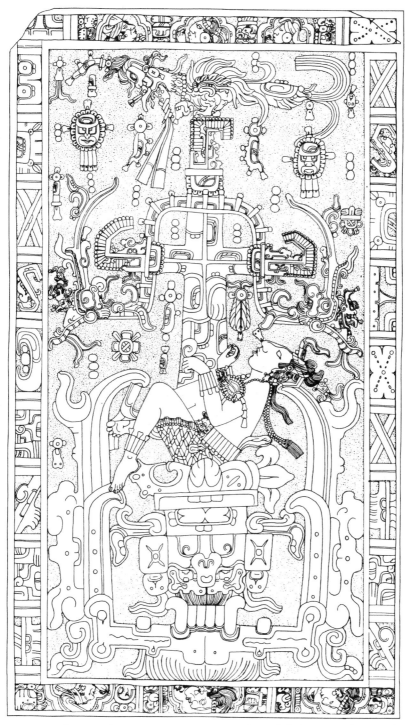

FIG. 3.34. Palenque, Chiapas, Mexico. Maya. Sarcophagus lid of King Pacal II, Temple of Inscriptions, stone, 146½" long x 86½" wide. Late Classic, A.D. 683. Drawing by Merle Greene Robertson, courtesy of Pre-Columbian Art Research Institute, San Francisco.

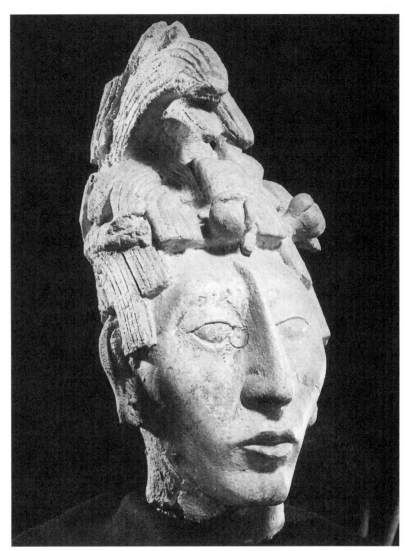

FIG. 3.35. Palenque, Chiapas, Mexico. Maya. Head of King Pacal II, Temple of Inscriptions crypt, stucco, 16⅞" high. Late Classic, A.D. 615–683. Mexico City: Museo Nacional de Antropología, 5–1031. Photo courtesy of Instituto Nacional de Antropología e Historia, Mexico.

royalty used a perishable material to artificially extend the line of their long noses up into the forehead, and this is visible on figure 3.35. The individuality achieved in royal portraits in the Classic period is similar to that attained by the Moche culture in Peru (see pl. 5). All the figures display a subtle flexibility and realistic attention to detail which characterize the outstanding works of early kingdoms during the Classic period throughout the Americas.

FOUR

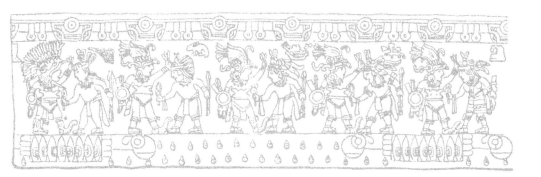

EMPIRES AND INTEGRATION

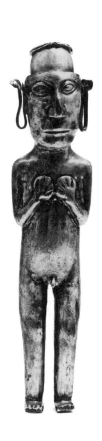

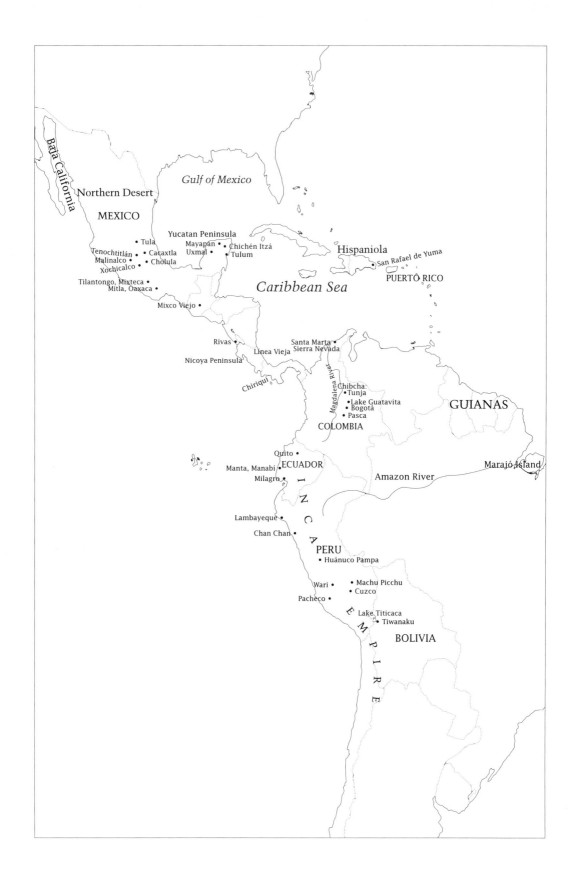

Baja California

Northern Desert

MEXICO

Gulf of Mexico

Yucatan Peninsula

• Tula
Tenochtitlán • Cacaxtla   Mayapán • • Chichén Itzá
Malinalco • • Cholula   Uxmal • • Tulum
Xochicalco •

Hispaniola

Caribbean Sea

• San Rafael de Yuma

PUERTO RICO

Tilantongo, Mixteca
Mitla, Oaxaca •

Mixco Viejo •

Rivas •   Santa Marta •
        Linea Vieja   Sierra Nevada

Nicoya Peninsula

Chiriquí •

Magdalena River

Chibcha
• Tunja
• Lake Guatavita
• Bogotá
• Pasca

COLOMBIA

GUIANAS

Quito •

Manta, Manabí •   ECUADOR

Milagro •

Amazon River

Marajó Island

I
N
C
A

Lambayeque •

Chan Chan •

PERU

• Huánuco Pampa

Wari •   • Machu Picchu
        • Cuzco
Pacheco •

E
M
P
I
R
E

Lake Titicaca
• Tiwanaku

BOLIVIA

IMPERIAL EXPANSION became a way of life for the states of Pre-Columbian America during the post-Classic era. The term "empire" refers to the state created as a result of conquest of other ethnic groups by a more powerful group. The empire therefore includes speakers of several languages. Usually the conquered groups kept their own ruling elite—even their kings—but they had to render tribute to the emperor of the conquering group and permit garrisons of soldiers and traders in their midst. During the Formative and the Classic periods, one ethnic group certainly conquered another, although this usually did not create a condition of permanent subjugation but rather a tributary status. Significantly, post-Classic artists became obsessed with the subjects of warfare and conquest, although both topics had certainly been treated before (see, for example, fig. 3.4). The Classic-period focus on religious and naturalistic subject matter was replaced by more realistic depictions of specific individuals and battles, although the Maya and the Moche had already inaugurated these two themes. Expressions of beauty were replaced by expressions of power. Even nonempires, polities quite small in scope, especially in the Intermediate Area (the region between Mesoamerica and the Central Andes), created similar images of military power. Architecturally, emphasis on religious structures gave way to construction of palaces and fortifications that expressed their defensive nature even when military attack was unlikely or inconceivable.

Here we will refer to this period as that of Integration because its major empires imposed a visual artistic unity throughout their domain, which then was reflected in adjoining areas. Although individual ethnic groups usually retained their own identity under the empire, the conquerors' garrisons of soldiers and sometimes even colonial settlements brought a far more pervasive influence to the conquered provinces than did the earlier trade networks. The beginning of the Integration period varies from region to region, starting about A.D. 600 in the Andes and in Ecuador and after A.D. 800 in lower Central America and Mesoamerica. The Integration period ends with the European conquest that spanned A.D. 1492 to 1538 in the major high-culture areas. In these areas, this period is known as the historic era because Spanish chroniclers documented what they saw and recorded native oral histories.

TOLTEC NAHUA, MEXICO: ABOUT A.D. 750–1150

The legendary history of the people later known as the Toltec emphasizes their emergence from a cave, their rude beginnings as nomadic hunters in the northern Mexican deserts, their conquest of civilized

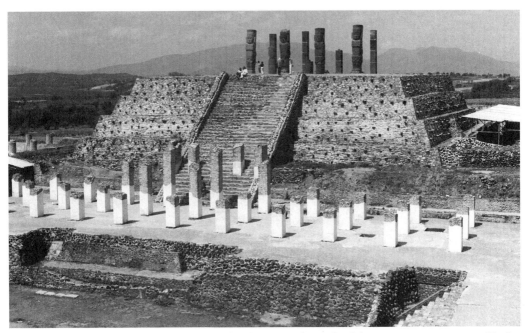

FIG. 4.1. Tula, Hidalgo, Mexico. Toltec. Pyramid and remains of Temple of the Morning Star, cut stone blocks, 131' wide. Integration, Early post-Classic, ca. A.D. 900–1000. Photo by John F. Scott.

peoples of central Mexico, and their triumph as a military state. Northwestern Mexico and the southwestern United States are the homeland of the Uto-Aztecan speakers, the southern branch of which is Nahua, the language of the Toltecs and the Aztecs. Many of the historic speakers of languages in this group remained nomadic until this century.

The city of Tula, located on the northern periphery of Mesoamerica, was not originally recognized as the capital of the legendary Toltecs because it had an unimposing, crudely constructed ceremonial center. It seemed an unprepossessing, provincial site, although much of its urban extent remained unrecognized because it was composed of low, secular structures. Its rapid growth between A.D. 750 and 950 (Diehl 1983: 48) follows the fall of Teotihuacán, the dominant site in that area during most of the Classic. The Toltecs may well have been partially responsible for Teotihuacán's fall. Its history parallels the pattern of Old World empires where a barbarian people first conquer and destroy the settled kingdoms, then emulate and absorb those kingdoms' cultures.

The best restored building at Tula is the Temple of the Morning Star (fig. 4.1). Its colonnade, a typical post-Classic feature, controls access to the pyramid's stairs. The stone columns supporting the temple roof, which would have been made of perishable materials, represent standing male figures, both in relief or in three-dimensions. Most figures are dressed like warriors. Each of the great columns in the first row of the temple is composed of four giant stone drums. These figures have the architectonic massiveness already seen in the sculptures of Teotihuacán (see fig. 3.20), but they are secular figures which subserviently supported the now-missing roof of the religious structure. The Tula column figures carry spearthrowers, the characteristic weapon of northern hunters, and hold bags in their other hands.

The low-relief carved slabs still surfacing a side and back of the temple (fig. 4.2) depict a procession of felines interspersed with a few coyotes on half the rows and eagles plucking at hearts on the intervening rows. At least two of these animals (eagles and jaguars) undoubtedly symbolize the same military orders later known among the Aztecs, who adopted many Toltec traits. Recessed within the eagle panels are frontal images of a skeletal human face in the open jaws of the earth monster. According to traditional interpretation, this image refers to the reemergence of the planet Venus as the "morning star" in the dawn sky after a period of invisibility below the horizon, symbolizing death and resurrection in Mesoamerica.

The carving style is coarse, abruptly changing from the plane of the animals to the sunken plane of the background. Details are simplified

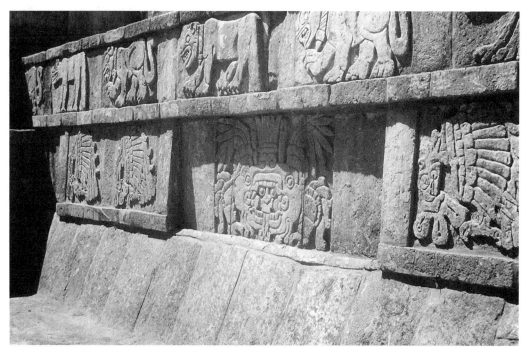

FIG. 4.2. Tula, Hidalgo, Mexico. Toltec. Processional Wall of Coyotes and Jaguars behind Temple of the Morning Star, stone, 25¼" high x 28" wide blocks. Integration, Early post-Classic, A.D. 900–1100. Photo courtesy of Visual Resources Center, University of Florida.

and heavy, typical of the lack of subtlety often found among newly civilized barbarians like the Hittites in the ancient Near East, who also adopted older styles of established civilizations. The Toltecs borrowed the style of Teotihuacán and other Mesoamerican cultures, including some aspects of the Maya. Emphasizing the rapacious nature of the animals rather than their beauty or grace, the style conveys the military brutality that the empire wished its soldiers to possess. Imperial scenes often render processions of unswerving servants of the empire bearing down on its enemies. Insistent repetition hammers home the message through quantity, not quality. Like the warrior columns that support the temple, these aggressive animals protect not a military but a religious structure through their menacing presence. Although most early kingdoms integrate political and religious power, the militarism of Mesoamerica is specifically related to "divine war," in which captives were taken to provide blood sacrifice to nourish their celestial gods.

Adjoining the temple at Tula, columned palace halls with central open patios—possibly meeting centers without living chambers (Diehl 1983: 65)—have numerous wide benches along the walls decorated with reliefs showing processions of feather-garbed male warriors. Sculptures in the round placed in front of altars depict a supine male figure with knees drawn up and raised head turned to the left; the container on his abdomen received sacrifices (fig. 4.3). The angular design and architectural qualities of this figure certainly recall the earlier Teotihuacán style, but the coarse execution and pockmarked vol-

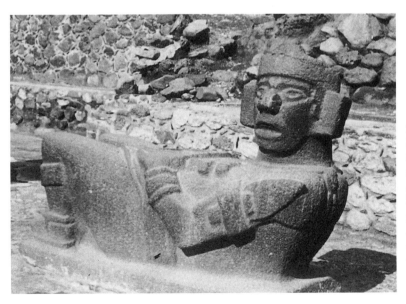

FIG. 4.3. Tula, Hidalgo, Mexico. Toltec. Chacmool from Burnt Palace, stone, 32" high x 43" long. Integration, Early post-Classic, A.D. 900–1100. Tula: Acosta Archaeological Museum. Photo courtesy of Visual Resources Center, University of Florida.

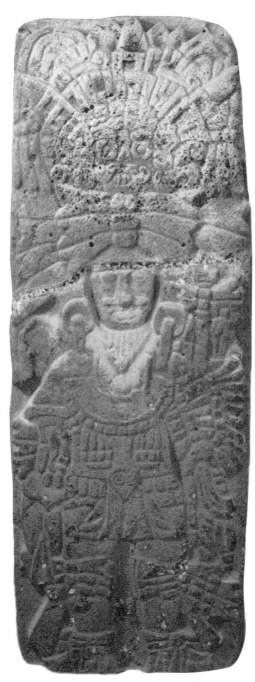

FIG. 4.4. Tula, Hidalgo, Mexico. Toltec. Stela 1, frontal ruler, stone, 72" high. Integration, Early post-Classic, ca. A.D. 900. Tula: Acosta Archaeological Museum. Photo by John F. Scott.

canic stone communicate a new brutality. Colors at Tula are often applied directly on the stone rather than on a smooth surface of stucco, as had been typical of Classic sculpture and architecture.

The kings of Tula are known through often contradictory legends which share only a few names in their dynastic lists of the Toltec rulers (Adams 1991: 273). A stone stela of what may be a ruler (fig. 4.4) shows a single frontal figure wearing a splay of feathers, rendered in a position borrowed from the Early Classic Maya (see fig. 3.30) but without the glyphs by which Maya stelae were identified and dated. Of the known rulers, the most important is 1 Reed Topiltzin Quetzalcoatl, whose last name is that of the feathered-serpent god. The "1 Reed" in his name refers to the day of his birth in the ritual calendar, since both gods and mortals have birthdays in that 260-day cycle. Topiltzin refers to the historic individual who inaugurated an era of peace and cultural flowering. Conflicts with a more militaristic faction led to the expulsion of Topiltzin Quetzalcoatl and his followers to the east, from where, by one account, he sailed east across the Gulf of Mexico on a raft of serpents.

TOLTEC MAYA, MEXICO: ABOUT A.D. 900–1200

Across the Gulf, directly east of Veracruz, lies the Yucatán Peninsula, the center of Maya culture after the collapse of the cities of the central Maya realm because of ecological stress and warfare. At the end of the Classic, already in the period here called Integration, the population had abandoned their cities in the tropical rain forests and migrated to the more arid north of the Yucatán Peninsula, swelling the population of secular cities that had existed in this area on a smaller scale for a thousand years. The increased population, undoubtedly including fine craftsmen from the old ruling elite further south, triggered the florescence of the northern Yucatec Maya. The capital of the area was Uxmal, ruled over by Lord Chac-Uinal-Kan around A.D. 900 (Kowalski 1987: 72). His major palace, today known as the Palace of the Governor (fig. 4.5), sits on an artificial mound opposite a smaller platform holding a throne in the form of two jaguars with torsos joined at the middle, a type known from Classic Maya paintings and relief sculptures. Thirteen openings in the palace wall, of which six can be seen in figure 4.5, relate this building to the sacred number of heavens in Mesoamerican belief. The façade is composed of a long central section and two flanking side sections, separated by recessed corbeled arches, structural features previously restricted to Maya interior supports. Inside, following Classic Maya tradition, space is created by paired corbeled vaults, each stone of which projects further toward the center of the space. On the exterior, above the cornice area where the corbeled vaults are hidden, an elaborate block mosaic of cut stone enriches the entire upper façade. Its stepped designs of long-nosed masks refer to both the serpent, who symbolized royal authority, and the Maya rain god Chac, who has the same name as the lord who built the palace. In the center, Lord Chac sits in a crescent which ascends to heaven on an inverted wedge of

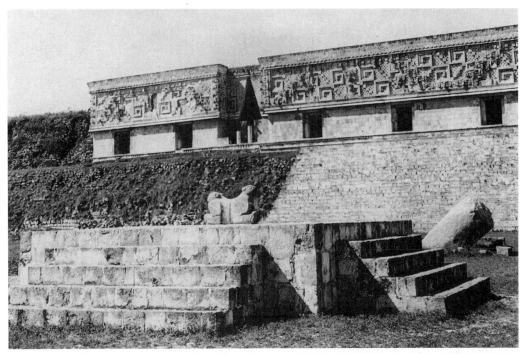

FIG. 4.5. Uxmal, Yucatán, Mexico. Palace of the Governor façade, cut limestone, with platform in front supporting stone double-headed jaguar throne. Integration, Terminal Classic, ca. A.D. 906. Photo by Roy C. Craven, Jr., courtesy of Center for Latin American Studies, University of Florida.

celestial serpent bars, symbols of rulership in Classic Maya iconography. At one time, high-relief portraits of the rulers, seated on thrones or cushions, also projected from the façade. Atypical of the Classic Maya style, however, are the stiff geometry of the three-dimensional sculpture of the figures and the lack of elegance; these features already reflect the impact of highland Mexican art.

About the time when Topiltzin Quetzalcoatl was reputed to have left Tula and sailed to the east (A.D. 899, by one correlation), the city of Chichén Itzá expanded by building a northern complex which controlled access to the sacred "well," a large natural limestone sinkhole into which numerous offerings (like fig. 4.6) were thrown over a long period of time. Several aspects of this new area of the city show stylistic similarities to designs at Tula. Numerous examples of the supine figure, called "chacmool" in Maya (fig. 4.7), are in positions identical to those at Tula (see fig. 4.3) but are executed in limestone with smoother, more finished surfaces, more angular knees, and more attention to detail, giving these Maya chacmools the illusion of larger scale and greater presence. They may be three-dimensional translations of earlier two-dimensional supine captives shown being trod upon by rulers in late Classic Maya stelae (Miller 1985: 14). Similarly, the processions carved in low relief along the base of many benches at Chichén Itzá are

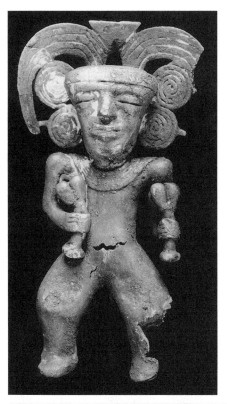

FIG. 4.6. Chichén Itzá, Yucatán, Mexico. Coclé-style figurine pendant, cast *tumbaga* (copper and gold alloy), 2⅞" high. Integration, Early post-Classic, A.D. 800–1200. Cambridge, Mass.: Peabody Museum—Harvard University, 10–71–20/C7694. Photo by Hillel Burger, courtesy of museum.

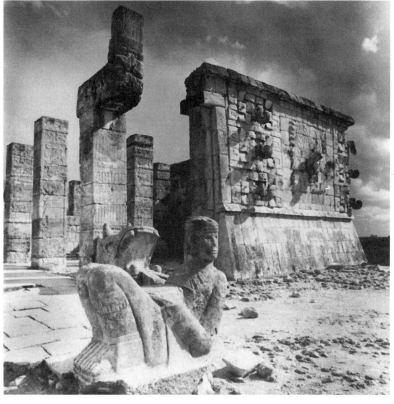

FIG. 4.7. Chichén Itzá, Yucatán, Mexico. Chacmool in front of Temple of the Warriors, stone, 42" high. Integration, Early post-Classic, A.D. 900–1200. Photo by Roy C. Craven, Jr., courtesy of Center for Latin American Studies, University of Florida.

far more skillfully rendered than those at Tula. Different platforms at
Chichén Itzá with stairs on their four equal sides include reliefs presenting eagles tearing at hearts, a frontal anthropomorphic face appearing in the jaws of the earth monster, and a seated (not striding) jaguar,
all creatures that appear together in the wall reliefs at Tula.

The massing and proportions of the Temple of the Warriors at Chichén Itzá (fig. 4.8) are so close to those of the Temple of the Morning
Star at Tula (see fig. 4.1) that one must have been consciously copied
from the other. They both have a rectangular plan, a single wide staircase with a colonnade in front, four stepped stages, and a columned
temple on the top. Inverted serpent columns supporting the main lintel
over the entrance of the Temple of the Warriors correspond to column
drums remaining at Tula. Interior rectangular columns in both structures have low-relief representations of striding warriors, many with
the distinctive horizontal nose bar of military leaders. Full-round male
figures serve as small supporting legs for the platform in the rear of
the Temple of the Warriors; larger ones in the older section of Chichén
Itzá, resembling the colossal Toltec figures, support a lintel with an
inscribed date in the year 879, corresponding quite closely to the pro-
posed time of arrival of Topiltzin Quetzalcoatl in the Yucatán. About
this time the Maya absorbed the god Quetzalcoatl into their pantheon
under the name of Kukulkan.

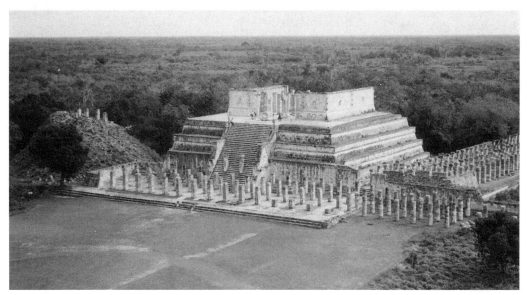

FIG. 4.8. Chichén Itzá, Yucatán, Mexico. Temple of the Warriors on four-tiered pyramid, cut stone. Integration,
Early post-Classic, A.D. 889–1100. Photo by Carl Feiss, courtesy of Visual Resources Center, University of
Florida.

The strong Toltec character of these features at Chichén Itzá and their lack of similarity to features at other contemporary Yucatan sites suggest that the influence came from central Mexico to the Maya. Many Maya features, however, were introduced into central Mexico toward the end of the Classic era, after the fall of Teotihuacán, and can be seen clearly at highland central Mexican sites such as Xochicalco and Cacaxtla. There was significant interaction between the Maya and the central Mexicans during the late first millennium, yet it is doubtful that either conquered the other. A strong Toltec presence at Chichén Itzá is undeniable, as is a greater militarism associated with an imperial state. This militarism is expressed in numerous battle scenes rendered in painted low relief and in fresco. An extensive cycle from the interior walls of the Temple of the Jaguars overlooking the Great Ball Court (largest in the Americas) represents the Toltec conquest of the Maya couched in celestial symbolism (Coggins 1984: 157). One fresco shows a raging battle underway outside a town composed of small thatched huts (fig. 4.9) of the kind still built by modern Maya of the Yucatán. The panorama rendered here is much more expansive than battle scenes depicted in the Classic period, even the Maya fresco in Room 2 at Bonampak; warriors carrying spears and shields advance in chevron diagonals peaking toward the center of the composition, where they punch into the enemy village. The Toltec prince Quetzalcoatl and his father Mixcoatl enter the fray from the upper right side, dressed in especially elaborate gear. Some slight overlapping helps depict depth in the scene, although, as in all Pre-Columbian art, the size of the figures and the brightness of color are undiminished in objects lying further back in the illusionistic scene; rather, the battle is conceived like a war map, with all the objects placed as if viewed from above yet individually rendered in side profile. The grandeur of the battle expresses the breadth of conquests achieved by the Integration empires and implies that the earthly victory is a reflection of heavenly power.

MIXTEC, MEXICO: AROUND A.D. 1200–1400

In the middle of its post-Classic period, Mesoamerica became divided into a number of minor states, each feuding and/or allying with the others. The Maya broke into small polities, loosely united in the Yucatan under the League of Mayapán (1224–1461). But the rubble stone walls that surrounded many of their cities, including Mayapán, the capital city of that league, emphasize the degree to which those states felt threatened. The same situation existed in the highland Maya area, as seen by the defensive hilltop city of Mixco Viejo in Guatemala, the

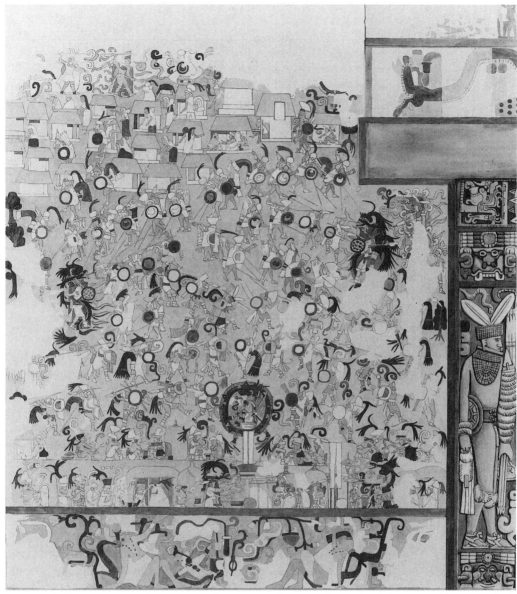

FIG. 4.9. Chichén Itzá, Yucatán, Mexico. Battle scene, southwest wall, Temple of the Jaguars, fresco, 131" high x 107" wide. Integration, Early post-Classic, A.D. 900–1200. Painted rendering by Adela Breton, 1904–1906. Cambridge, Mass.: Peabody Museum—Harvard University. Photo by Hillel Burger, courtesy of museum.

capital of the Quiché Maya, whose version of their history, called the *Popul Vuh*, is the most complete account of Maya mythology known to have survived the Conquest. Further north, in the mountainous state of Oaxaca, the Mixtec-speaking cities formed numerous competing kingdoms, each proudly proclaiming its royal lineage in accordion-paged screenfold manuscripts executed by painting on continuous strips of smooth plaster-covered deer hide folded horizontally into rectangular pages. The content of these manuscripts was primarily genealogical, recording who married whom and begat which heir. Major battles and treaties are also dated and their participants named. One page in the finest Mixtec genealogical manuscript, the Codex Zouche-Nuttall (pl. 11), shows their greatest king, named by glyphs as 8 Deer Tiger Claw, receiving the horizontal nose bar designating him as a lord. This event probably took place in 1052 in the imperial city of Tula; only the emperor of the Toltecs was grand enough to bestow this honor upon the Mixtec king. In this manuscript the events are depicted in a right to left sequence, the reading order guided by red lines acting like fences. People's names and birth dates, the place names of towns conquered or allied with, and year dates when events took place, all are carefully recorded with glyphs next to the depictions to which they refer. The content of Mexican writing such as this is limited to such numbers and proper names; only the Maya could write full texts. Stylistically the figures are drawn with firm, even outlines bordering flat, bright colors; the figures are contained within an approximate square—slightly taller than square in the Zouche-Nuttall but squatter in later manuscripts. Appendages bristle out from the center, creating a very aggressive outline emphasized by sharp points.

This style was widely spread via similar manuscripts, mainly containing religious auguries and rituals. It also appeared in other contexts such as architectural reliefs, pottery, and fresco painting. Its heartland seems to be the area where the Mixtec lived (the "Mixteca" of western Oaxaca state) and the polyglot region in the southern half of Puebla, centering on the great religious center of Cholula, the main pyramid of which was enlarged during the post-Classic to become the most massive structure in all of the Americas. The style produced in this region is known as Mixteca-Puebla. It spread to the northwest Mexican frontier area on the mainland opposite the tip of the Baja California peninsula, and it expanded south throughout the Maya area and even into lower Central America.

A tripod vessel representing an eagle (pl. 10), symbolizing a warrior cult, embodies the high quality of Mixtec polychrome pottery. Its three elongated legs express the bristly quality noted in manuscript painting and seen here as well in the sharply painted details of the eagle. Although not as ferocious as its Toltec forebear (see fig. 4.2), the eagle expresses the same aggressiveness and intensity, but with a greater aesthetic skill consistent with its production in an older cultural center of Mesoamerica.

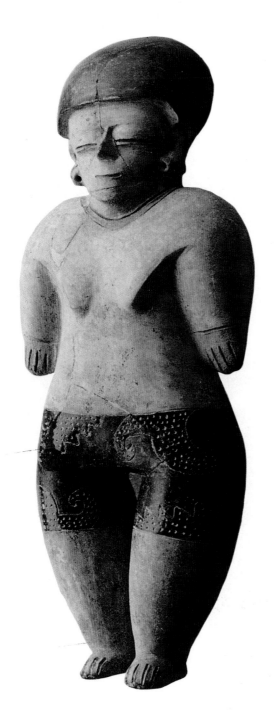

PLATE 1. Pinpicuasi, Manabí, Ecuador. Chorrera. Figure with closed eyes, hollow white-slipped ceramic with black and red paint and incisions, 16½" high. Formative, 1000–300 B.C. Guayaquil: Museo del Banco del Pacífico, Ch-115. Photo by John F. Scott.

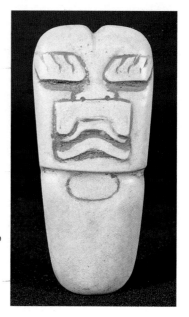

PLATE 2. La Venta, Tabasco, Mexico. Olmec. Axe head with everted-mouth jaguar, jade with red cinnabar pigment, 4¾" high. Middle Formative, 1000–600 B.C. Mexico City: Museo Nacional de Antropología, 13–435. Photo courtesy of Instituto Nacional de Antropología e Historia, Mexico.

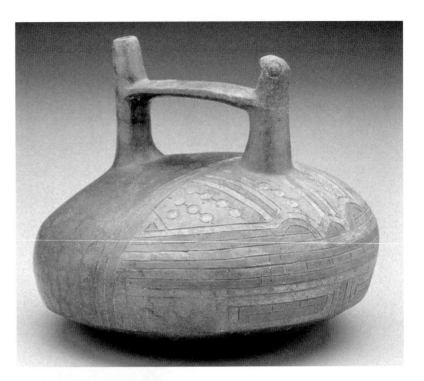

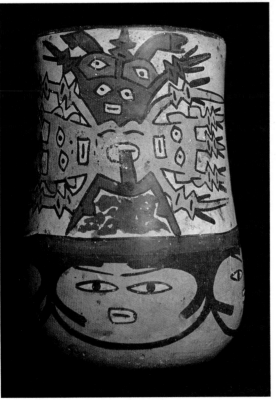

Above: PLATE 3. Ica Valley, Ica, Peru. Paracas. Bridge-handled double-spouted bottle with feline mask, negative painted orange pottery with traces of postfired red and white paints, 5¼" high x 6½" diameter. Formative, Early Horizon, ca. 500 B.C. Charlotte, N.C.: Mint Museum of Art, 94.106.69, gift of Dr. and Mrs. Francis Robicsek. Photo courtesy of museum.

Left: PLATE 4. Ica Department, Peru. Late Nazca. Vase with human heads painted around base, polychromed pottery, 5¼" high. Classic, Early Intermediate Period, A.D. 300–600. Gainesville: Collections of the Anthropology Department of the Florida Museum of Natural History, FLMNH 94750, gift of Mr. and Mrs. Francis Jack III. Color transparency by Kathryn Reed, courtesy of museum.

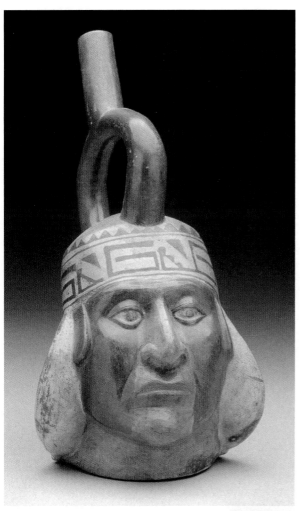

Left: PLATE 5. La Libertad, Peru. Moche. Stirrup-spout portrait jar, slipped pottery, 11⅞" high. Classic, Early Intermediate Period, A.D. 300–500. Charlotte, N.C.: Mint Museum of Art, 94.106.124, gift of Dr. and Mrs. Francis Robicsek. Photo courtesy of museum.

Below: PLATE 6. Recuay, Ancash, Peru. Spouted standing male effigy jar, negative black and red on cream pottery, 8" high. Classic, Early Intermediate Period, A.D. 300–600. Orlando, Fla.: Orlando Museum of Art, 80.93, gift of Howard Campbell, 1976. Photo courtesy of museum.

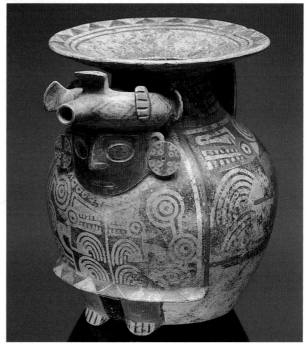

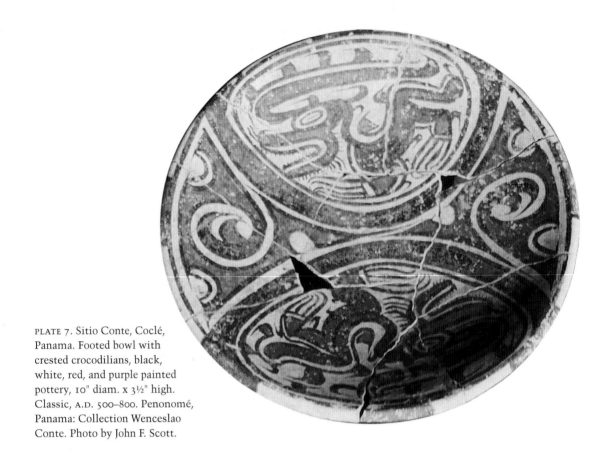

PLATE 7. Sitio Conte, Coclé, Panama. Footed bowl with crested crocodilians, black, white, red, and purple painted pottery, 10" diam. x 3½" high. Classic, A.D. 500–800. Penonomé, Panama: Collection Wenceslao Conte. Photo by John F. Scott.

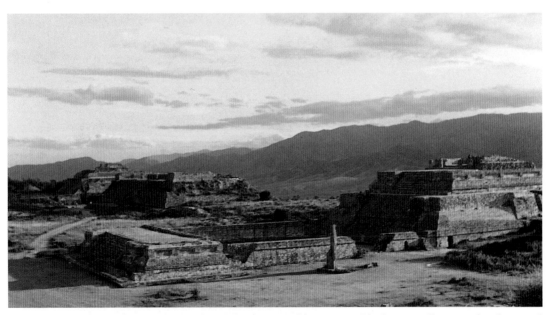

PLATE 8. Monte Albán, Oaxaca, Mexico. System IV plaza, roughly cut stone blocks originally covered with painted plaster, ca. 410' long. Middle Classic, A.D. 500–700. Photo by John F. Scott.

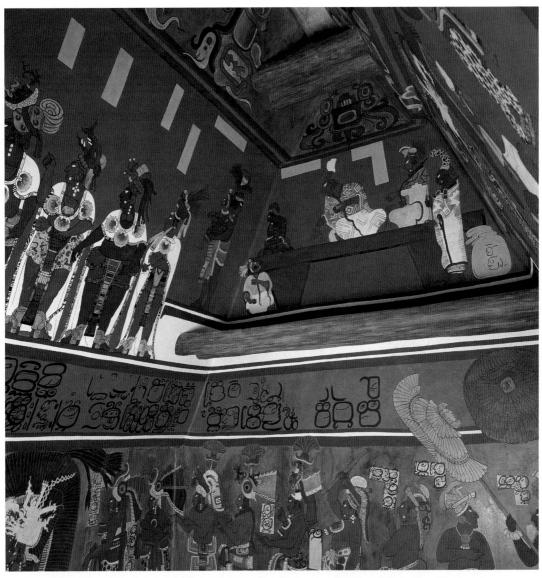

PLATE 9. Bonampak, Chiapas, Mexico. Maya. Room 1, detail of west end wall and vault. Late Classic, after A.D. 792. Reconstruction made by Felipe Dávalos at the Florida Museum of Natural History, Gainesville. Photo by Kathryn Reed, courtesy of museum.

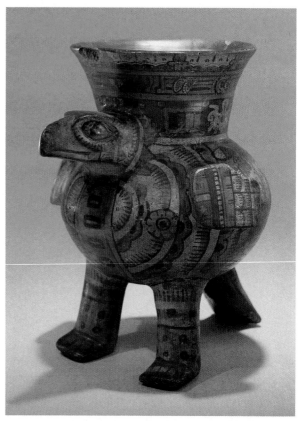

Right: PLATE 10. Oaxaca, Mexico. Mixtec. Eagle tripod, polychrome pottery, 8¼" high. Integration, Late post-Classic, A.D. 1200–1400. Los Angeles, Calif.: Natural History Museum of Los Angeles County, Anthropology Section, FA.1059.71–1. Photo courtesy of museum, negative NN–0000–834.

Below: PLATE 11. Tilantongo, Oaxaca, Mexico. Mixtec. Codex Zouche-Nuttall, page 52, deer hide covered with gesso and painted, 10" wide x 7⅜" high: "8 Deer receiving his nose plug at Tula," lower left. Integration, Late post-Classic, ca. A.D. 1350. London: British Museum. Photo of facsimile by Zelia Nuttall, used with permission of Arthur G. Miller.

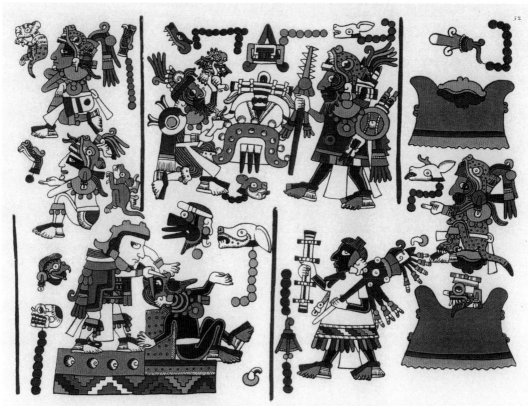

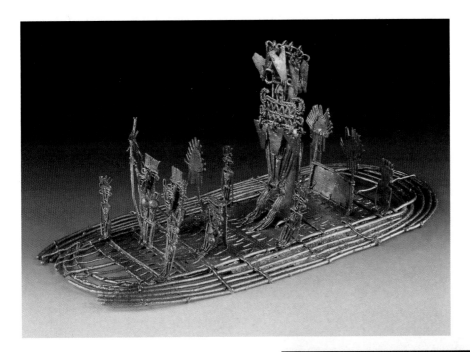

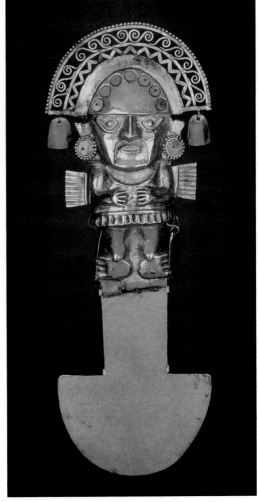

Above: PLATE 12. Pasca, Cundinamarca, Colombia. Chibcha. Votive offering of El Dorado on raft, cast *tumbaga* (gold and copper alloy), 7¼" long. Integration, Late Period, A.D. 1200–1538. Santafé de Bogotá: Museo del Oro, Banco de la Republica. Transparency courtesy of museum.

Right: PLATE 13. Lambayeque Department, Peru. Sicán. Ceremonial knife depicting Naymlap, hammered and repoussé gold with turquoise inlay, 13½" high. Integration, Middle Horizon, A.D. 850–1050. Chicago: Art Institute, 1963.841, Ada Turnbull Hertle Fund. Photo by Christopher Gallagher, © 1996, The Art Institute of Chicago. All rights reserved.

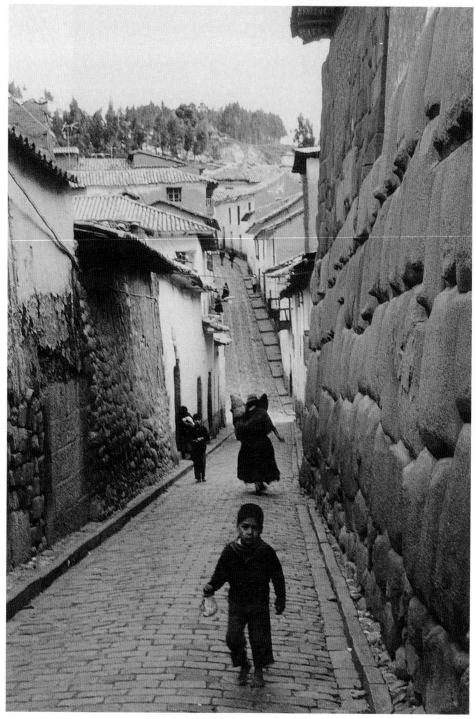

PLATE 14. Cuzco, Peru. Hatunrumiyoq Street. Inca. Polygonal stone Inca wall with Spanish colonial construction on top. Photo by John F. Scott.

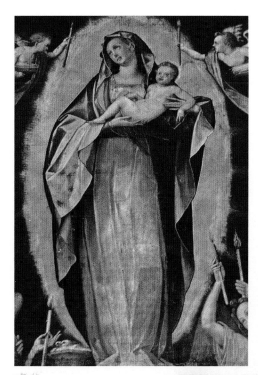

Left: PLATE 15. Bernardo Bitti, painter. *Virgin of La Candelaria,* oil on canvas, detail, sacristy of Church of San Pedro, Lima, Peru, life-size, 1576–1882. Photo by José de Mesa and Teresa Gisbert, used with permission.

Below: PLATE 16. Father Carlos, sculptor? *Apostle James,* partially gilded wood and lacquered paint, life-size, sometime between 1620 and 1680. Quito: Museo del Banco Central. Photo by John F. Scott.

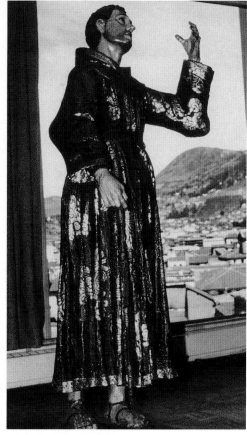

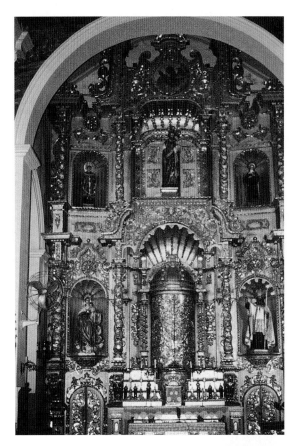

Left: PLATE 17. Anonymous. Golden Altar, wood and gold leaf, San José church, Panama City, Panama, before 1671. Photo by John F. Scott.

Below: PLATE 18. Francisco Guerrero y Torres, architect. Pocito chapel, Guadalupe Basilica, Mexico City, 1777–1791. Photo by John F. Scott.

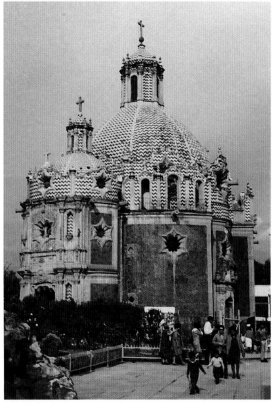

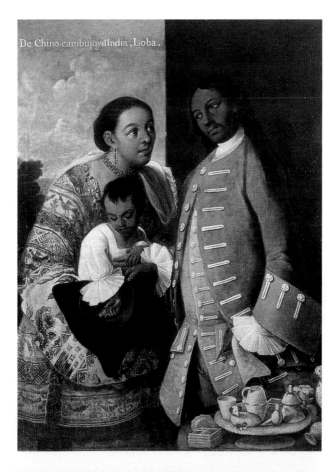

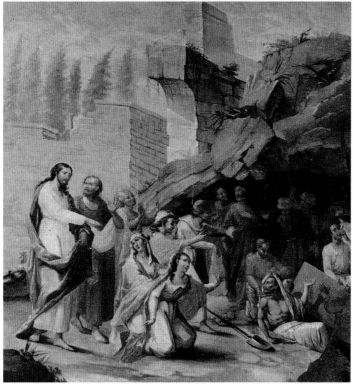

Above: PLATE 19. Miguel Cabrera, painter. *From Sambo and Indian Woman, Wolf-Girl,* oil on canvas, 52" high x 39¾" wide, 1763. Madrid: Museo de América. Photo courtesy of museum.

Left: PLATE 20. Eduardo Tresguerras, architect and painter. *Resurrection of Lazarus,* mural fresco in transept chapel, about 10' x 12'. El Carmen church, Celaya, Guanajuato, Mexico, 1803–1807. Photo by John F. Scott.

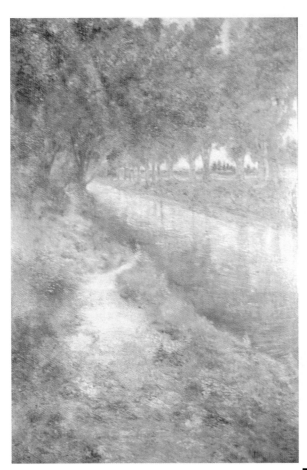

Left: PLATE 21. Joaquín Clausell, painter. *Canal of Santa Anita,* oil on canvas, 50" high x 33¼" wide, ca. 1900. Mexico City: Museo Nacional de Arte. Photo courtesy of Instituto de Investigaciones Estéticas photo archive, Universidad Nacional Autónoma de México.

Below: PLATE 22. Leopoldo Romañach, painter. *On the Way to Mass,* oil on canvas, 39" high x 31" wide, early 20th century. Daytona Beach, Fla.: Cuban Foundation Collection of the Museum of Arts and Sciences. Photo courtesy of museum.

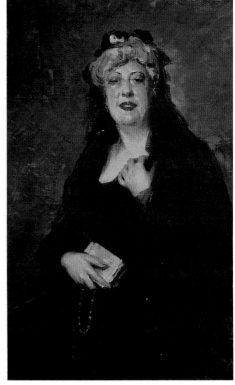

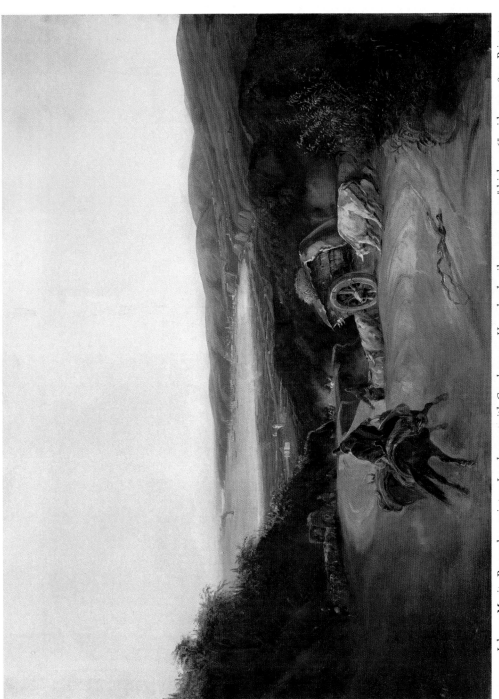

PLATE 23. Johann Moritz Rugendas, painter. *Landscape with Cowboys on Horseback*, oil on canvas, 27" high x 36" wide, ca. 1834. Private collection. Photo courtesy of Sotheby's, New York.

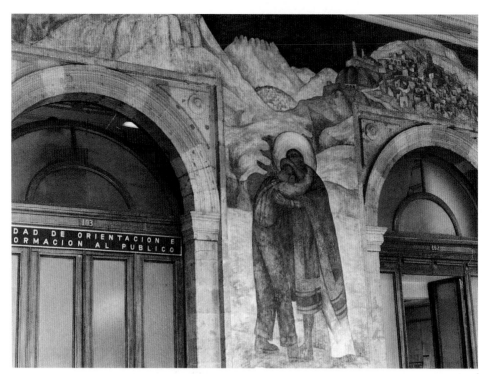

PLATE 24. Diego Rivera, painter. *The Embrace,* fresco on plaster wall, first floor, Ministry of Public Education, Mexico City, 1923. Photo by John F. Scott.

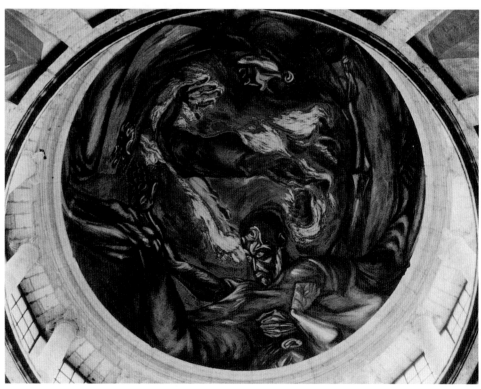

PLATE 25. José Clemente Orozco, painter. *Man of Fire,* dome fresco painting, Hospicio Cabañas, Guadalajara, Jalisco, Mexico, 1939. Photo by John F. Scott.

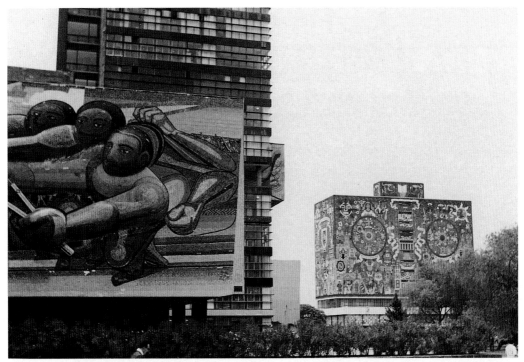

PLATE 26. Enrique del Moral and Mario Pani, architects. Rectory, left, 1949–1954, with *The People to the University, the University to the People*, right half of relief mural by David Alfaro Siqueiros, 1952–1956; and University Library in distance with mosaic mural by Juan O'Gorman, 1953. Photo by John F. Scott.

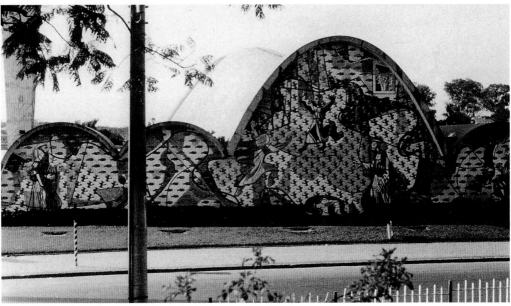

PLATE 27. Oscar Niemeyer, architect. São Francisco Church, Pampulha, Minas Gerais, Brazil, with glazed tile mural by Cândido Portinari, 1943. Photo by Roy C. Craven, Jr., courtesy of Visual Resources Center, University of Florida.

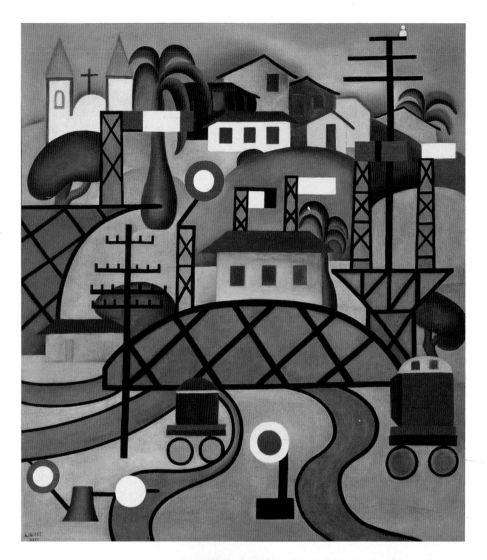

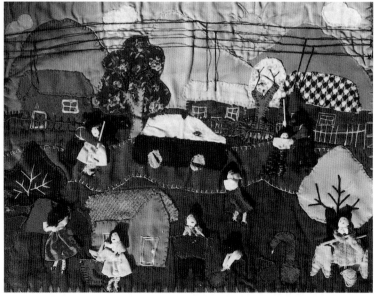

Above: PLATE 28. Tarsila do Amaral, painter. *EFCB* (Central Railroad of Brazil), oil on canvas, 56" high x 50" wide, 1924. São Paulo, Brazil: Museu de Arte Contemporánea da Universidade de São Paulo, 63.3.392. Photo by Romulo Fialdini, courtesy of museum.

Right: PLATE 29. Anonymous Chilean woman. *Police Beating Dissidents in Poor Neighborhood, arpillera,* sticks and wool embroidered on stitched cotton cloth fragments backed with burlap, 18¾" wide x 14⅞" high, 1979–1980. Gainesville, Fla: Hernán Vera collection. Photo by John F. Scott.

CHOROTEGA, NICARAGUA-COSTA RICA: ABOUT A.D. 800–1500

A southern provincial relative of the Mixteca-Puebla style was produced in the Rivas area of southwestern Nicaragua and the Nicoya
Peninsula of Costa Rica, a region only marginally part of Mesoamerica
and inhabited at the time of the Conquest by the Chorotega, linguisti-
cally related to the Mixtec. However, enclaves of people speaking other
Mesoamerican languages, including the Nahua-speaking Nicarao, apparently settled during the post-Classic period along the Pacific coast
of Central America and may have brought with them their art forms
and trade networks. Their earlier cultural links had been with the Maya
during the Classic and the heirs of the Olmec in the Late Formative (see
fig. 2.9). A Costa Rican jar with a modeled jaguar head projecting from
its body (fig. 4.10) has many of the same stylistic features as the Mixteca-Puebla eagle tripod (see pl. 10): bright, contrasting colors arranged
in bands and panels, bristling forms both painted and modeled, especially the three legs, and the overall shape of the vessel.

The artistic influences also traveled in the opposite direction. Miniature men and animals of cast *tumbaga* (an alloy of gold and copper)
worked in a technique not known to Mesoamerica during the Classic
except by trade, were found in the sacred well at Chichén Itzá (Coggins
1984: 62–65). Their style indicates they were imported from lower
Central America, particularly the Chiriquí and Coclé regions of western Panama (fig. 4.6). In the post-Classic period, metallurgy was widely
adopted in Mesoamerica, from the northwestern frontier to the Maya
area, especially for casting small copper bells. The Mixtec picked up
this medium with gusto to model small images of their gods. They
preferred flat surfaces that permitted greater detail executed by rolled
wax fillets, which then were converted into gold by melting out the
wax and replacing it with molten metal. Although this "lost wax"
technology was imported from the Intermediate Area and the forms
even retained some characteristics—like flat frog-foot flanges—derived
from lower Central America, the workmanship and iconography of the
Mixtec objects are purely Mesoamerican.

Along the Caribbean watershed of Costa Rica, Chibchan-speaking
tribes carved numerous medium-size stone sculptures of nude men
and women apparently representing their deceased ancestors. These
sculptures were erected in front of earthen burial mounds arranged in
rectangular plazas. To express their potency, the female figures promi-
nently display their breasts and vulvae, and the men flaunt their geni-
tals and well-defined chest muscles. In addition, many male figures

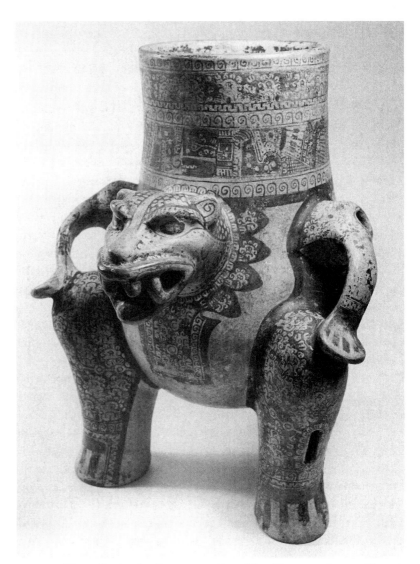

FIG. 4.10. Nicoya Peninsula, Guanacaste, Costa Rica. Chorotega. Jaguar effigy tripod urn, polychromed pottery, 12½" high. Integration, Middle Polychrome Period, A.D. 800–1200. Lakeland, Fla.: Polk Museum of Art, 83–2–1. Photo by Roy C. Craven, Jr., courtesy of museum.

carry weapons and trophy heads to show their masculine prowess in the art of war (fig. 4.11). The coarse surface of the images, made of pockmarked volcanic stone like that preferred by the Toltecs, stresses the militaristic brutality of these figures. They are, however, more abstract than the Toltec-era figures of Mesoamerica: the energetic curves of the limbs and torso and their sharp definition of parts recall the conceptual stylization of recent African wood sculpture. Thus, both Mesoamerica and Costa Rica express the new military content through their aggressive realism. Although not all cultures maintained empires—the political control of the Central American Chibchan chiefs and the Mexican Mixtec states was quite small—all reflect the dominant militaristic aesthetic created by empires such as the Toltec.

AZTEC, MEXICO: A.D. 1375–1521

The largest documented Pre-Columbian empire in the northern hemisphere of America was created by the successors of the Toltecs, whose migration legend is surprisingly similar. They first called themselves the Aztecs, the people from the place of the herons (perhaps somewhere in western Mexico), but they later called themselves the Mexica, from which the name of the modern state is derived. But the empire of the

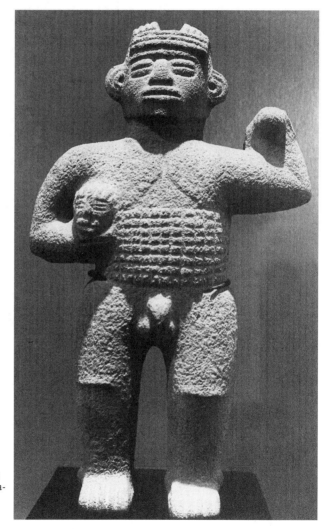

FIG. 4.11. Línea Vieja region, Limón, Costa Rica. Standing male holding trophy head, volcanic stone, 24" high. Integration, Late Middle Polychrome Period, A.D. 1000–1200. San José, Costa Rica: National Museum, 11697. Photo by Curtis Craven.

Aztecs (or Mexica) was much more restricted than the present extent of modern Mexico. It straddled the central zone from coast to coast, but extended its political domination only into selected regions of southern Mesoamerica, although its trade network no doubt strongly influenced many other areas economically and culturally. The great capital city, called Tenochtitlán by the Aztecs—now the core of modern Mexico City—was laid out in a grid plan on the small island where they as mercenary nomads had been allowed to settle after A.D. 1325. Their prophesy that they were to settle where an eagle devoured a serpent on a cactus compelled them to claim this inhospitable island where they observed this phenomenon. The main avenues of their capital city, extending onto causeways across a shallow lake to connect the city to the mainland, were oriented to the cardinal directions; only the east lacked such a thoroughfare, no doubt because the lake was too wide at that point for one to reach the eastern shore. In the center was the ceremonial precinct, the "heart of the one world," surrounded by a crenelated wall and a sculptural rendering of an intertwined rope of serpents acting as fierce protective animals to guard the precinct. They express the Aztec militaristic determination to safeguard their culture against all enemies, physical and spiritual. Outside the sacred enclosure were the palaces of the emperors, the last belonging to the ill-fated Montezuma II, who was captured by Cortes. Thus, sacred and secular became separated physically, and the isolation of the temples, already suggested by the colonnades in front of the temple at Tula, now became more vigorously emphasized.

In the mid-1970s, excavations in the center of Mexico City unearthed the Great Temple which once dominated the sacred enclosure, and in turn, the entire capital city. Formerly known only from conquistadors' descriptions and chroniclers' paintings, it now has been revealed as a sequence of structures dating to the late fourteenth century, when the Aztecs had settled the island in the lake. From the beginning, the Great Temple was dual, dedicated to both the old Mesoamerican Rain God, whom the Aztecs called Tlaloc, and their own tribal war deity, the vigorous Huitzilopochtli. Staircases leading up both sides of the single pyramid structure had serpent heads at their bases, steep stairs, and the characteristic imperial Aztec balustrade that changes its slope at the top to an even steeper angle, emphasizing the dizzying ascent required and the awesome height of the gods.

On one of these temples within the sacred precinct stood the colossal idol of the goddess Coatlicue, "she of the serpent skirt" (fig. 4.12). Because she was the mother of the supreme War God, Huitzilopochtli,

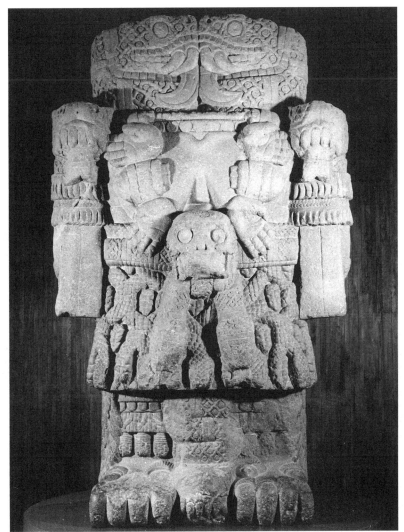

FIG. 4.12. Tenochtitlán, Federal District, Mexico. Aztec. Coatlicue, olivine basalt, 99" high. Integration, Late post-Classic, A.D. 1500. Mexico City: Museo Nacional de Antropología. Photo courtesy of Instituto Nacional de Antropología e Historia.

she probably stood on his half of the great double temple. Spanish conquistadors described how such idols were smeared with blood from the sacrifices performed on top of the pyramids. This idol presents a horrific image, at once intensely realistic and fantastically otherworldly. More than 8 feet high, she looms above the viewer, overwhelming in her massiveness. Tangibly realistic details range from the minuscule to the gigantic, creating a sense of colossal scale. Coatlicue's forms are turgid with life, swelling as if about to burst. She is represented as a standing female, her sagging breasts covered with a necklace of human hands and hearts with a central skull pendant. She is named for her serpent skirt composed of intertwined rattlesnakes, whose diamond-shaped scales add a harsh texture to the surface. The goddess's head appears as an illusion created by the heads of two confronting serpents, which together form the image of one face. Giant claws as feet turn into heads by the addition of eyes, all the more impressive for being so close to the viewer. At first glance, her hands also appear to be claws, but they are really serpent heads with fangs which look like fingers. These heads emerge from what are obviously severed appendages, created when Coatlicue's older children, the moon and the stars, conspired against her for becoming pregnant with Huitzilopochtli. As they killed her, Huitzilopochtli sprang forth full-grown from her womb and slew them. A recently discovered colossal stone disk at the base of the steps on Huitzilopochtli's side of the Great Temple renders the dismembered body of the moon goddess, Huitzilopochtli's treacherous half-sister. These myths are made palpably real, like Baroque sculpture, through the skill of the imperial artists. Gone are the crudities of Toltec sculpture, although many Aztec sculptors still preferred the coarse volcanic rock as their raw material. But the greater modulation of surface and subtlety in rendering the realistic details set Aztec sculpture apart and create a powerful expression of imperial might similar to that conveyed by Assyrian sculpture in the ancient Near East.

A rock-cut sanctuary in Malinalco, some seventy miles southwest of Tenochtitlán, served as a sacred retreat for eagle and jaguar warriors who fought for the Aztec empire. Their role was not only to expand and maintain the empire and its tributary states but also to wage continuous battle required to obtain captives to sacrifice to the gods. Those very gods had already sacrificed themselves so that the present creation (called the "fifth sun") would take place. The warrior cults conveyed this sacred responsibility to the elite brotherhoods of eagle knights and jaguar knights. These cults used attributes of those animals as part of their battle dress, and although the quilted cotton armor of this garb provided some small protection, its greatest benefit was spiritual. Even they, the elite of the society, knew that their life would be brief, and a glorious abode in the highest heaven awaited those who died for the sun god. (Women who died in childbirth were similarly rewarded by going to the highest heaven, for their battle was just as intense and their goal as noble.)

With the above mind-set, the eagle and jaguar warriors approached the rock-cut temple via its steep flight of steps guarded by two stone coyotes and flanked by the characteristic Aztec double-angle balustrades. At the top of the staircase, the initiates entered the temple proper through an earth-monster mouth. Inside they found a circular chamber like a prehistoric Southwestern Pueblo *kiva* with a shallow raised bench surrounding the space. Carved monolithically on the bench are three pelts—two eagles and one jaguar—the latter spread out but still snarling fiercely. A high-relief carving of a nesting eagle guards a ritual hole into which blood was shed. The vigorously modeled texture of the eagle's feathers reveals an understanding of the underlying anatomy. The ritual cavity is similar to that in the first Mesoamerican men's society building (see fig. 1.16), a communication channel with the spirit world much like the *sipapu* of a Pueblo kiva, also a men's society house. For the Aztec warriors, entering and exiting from the jaws of the earth monster symbolized a spiritual death and rebirth (fig. 4.13).

In another part of Malinalco, excavated murals depict the inexorable marching procession of warriors (fig. 4.14) typical of imperial art the world over. Each figure repeats the posture of the others: far foot strongly striding forward, near arm raised back holding a spear, causing the shoulder to be seen in full width. The entire figure re-creates the so-

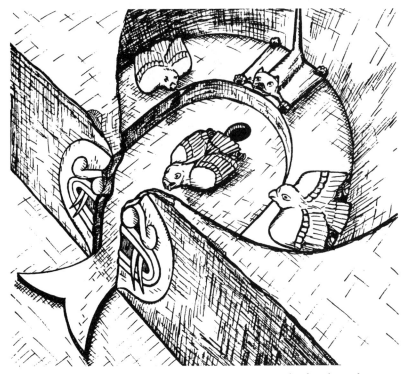

FIG. 4.13. Malinalco, State of México, Mexico. Aztec. Temple of Eagles and Jaguars, rock-cut, ca. 10' wide interior. Integration, Late post-Classic, A.D. 1501–1515. Drawing after Karl Luckert.

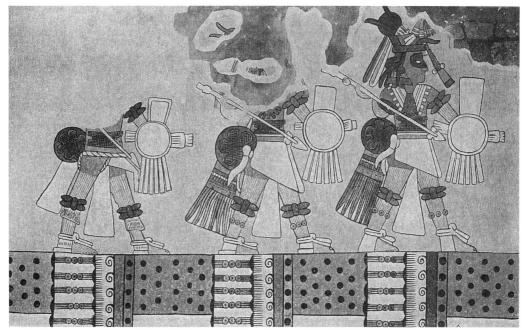

FIG. 4.14. Malinalco, State of México, Mexico. Aztec. Mural procession of hunters or warriors dressed like Mixcoatl, now destroyed, ca. 27" high. Integration, Late post-Classic, A.D. 1440–1521. Painted copy by Miguel Angel Fernández, reproduced courtesy of Instituto Nacional de Antropología e Historia, Mexico.

called Egyptian canonical posture commonly found in conceptualized art everywhere, a view preferred because it renders the distinctive parts of the body in the clearest view. Even the shield carried in the far hand and the feather bustle worn on the back of the belt are rendered fully frontal. The proportions of the parts of the body, however, are completely correct, unlike the squat figures in Mixteca-Puebla paintings (see pl. 11). This Malinalco mural, which has now been washed away, had been the only securely documented Pre-Columbian example of Aztec figure painting, and as such establishes the precedent for the early post-Conquest native manuscript style such as that in the Codex Borbonicus.

Colonial manuscripts painted by native scribes provide extensive references to the Aztec emperors, but royal portraits are quite rare in Aztec art before the Spanish Conquest. Those few which do render the ruler identify him primarily by glyphs of his name placed near his head. For example, on the relief frieze carved around the Stone of Tizoc (fig. 4.15), the emperor Tizoc (reigned A.D. 1481–1486) is identified by the leg glyph to the left of his head. Otherwise he looks almost the same as the other military leaders, who also hold captives by the forelock. The left foot of each of the conquering Aztecs has been replaced by a smoking mirror, a divine attribute of the god Tezcatlipoca. Tizoc does wear a more elaborate feathered headdress than the other warriors, however, which may be another divine attribute, this time of Huitzilopochtli,

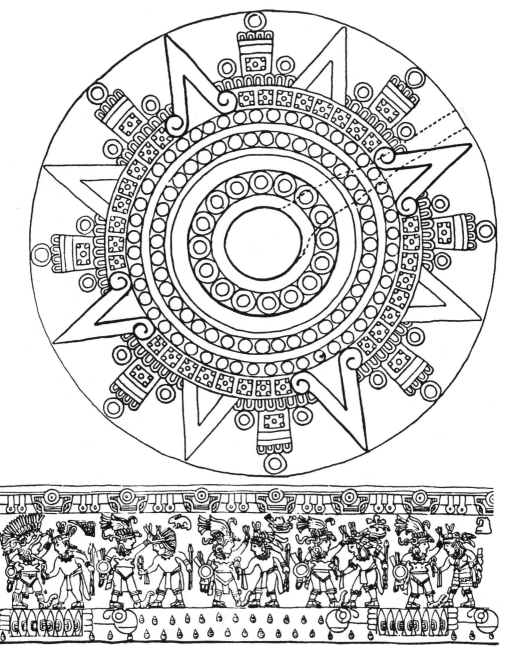

FIG. 4.15. Tenochtitlán, Federal District, Mexico. Aztec. Cylindrical monument of Emperor Tizoc, basalt, 34"
high x 104½" diam. Integration, Late post-Classic, A.D. 1481–1486. Mexico City: Museo Nacional de
Antropología. Line drawing after Manuel Orozco y Berra.

whose name means "hummingbird on the left" (Townsend 1979: 46).
One such huge feathered headdress, attributed to the Emperor Montezuma II, made of tail plumes from the quetzal bird imported from the
southern rain forest, has survived unburied since the Conquest; this
rare treasure now resides in the Museum of Ethnology in Vienna, home
of the Hapsburg dynasty which included the king of Spain at the time
of Cortez.

The actions of Tizoc and his captains take place below a sky band
encircling the top of the vertical frieze which then merges with the sun
disk carved in rounded relief on top of the stone. The sun image, so
well-known on other Aztec monuments such as the so-called Calendar
Stone of the Fifth Creation, has four major rays pointing in the cardinal
directions and smaller intermediate rays coming out of precious greenstone and turquoise symbols forming concentric circular bands. The
central hole may have been used to tie a ranking, valorous captive, who
would have to defend himself from obsidian-lined weapons with only
a feather-lined wooden one. His blood, then shed on the sun disk, would
pool in the concavity in the center and nourish the sun, much as the
captives taken in the frieze would ultimately be sacrificed for the same
end. In this way the Aztecs believed the cosmos would continue and
they would repay the blood debt to the gods who sacrificed themselves
to make the fifth creation.

INTERMEDIATE AREA CHIEFDOMS: A.D. 800–1500

Throughout the area between Mesoamerica and the Central Andes,
major chiefdoms were established during this late period. They were
not truly empires, since they ruled only over speakers of the same
language family as their own. But by conquests and alliances with
neighboring ethnic groups, they established a dominant style for their
region which had as an important theme the enhancement of the chief
and his relatives. But these chiefs had neither the population nor the
power to demand the unlimited labor from their subjects as did kings,
so their monumental artistic production was slight. Craftsmen working for these chiefs did not build permanent architecture or carve large-
scale sculpture.

Some tropical forest people possessed ranked chiefdoms, counteract-
ing the earlier idea that their societies were all egalitarian. The culture
on Marajó Island, at the mouth of the Amazon River, beginning in the
later Classic period built large villages on artificially raised terraces
above the rich floodplain on which the population raised its crops
(Roosevelt 1989). Individual dwellings retained the oval plan known

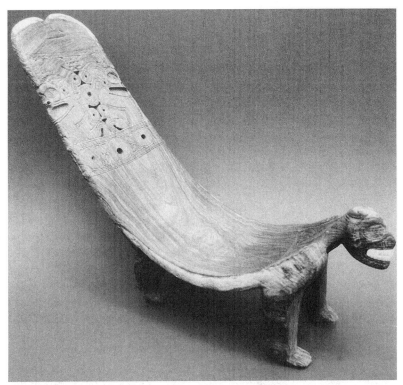

FIG. 4.16. San Rafael de Yuma, Altagracia, Dominican Republic. Taíno. *Duho* (seat) of chief, wood with shell teeth, 11½" high x 14¼" long. Integration, A.D. 1300–1500. Santo Domingo: Museo del Hombre Dominicano. Photo by Roy C. Craven, Jr., courtesy of Center for Visual Resources Center, University of Florida.

from much earlier times at Real Alto in Ecuador and sheltered extended families, much like the houses of historic Amazonian tribes. Their finest art products were trichrome pottery urns in the form of stylized female shamans in which their male leaders were buried. This culture disappeared around A.D. 1300, and the historic pattern of smaller egalitarian groups with shifting residences replaced it in the Amazon and the Caribbean lowlands from Colombia to the Guianas.

TAINO, WEST INDIES: A.D. 1000–1492

On the major islands of the Caribbean Sea, especially Hispaniola and Puerto Rico, the Taino people also developed major chiefdoms, although their ancestors had been egalitarian Arawak-speaking farmers from the tropical forest of South America. Their folk pottery, produced in abundance, retains a style known from the earliest pottery in the Americas (like fig. 1.6). More impressive items of rank, however, stress the supernatural images that support the role of the chiefs. Wooden stools, called *duhos* by the Taino, elevated the seated chief above the ordinary citizen, who simply squatted on the ground. Elegant carved circular motifs energize the surface of the example in figure 4.16 with supernatural force, much like the pottery, while the fierce face of the spirit grimaces at the viewer seated opposite the august personage. The potent flex of the legs suggests the creature would spring to the aid of the chief who sat upon it, and yet the spirit's acquiescence to being subordinated in that fashion reveals how the chief dominates even the

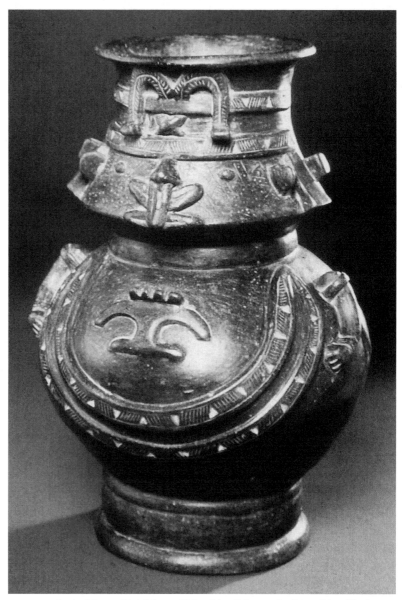

FIG. 4.17. Santa Marta, Magdalena, Colombia. Tairona. Sculptural jar, blackware pottery, 15¼" high. Integration, Late Period, A.D. 1250–1500. Ocala, Fla.: Appleton Museum of Art, G1986.3. Photo courtesy of museum.

spirit world. Stools are important images of leadership throughout the Intermediate Area during the Integration period, although their use was already documented in the Classic (see figs. 3.9, 3.16).

TAIRONA, COLOMBIA: ABOUT A.D. 1200–1500

Among the most versatile artisans in ancient America were the Tairona, a group of Chibchan-speaking chiefdoms organized into in a confederation around the area of the Sierra Nevada de Santa Marta, a snow-capped volcanic range abutting the Caribbean in northeastern Colombia. The skill of these artisans in lapidary jewelry, architecture, gold, and pottery is unsurpassed in the Intermediate Area. A magnificent sculpture on a Tairona burnished black pottery jar (fig. 4.17) shows formal and iconographic features similar to Manteño (Ecuador) images (see fig. 4.20): the use of blackware for ritual sculptures, powerful facial features, and a prominent crescent-shaped nose ornament, which we know—from actual examples found in the area—to represent gold. Crisp, delicate details played off against large, smoothly modeled forms create a sense of imposing scale also seen in Manteño figures. Only the non-naturalistic rendering of the torso in the Tairona pieces signals an important difference between these two cultures.

Among the Tairona, goldwork clearly signals luxury and status, as it does in much of America during the Integration period, but it also refers to divine imperishability. A pendant representing an anthropomorphic Bat God (fig. 4.18) shows a husky figure supporting a semicircular solar headdress. Its powerful forms and its large scale (notwithstanding its small size) communicate power and monumentality, comparable to those qualities found on much larger Aztec stone sculpture (see figs. 4.12 and 4.15), in spite of the modest absolute size of the gold object.

The surviving circular foundations of the Tairona perishable village structures, located on irregular, sloping terrain, are exquisitely made, with precisely cut slabs forming terraces and stairs leading up to circular house bases. So well made are they that in recent years the Colombian government used the circular bases of a recently discovered "lost city" for helicopter landing pads while intercepting drug traffickers in the surrounding jungle. The handsome cut stone foundations recall the stonework in monumental buildings of the Tiwanaku (see fig. 4.22) and Inca empires of the Central Andes and those of Yucatecan Maya cities (see fig. 4.5).

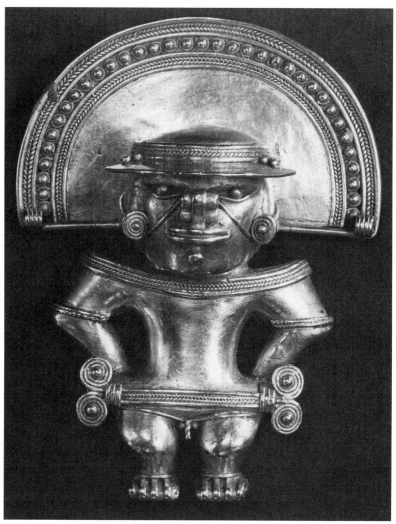

FIG. 4.18. Santa Marta, Magdalena, Colombia. Tairona. Bat God, cast gold, 2½" high. Integration, Late Period, A.D. 1250–1500. Washington: Dumbarton Oaks Research Library and Collections, B-393.CG. Photo courtesy of Dumbarton Oaks Research Library and Collections, Washington, D.C.

CHIBCHA, COLOMBIA: ABOUT A.D. 1200–1538

An even more powerful polity, approaching a true empire, was created by a confederation of great chiefs of the Chibcha (also called Muisca) on the high grassy plateau east of the Magdalena River. One major chiefdom was centered in modern Bogotá (ancient Bacatá), while the other capital was at Tunja, to the north. To display his wealth and keep the support of the gods, the Bogotá chief would cover his body with gold dust and be paddled by raft to the center of the volcanic Lake Guatavita, where he would dive in and thereby sacrifice the gold adhering to his body. Spaniards hearing this story called him "El Dorado" (the gilded man); this concept became the subject of many rumors driving the conquistadors in search of gold as far north as the southwestern United States. Such sacrifice of gold was common among chiefdoms of Central America, whose gold objects were traded as far north as the sacred well of Chichén Itzá. A magnificent Chibcha offering cast in *tumbaga* (the gold alloy also used to manufacture fig. 4.6) appears to depict "El Dorado" on his raft (pl. 12). Each figure is a very standardized flat frontal silhouette with fillets outlining the facial features, limbs, and decorative adornments. The standardization of these figures recalls that of processional warriors rendered by Mesoamerican empires such as the Aztec (see figs. 4.14, 4.15). Pottery urns modeled by the Chibcha have more bulk than the *tumbaga* figures, although the strong geometry of detail indicates a stylization of the human form and a lack of individuality. The small supporting heads attached to the front of the stool in figure 4.19 probably refer to trophy heads taken in battle by which the

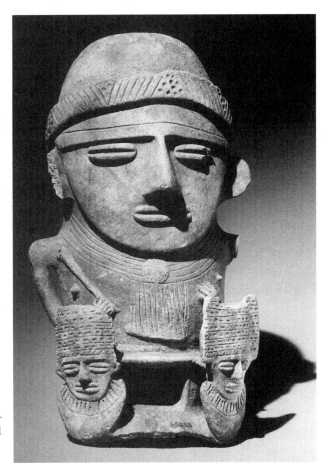

FIG. 4.19. Cundinamarca Department, Colombia. Chibcha. Jar lid representing chief's mummy placed on stool flanked by two trophy heads, buff pottery, 13½" high. Integration, Late Period, A.D. 1200–1538. Chicago: Field Museum of Natural History, 65023. Photo © The Field Museum, Chicago, Ill., neg. #A97622.

chief accumulates power. The incomplete body of the chief, placed clothed on the stool, and the closed eyes and masklike face, suggest a mummified body such as those preserved in their temples.

MANTEÑO, ECUADOR: A.D. 1100–1500

Along the coast in modern Ecuador, two archaeologically identifiable cultures—Manteño and Milagro—brought together previously distinct ethnic groups during the Integration period (A.D. 600–1500). The capital city of Manta was extremely large, as reported by early Spanish conquistadors; its culture, called Manteño after the inhabitants of that city, conquered the areas of the old Regional Developmental coastal cultures extending from Guangala to Jama-Coaque. In the Manteño kingdom, large stone statues of standing men, with architectonic shapes much like the Tiwanaku monoliths, apparently represent the rulers but with no features which could be considered divine. Ceramic lids made of burnished blackware, a medium much favored by north-coastal Peruvian empires during the Integration period for ritual images (like fig. 4.28), show males seated on benches, traditional symbols of leaders in the Intermediate Area (fig. 4.20). The torso is full and powerful, a sign of the chief's strength. Incisions on part of the torso suggest body painting or tattooing; they create the illusion of large scale because of the contrast between the large smooth surfaces of part of the body and the small, delicate designs of the decoration. The facial features, especially the nose, are heavy modeled and large, emphasizing the strong personality of the chief. Modern inhabitants of Manabí, although completely acculturated, still preserve these strong features. A gold crescent-shaped nose pendant still remains in this pottery figure's septum, suggesting the importance of this elite piece of jewelry in identifying the nobleman.

Stone benches of the kind rendered on the sculpture in fig. 4.20 actually existed among the Manteño, placed about 20 feet apart along the interior walls of the meeting houses and temples. A typical human-supported "Savonarola"-type chair (fig. 4.21) expresses domination of their people by the leaders who sat on these benches. These carvings simplify the shape of the crouching man to emphasize turgid curving lines and sharpen the carving. The thick proportions and the stability of the sleigh-shaped seat suggest firmness and permanence—just those qualities one looks for in a leader.

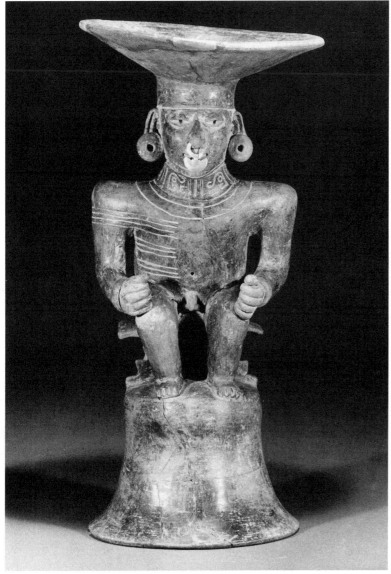

FIG. 4.20. Central Manabí Province, Ecuador. Manteño. Seated male figure on lid, blackware pottery with gold nose ring, 21" total height. Integration, A.D. 1100–1470. Ithaca, N.Y.: The Herbert F. Johnson Museum of Art, Cornell University, 74.53.39, gift of Margaret and Tessim Zorach. Photo courtesy of museum.

TIWANAKU, BOLIVIA: ABOUT A.D. 400–1000

Imperial art in the Central Andes began in the high plateau of modern Bolivia at Tiwanaku (also spelled Tiahuanaco), near the southern shore of Lake Titicaca, about A.D. 400. By that time the semisubterranean court was built (fig. 4.22); its cut stone walls include tenoned stone heads projecting from its even surface. These fully human heads, executed in various styles, perhaps represent the trophy heads of con-

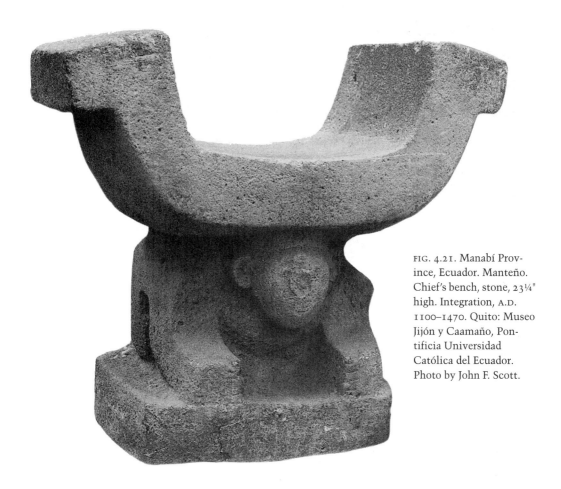

FIG. 4.21. Manabí Province, Ecuador. Manteño. Chief's bench, stone, 23¼" high. Integration, A.D. 1100–1470. Quito: Museo Jijón y Caamaño, Pontificia Universidad Católica del Ecuador. Photo by John F. Scott.

quered areas around the southern highlands. Although the construction is similar to the temple at Chavín de Huántar, from the Early Horizon, the meaning of the tenoned heads is different, since at Chavín they represented supernatural beings, part human, part animal (see fig. 2.12). Crudely sculpted standing figures near the center of the court show humanlike features rendered in low relief wrapped around the surface of the stone.

Directly opposite the court to the north is a large artificial mound with a sunken central depression containing water which once was channeled to the different terraces and a surrounding moat, symbolizing a sacred island (Kolata 1993: 111). The contrast between sunken and elevated portions corresponds to ancient Andean practice, as exemplified by coastal ritual centers like Sechín Alto (see fig. 2.10). To the west of the sunken court lies a great enclosure, named the Kalasasaya (from *kala sayasaya*, "scattered standing stones" in the local Aymara language probably spoken by the builders), which once served to commemorate the ancestors of the royal lineage, with rooms dedicated to each one opening onto the somewhat sunken central patio (Kolata 1993: 145–147). Raised slightly above the level of the surrounding treeless plain, its walls were constructed by alternating large irregular vertical stones and small smoothly cut stone blocks.

Within the Kalasasaya, monolithic sculptures stand like lightning rods to channel the forces of the enormous surrounding space (fig. 4.23). Most are in the shape of standing men, yet their raised squarish eyes and the incised patterns on their clothing and skin make them seem supernatural. In one hand they carry a ritual cup of the type that later Incas used ceremonially to drink the sacred beer *chicha*; the contents of a matching cup could be offered to a deity. These statues can represent rulers acting as priests and dressed in the deity's insignia. Their colossal size and architectonic form recall the warrior columns from Tula (see fig. 4.1).

Now isolated within the enclosure stands a ceremonial gateway made of a single block of stone (fig. 4.24). Its opening is surprisingly small compared to the enormity of the enclosure and its functional gateways. Niches on one side are of the kind long used in ritual buildings in the Central Andes (see fig. 1.15). Above the opening, depicted in high relief, the radiant sun deity with squared features stands astride a stepped mountain and holds straight out to his side two staffs with bird-head

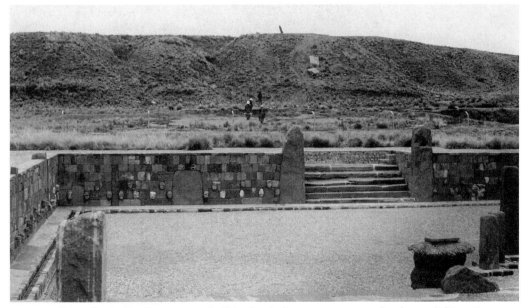

FIG. 4.22. Tiwanaku, La Paz Department, Bolivia. Semisubterranean courtyard and monolithic staircase towards Akapana. In situ. Classic, Early Intermediate Period, ca. A.D. 400. Photo by John F. Scott.

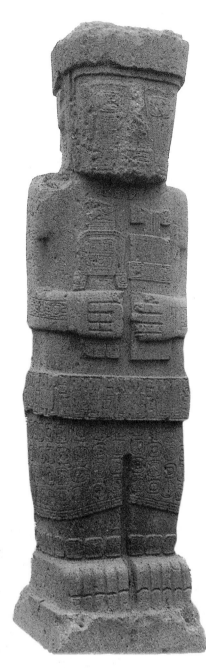

FIG. 4.23. Tiwanaku, La Paz Department, Bolivia. Ponce monolith, stone, 120" high. In situ in Kalasasaya. Integration, Middle Horizon, ca. A.D. 600. Photo by John F. Scott.

bases and bifurcated tops. The image is descended from the Staff God of Chavín (see fig. 2.14). In flat relief, flanking this raised central figure, kneel three rows of winged figures: the top and bottom rows human, the middle row with bird heads turned upward. They too carry staffs of similar design. With their repetition, they clearly form a procession characteristic of other imperial art styles. On a base frieze, serving as a lintel over the opening, are trapezoidal-faced suns with serpents and birds radiating like a nimbus around their heads—they have no bodies. The traditional name of this whole carving is the "Gate of the Sun," not only because of the radiant central deity but also because its design served as a kind of annual solar calendar. The impact of this design is enormous, although details later rendered in isolation lack the full context given here.

WARI, PERU: ABOUT A.D. 600–1000

The expansion of the Wari empire, whose duration defines the Middle Horizon (A.D. 600–1000) in the Central Andes, spread Tiwanaku imagery, which they revered, throughout most of Peru. Colossal painted pottery urns from the south coastal site of Pacheco (fig. 4.25), some others of which take the shape of ritual cups like those used by the Incas, repeat these major motifs from the Tiwanaku highland site. The radiant figure with outstretched arms holding staffs resembles the cen-

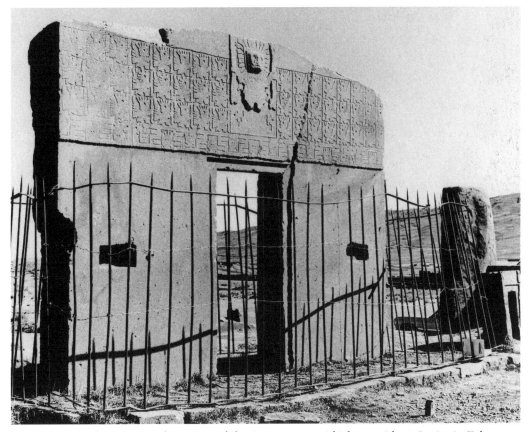

FIG. 4.24. Tiwanaku, La Paz, Bolivia. Gate of the Sun, stone, 120" high x 150" long. In situ in Kalasasaya. Integration, Middle Horizon, ca. A.D. 600. Photo by Roy C. Craven, Jr., courtesy of Center for Latin American Studies, University of Florida.

tral figure on Tiwanaku's Gate of the Sun. His staffs and associated appendages are more often vegetative, suggesting that the Wari rulers encouraged his association with plant fertility rather than purely with the sun (Moseley 1992: 220). The rich, warm earth colors reflect this vessel's origin in the homeland of the earlier Nazca culture (see fig. 3.1). Fragments of a textile shirt with finely woven designs, probably from the same area, adapts the running-kneeling profile figures (looking like angels) from the Gate of the Sun, renders them in color, and compresses or stretches the design laterally (see Sawyer 1963), making it at times almost illegible (fig. 4.26). This design recalls the abstraction of the

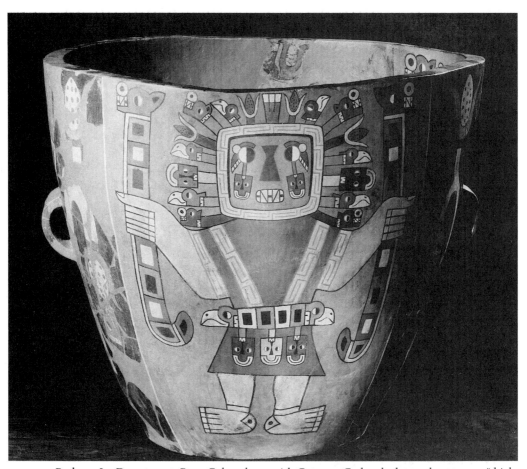

FIG. 4.25. Pacheco, Ica Department, Peru. Colossal urn with Gateway God, polychromed pottery, 29" high. Integration, Middle Horizon, A.D. 600–800. New York: American Museum of Natural History, 41.0/5314. Photo by Dutcher and Rice, neg. No. 411347, courtesy of Department of Library Services, American Museum of Natural History.

FIG. 4.26. Ica Department, Peru. Wari. Textile fragments of running-kneeling bird figures, wool, total width warp 22½", weft 18½" high. Integration, Middle Horizon, A.D. 600–800. Washington, D.C.: The Textile Museum, 1962.51.1, gift of Dr. Junius Bird. Photo courtesy of museum.

feline during the Early Horizon in this same south coastal area (see pl. 3) by transforming the figure into bands: horizontal in that time, vertical here. The multiple versions of this figure often have the color switched and the orientation changed—sometimes facing each other, sometimes upside down—to add variety to the repeated designs. Such color and direction alternation was found on earlier embroidered Paracas textiles, but those exhibited a greater variety of figures (see fig. 2.16). The woven technique encourages a sameness in the figures, making them more like imperial processions. When the repetition is more insistent, as in this case, it communicates the more rigid control of a centralized empire.

SICÁN, PERU: ABOUT A.D. 850–1050

During the waning days of the Wari Empire, which controlled most of Peru from its central highland capital of Wari, a new kingdom arose in the far north coast of Peru. Its art continues to use imperial images, bridging the true empires of Wari and Chimú. Better known by the name of Lambayeque, the modern city near which it was centered, the culture recently has been renamed Sicán after the ancient name of its major site (Carcedo and Shimada 1985: 62). A legendary history recorded by an early Spanish priest Cabello Balboa states that the dynasty was founded by Naymlap, who then disappeared, supposedly having sprouted wings and flown away (Means 1931: 52). A ritual knife with a figure on its handle has traditionally been said to represent Naymlap, although it has the features of a celestial deity (pl. 13). The figure in frontal face exhibits characteristic teardrop-shaped eyes and a semicircular headdress that suggests a half-moon or a rising sun surrounded by wave patterns on the outer grillwork. Small wings jut horizontally from his shoulders, a specific reference to Naymlap's flight. Note the parallels in this story to the legend of Topiltzin Quetzalcoatl summarized at the beginning of this chapter. The knife, which is cast in gold and inlaid with turquoise, is the same shape as that carried by the decapitator on the Moche gold and turquoise nose ornament found at the far northern site of Loma Negra (fig. 3.5). The teardrop-shaped eyes, the semicircular headdress, and the radiance emitted from his body derive from a style of rendering divine figures at the end of the Moche civilization (A.D. 600–700). The figure on the Sicán knife lacks the divine fanged mouth, however, and so we infer he is human rather than a god. Yet Naymlap and his immediate heir both feigned their disappearance from the earth "so that posterity might regard [them] as immortal and divine" (Means 1931: 52). In fact, many early kings, such as the Maya rulers, were considered deified after their deaths. The Inca, who considered their kings sons of the sun god, mummified their rulers, kept the mummies in accessible places like caves or specific rooms, and treated them like living beings during ceremonies.

Masks with the same facial features as those on the knife covered mummy bundles of the Sicán elite (fig. 4.27). Very different from the naturalism of the Moche funerary masks, this mask depicts not the specific leader but the mythical king Naymlap, whose actions founded the dynasty and whose spiritual power gave the later occupant the right to rule. Although made of gold, this mask was covered with red pigment and colored feathers to make a dazzlingly rich, layered image. Its

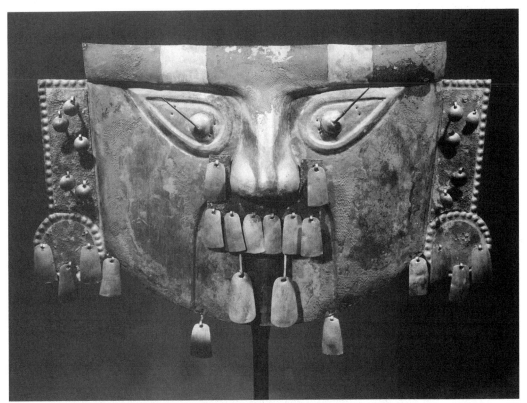

FIG. 4.27. Lambayeque Department, Peru. Sicán. Mask of lord, hammered gold with red paint, 11½" high x 19½" wide. Integration, Middle Horizon, A.D. 850–1050. New York: The Metropolitan Museum of Art, 1974.271.35, gift and bequest of Alice Bache. Photo courtesy of museum.

breadth, much greater than that of a normal face, is in proportion with the thick bundle of mantles in which noble persons were buried.

This personage is also represented on lustrous blackware pottery and can be shown as just a head rendered on the strap-handled spout (fig. 4.28). The body of the vessel may have been visualized as the mummy bundle on top of which the mask was placed (Carcedo and Shimada 1985: 65). The pottery style employs the same sharp, angular forms as the gold, suggesting that metallurgy was the dominant artistic medium.

CHIMÚ, PERU: ABOUT A.D. 1050–1470

The successors to the Lambayeque kingdom on the north coast of Peru were the Chimú, who founded the Kingdom of Chimor, as it is known in the Spanish chronicles. This mighty state created an extensive empire that stretched along the northern half of the Peruvian coast and undoubtedly interacted with the peoples of the highland Peruvian interior and the Ecuadorian coast. The royal art depended on the imagery

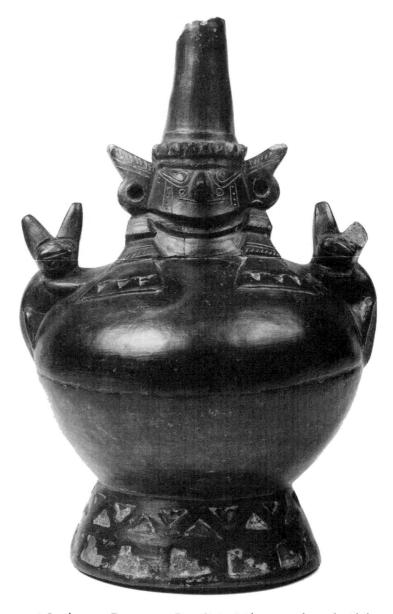

FIG. 4.28. Lambayeque Department, Peru. Sicán. Bridge-spouted vessel with foxes flanking lord, blackware pottery, 9¼" high. Integration, Middle Horizon, A.D. 850–1050. Gainesville, Fla.: Harn Museum of Art, C–73–127, anonymous gift in honor of Professor Philip A. Ward in appreciation of his encouragement and interest. Photo courtesy of museum.

of the Naymlap dynasty, as can be seen in carvings on the back of a wooden litter upon which their elite would be carried (fig. 4.29). The frontal figures in low relief descend from the Naymlap image (see pl. 13), but they lack the distinctive teardrop eyes and wings of the former. The headdress is shaped like an inverted knife of a form worn earlier by Moche warriors. Very significantly, as this figure is multiplied, it loses its mythic meaning but proliferates as a warrior image protecting the ruling class. Litters can be documented earlier as a means of transporting leaders, even in defeat (on the reverse side of fig. 3.4). Repeated images of frontal warriors also appear in Chimú and Inca textiles (fig. 4.30), sometimes arranged in step patterns like pyramids, suggesting imperial control of the mountains. Often these textiles are rendered with a mosaic of exotic feathers imported from the Amazonian side of the Andes, but sometimes, as depicted in figure 4.30, representations of feathers are woven into the cloth. Although posed frontally, the placement of the figures of this garment recalls the inexorable processions typically associated with imperial art.

A row of similar frontal figures supporting the authority of the king of Chimor were found in niches flanking the entryway to one of the royal compounds of the Chimú kings in the capital city of Chan Chan, on the opposite side of the river valley from the site of the Moche capital at Cerro Blanco. In two niches wooden figures stand staring rigidly out

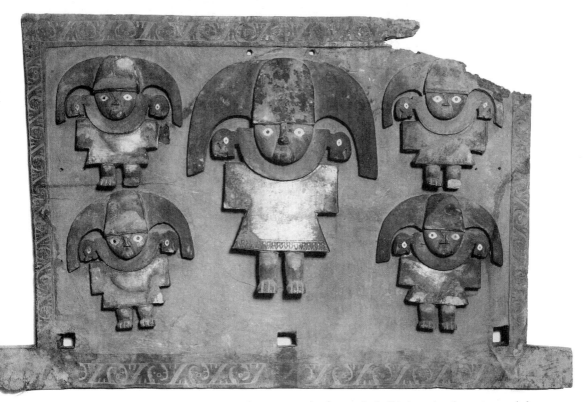

FIG. 4.29. Lambayeque Department, Peru. Chimú. Litter back, wood, shell inlay, cinnabar paint, and sheet metal, 23¾" high x 37⅜" wide. Integration, Late Intermediate Period, A.D. 1200–1350. Cleveland, Ohio: The Cleveland Museum of Art, 1952.233, John L. Severance Fund. Photo © The Cleveland Museum of Art, 1998.

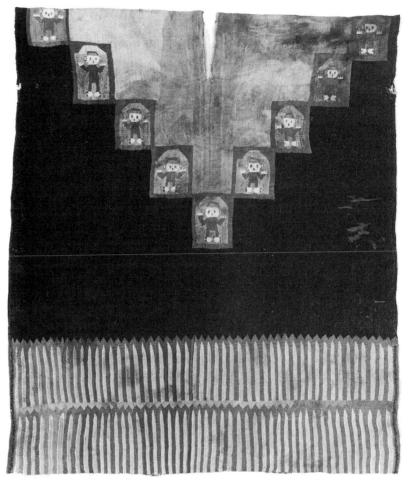

FIG. 4.30. Coastal Peru. Inca. Tunic with geometric frontal figures, wool and cotton, 35" high x 29½" wide. Integration, Late Horizon, A.D. 1438–1530. Washington: Dumbarton Oaks Research Library and Collections, B-505.PT. Photo courtesy of Dumbarton Oaks Research Library and Collections, Washington, D.C.

into the entry corridor; the best preserved (fig. 4.31) wears a short kilt and a peaked hat. Nude wooden figures occur in other Chimú contexts; presumably they would have been dressed in appropriate costume for the various provincial capitals in which the king's authority was to be exercised and represented.

The royal city of Chan Chan is composed of ten great citadels, each of which has been attributed to a different dynastic ruler of the Chimú (Day 1982: 63); today, however, each citadel is named for an early archaeologist active at the site. A recently excavated compound (fig. 4.32), named after the early Peruvian naturalist writer Mariano de Rivero, has multiple high adobe walls limiting access not only physically but also psychologically. They express a siege mentality even in the heart of the empire, where presumably they would not be needed.

They also communicate restrictiveness, keeping out the ordinary citizens who did not have business with the rulers. Those who did had to enter through narrow roofless corridors into a large courtyard, where major ceremonies could be held. Behind the courtyard are the audience chambers, each with a thick-walled niche in the center. Even further behind are the royal chambers, a water-collection reservoir, and, off to one side, a stepped pyramid intended for the burial of the monarch who built the citadel. Upon his death, the whole enclosed citadel ceased to exist for the living and became the shrine of the spirit of the now divine king. Only a few great pyramids exist on their own at Chan Chan; the rest are incorporated into the royal shrines. These free-standing monuments to divinity are also closed off by the multiple walls, creating restricted access similar to that seen in Toltec architecture (see figs. 4.1, 4.8).

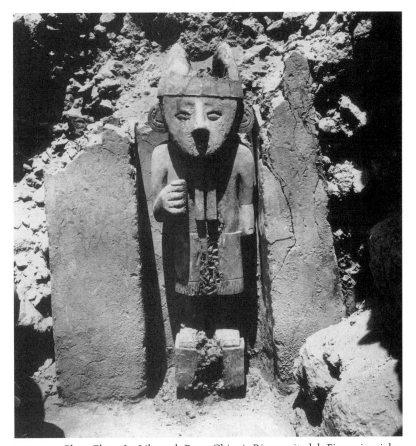

FIG. 4.31. Chan Chan, La Libertad, Peru. Chimú. Rivero citadel. Figure in niche, wood, excavated in situ, 24" high, on top of 20" high buried base. Integration, Late Intermediate Period, A.D. 1400–1470. Photo courtesy of Michael E. Moseley.

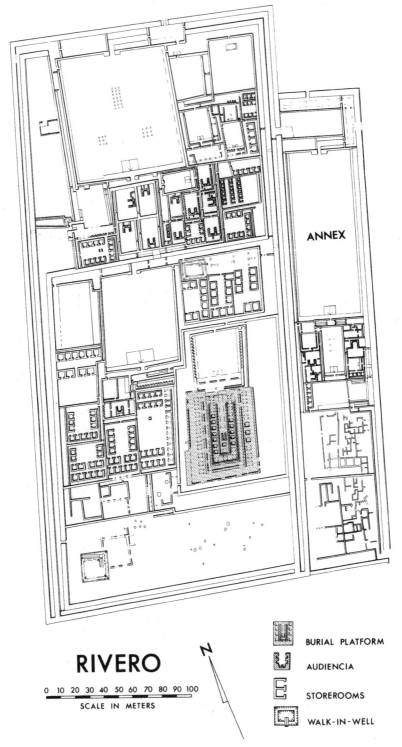

RIVERO

0 10 20 30 40 50 60 70 80 90 100
SCALE IN METERS

N

ANNEX

🪟 BURIAL PLATFORM

🪟 AUDIENCIA

E STOREROOMS

🪟 WALK-IN-WELL

FIG. 4.32. Chan Chan, La Libertad, Peru. Chimú. Plan of Rivero citadel, ca. 1340' long. Integration, Late Intermediate Period, A.D. 1400–1470. Drawing courtesy of Michael E. Moseley.

The greatest imperialists of the New World were the Inca, who expanded from their original homeland around Cuzco, Peru, to conquer all of Peru, Bolivia (except the tropical forest to the east), Ecuador, the northern two-thirds of Chile, and northwestern Argentina. They imposed their Quechua language on many of these conquered territories through systematic resettlement, so that in many cases we know very little about the original languages of important pre-Inca cultures. Like previous Andean people, the Inca had no writing, but kept records and communicated long-distance by means of a *quipu*—a textile strand with aligned cords, the different knots and colors of which indicated number and identity of goods being counted. They imposed artistic uniformity over their vast territory: the extensive presence of finely cut stone architectural blocks and thin-walled, necked storage jars, traditionally called *aryballoi* after a somewhat similar Greek form, provide ready examples. Design standardization of textiles and figurines suffocated the inventive variation of previous cultures. A good example is the silver figurine (fig. 4.33) representing a man of the noble class, identifiable by his long perforated earlobes. A wad in his left cheek indicates he is chewing coca leaves, still a common practice in the Andes to alleviate fatigue. Like so many others found throughout the Inca realm, this nude figurine, with its oversized head and undersized appendages, does not have a commanding presence. Its expressionless face, with wide, staring eyes, and rigid frontality, bespeaks an acquiescent pawn in an imperial chess game played across the length of the Andes. Other such figurines placed with children sacrificed on sacred mountaintops wear enveloping garments that prefigure the rich folk weaving still seen today in the southern highlands of Peru and Bolivia.

Standardized weavings were used to establish the rank of the wearer within the Inca hierarchy. The frontal figures already seen in Chimú designs were incorporated by the Inca into their tunics (see fig. 4.30). The whole design is stolidly geometric and symmetrical, each figure contained in its little niche like so many interchangeable subjects. One common design of tunics suggests a chessboard, although the actual game of chess, with its imperial association of pawns and rulers, was introduced by the Spaniards.

The rigidity noted in the visual arts is surprisingly absent in Inca monumental architecture. Powerful walls of important Inca buildings are made of huge stones individually shaped to fit their particular place with no use of mortar. While lesser buildings have regularly cut, four-

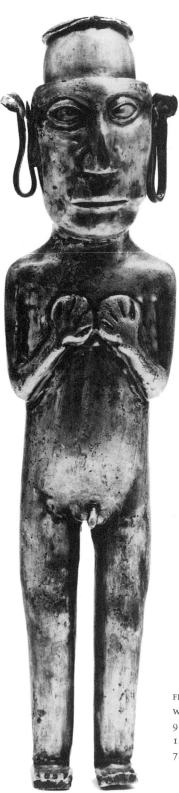

FIG. 4.33. Peru. Inca. Standing nude male with long perforated ears, cast hollow silver, 9" high. Integration, Late Horizon, A.D. 1480–1530. Madrid: Museo de América, 7431. Photo courtesy of museum.

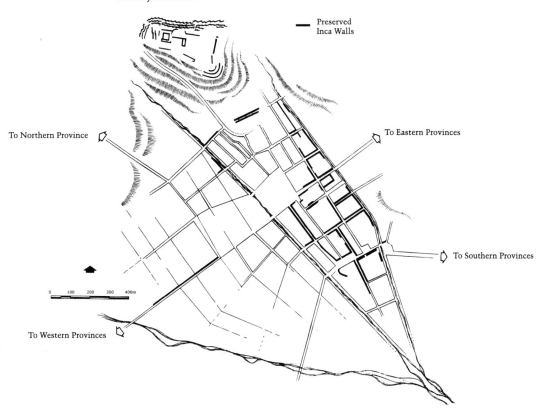

Sacsayhuaman

Preserved Inca Walls

To Northern Province

To Eastern Provinces

To Southern Provinces

To Western Provinces

0   100   200   300   400m

FIG. 4.34. Cuzco, Cuzco Department, Peru. Inca. City plan in shape of puma, including Sacsayhuaman ceremonial center. Integration, Late Horizon, before A.D. 1532. Line drawing after Graziano Gasparini and Luise Margolies.

sided stones, even they have a swell to their surfaces that suggests organic matter rather than inert rock (pl. 14). Some stones literally become animated with small creatures, executed in low relief, skittering across their surfaces. Finally, the plan of the royal capital, Cuzco, takes the shape of a giant puma, although the individual city blocks are generally rectangular (fig. 4.34), similar to the grid plan imposed on European planned cities (see chap. 5). The puma plan is adapted to the irregularities of the terrain, its tail formed by the juncture of rivers, its head by the massive-walled ceremonial center of Sacsayhuaman, which still overlooks modern Cuzco.

The anonymity of most Inca citizens disappears when we look into the unique face of one of the emperors (fig. 4.35), a stone sculpture found under the colonial church of La Compañía (see fig. 5.23). The strong depiction of character comes from the deep yet animated wrinkles around the eyes and mouth. It is identifiable as the emperor

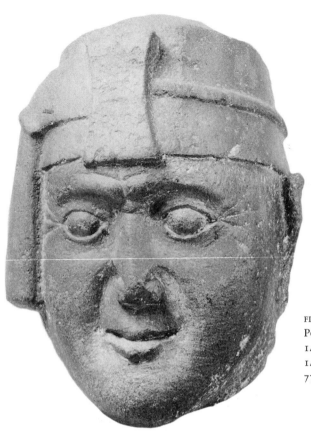

FIG. 4.35. Cuzco, Cuzco Department, Peru. Inca. Head of Inca emperor, stone, 14⅜" high. Integration, Late Horizon, A.D. 1438–1533. Madrid: Museo de América, 7799. Photo courtesy of museum.

(or "Inca") by the distinctive headdress, including the asymmetrical tassel of royalty. Larger than life size, this head must have been part of an impressive statue, although no such sculptured bodies have survived. Yet previous imperial sculptures provide prototypes, such as Manteño standing stone males or even Tiwanaku monoliths (see fig. 4.23). The royal Inca were believed to possess divinity via their descent from the sun god. This head does not emphasize divinity; rather it exhibits the strong individuality of earlier Tiwanaku and Moche rulers as communicated in their portrait jars (see pl. 5). Only the heroic scale of the sculpture suggests the political power this figure possessed. Yet because of conflict with a half-brother who controlled the secondary Inca capital in Quito, now capital of Ecuador, the last Inca was vulnerable to defeat by the Spaniards, who revealed him to be only human, as this portrait attests.

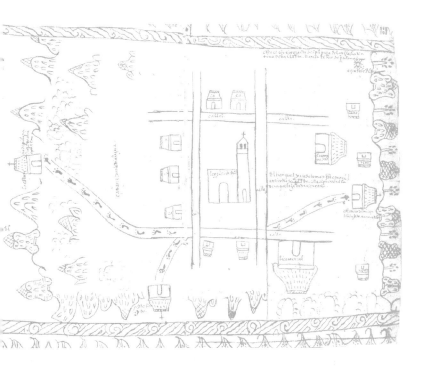

FIVE

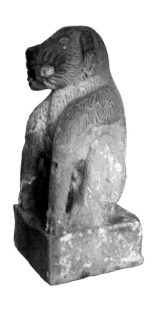

COLONIAL ART OF THE
AMERICAN VICEROYALTIES

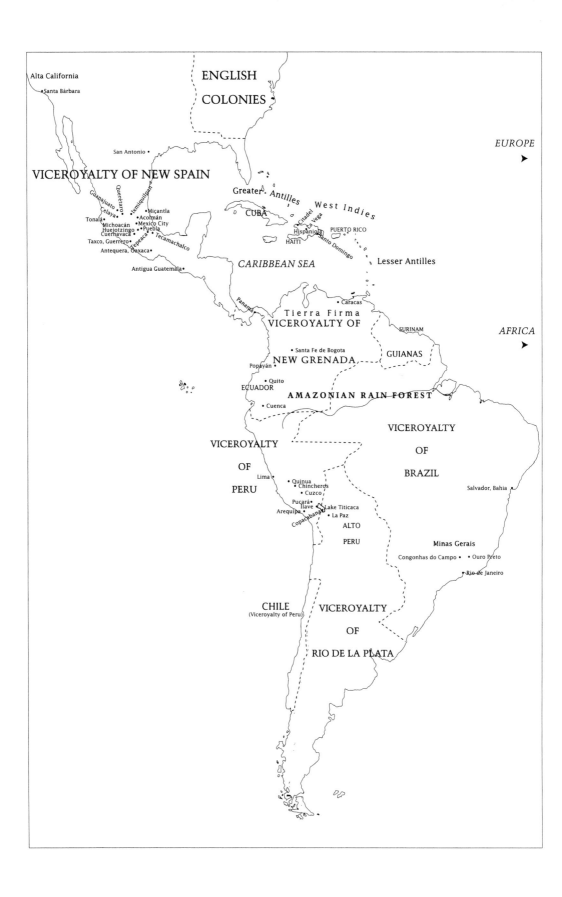

THE IMPLANTATION OF Iberian culture in the Americas with relatively little resistance must by seen as the most complete "spiritual conquest," to use Robert Ricard's phrase (1966), in the history of the world. This conquest was most complete in the upper levels of society, which had been responsible for awarding artistic commissions of major significance. Although there was an initial period of physical merging—called *mestizaje* in Spanish—between the native population and the Spanish conquistadors, the native cultural component became thoroughly suppressed in subsequent generations among the ruling classes. It is mainly in the lower levels of society that a great deal of native blood and ways still remain. The leading art media of the Pre-Columbian cultures were considered marginal by the Iberian cultures which supplanted them, relegated at best to minor arts and at worst dismissed as folk crafts: metalworking, lapidary, pottery, weaving, and manuscript illustrations. This discussion will make only passing references to the arts of these subcultures, mainly at the end of this chapter, but instead will concentrate on the arts which received the attention of the societies as a whole and their leaders.

Not coincidentally the areas of the greatest artistic production in the colonial times are those of the highest Pre-Columbian civilizations. Two reasons for this can be offered: first, the Spanish administration settled where the Inca and the Aztec empires already were located and to which the greatest amount of tribute was being sent; and second, both Mesoamerica and the Central Andes were the only areas in the Americas to produce permanent stone architecture and had long traditions of fine artistic craftsmanship in all media. By the mid-sixteenth century the centers of the two Spanish viceroyalties (New Spain and Peru) dominated those two areas where Pre-Columbian traditions of the skilled craftsmen had flowered.

Areas of lower culture were either bypassed initially or subsequently abandoned in all but name. In those areas, conquest of one small group did not cause submission by other neighboring groups. Their leaders did not wield nearly so much power as did the rulers of the high civilizations nor did they control the distribution of valuable goods over a wide area. In these areas the Europeans had to create their own distribution network, and they imposed on the natives a form of centralized control which they had not previously known and which they resisted either actively or passively. Areas inhabited by native nomads, such as northern and western North America and eastern and southern South America, were not seriously settled by Europeans until relatively late in the colonial era or even after independence.

Chiefdoms of the Circum-Caribbean area were the first encountered by Columbus between 1492 and 1502, both on the West Indies and on Tierra Firma—present-day Venezuela, Colombia, and lower Central America. Their populations, while subordinate to their chiefs and quite peaceable, had not had heavy demands placed upon them for either goods or services. The crafts at which they excelled—pottery modeling, shell- and woodcarving—were not highly prized by the Spaniards. However, at La Vega on Hispaniola (now the Dominican Republic) local potters made utilitarian jars and even some decorated wares for the Spaniards. The indigenous Taino decoration of small spirit faces modeled on vessels was rejected by the Catholic conquerors. Instead they requested that the potters copy Spanish vessel forms and geometric painted decoration by then known from the Mixtec style of Mesoamerica (see pl. 10). This hybrid style lasted only a generation until it died out, probably along with the Taino, who were its makers. Subsequent pottery was either totally utilitarian when it was made locally or fine decorated earthenware first imported from European centers (although a few cities came to specialize in reproductions of European styles). Like all Pre-Columbian peoples, the potters of the Greater Antilles had known neither the wheel, which would have permitted faster production and a more predictable product, nor glazes, which would have sealed the vessel more effectively. The indigenous Circum-Caribbean groups did not erect permanent stone architecture but built their structures of wood and light vegetative materials. Only their ritual spaces were outlined primarily with unworked stones. Thus, the permanent architecture which would subsequently be built on the islands could not employ any existing crafts from Pre-Columbian times. The skilled work of small objects such as amulets and stools could not immediately be transferred to Spanish needs. Once the belief in a spirit world which animated the decoration of these objects was destroyed by conversion to Roman Catholicism, the reason for them evaporated, to be replaced by images of Christian saints and symbols to venerate.

The more developed civilizations of Mesoamerica and the Andes attracted the primary attention of Spaniards in the 1520s after they came to realize the existence of those civilizations. The work specialization typical of civilizations produced artists who were full-time practitioners in one craft. Large-scale building projects organized according to a master plan taught the laborers how to follow directions and gave them skills in stone-cutting and architectural relief-carving. Paintings on plaster walls communicated with the building's users.

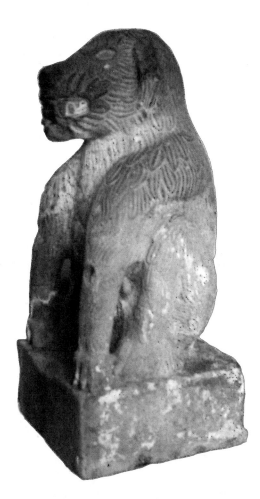

FIG. 5.1. Anonymous native sculptor. Seated lion from Tepeaca, Puebla, Mexico, stone, 43¼" high, 16th century. Tepotzotlán, Mexico: Viceregal Museum. Photo by John F. Scott.

Although there was considerable overlap, the different cultures had the following specializations which continued into the Hispanic period:

1) The Aztec centers in Mexico of the Late post-Classic Period, while co-opting many craftsmen from surrounding provinces, produced the finest Mesoamerican stonecarving in the round, a continuation of which can be found in a number of sixteenth-century highland towns, such as a fountain conceived as a lion but resembling an Aztec feathered coyote (fig. 5.1).

2) Featherworking was a highly esteemed craft among the Aztecs, as revealed in the accounts of Fray Bernardino de Sahagún and as attested by the preserved objects brought back to Europe at the time of Cortez. Sixteenth-century examples of mosaic featherwork after the Conquest are known, both from central Mexico and the old Tarascan empire in Michoacán, where it may have been introduced as an occupational craft from central Mexico by the utopian Bishop Vasco de Quiroga.

3) Aztec city planning is distinguished by the regularity of its design, notably in the capital city of Tenochtitlán, on which the modern Mexican capital of Mexico City was established in 1522. Straight causeways

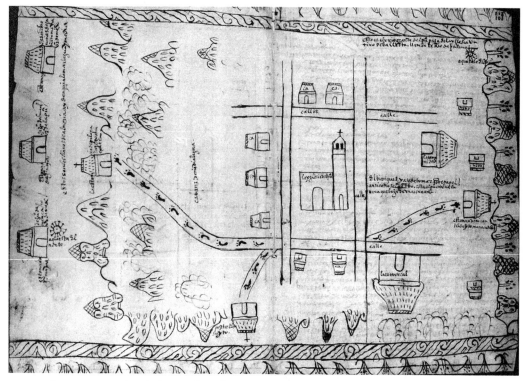

FIG. 5.2. Anonymous native draftsman for Sebastián de Arteaga. Map of Miçantla, Veracruz, Mexico, from *Relaciónes Geográficas*, ink on European paper, ca. 24" wide, 1579. Austin: Benson Latin American Collection, General Libraries, The University of Texas at Austin. Photo by John F. Scott.

which separated various bodies of water led into a city with a network of canals and streets intersecting at right angles, the kind of plan later recommended by the Spanish Laws of the Indies for the colonies around 1573. An early copy of a Pre-Columbian map of a section of such an area indicates that the Aztec state divided this rich agricultural property into regular administrative units (Robertson 1959: 83). This map on native maguey-leaf fiber provides an example of a bird's-eye view of a town with small houses and seated heads of households rendered in profile view, a convention continued in the colonial plans done on European paper beginning in 1579 to illustrate the *Relaciones Geográficas* (fig. 5.2).

4) The Mixteca-Puebla style lent the Aztec culture tradition of painted pottery, goldworking, and manuscript painting. Manuscript painting is best known from the Mixtec area (see pl. 11). No manuscript has been securely dated to the Pre-Columbian Aztec, although the Codex Borbonicus is mainly pre-Hispanic in style. Aztec and Mixtec painting differ in the sizes of the figures, the Aztec showing more naturalistic proportions and therefore taller figures (like fig. 4.14) than the Mixtec, which were squarish. Aztec compositions, less densely packed

than those in Mixtec manuscripts, often use the entire page as one large field, giving Aztec manuscript painting a sweep such as one most often sees in the early colonial manuscripts like the Codex Mendoza commissioned by the Spanish authorities.

5) Painting on ceramics done in the Mixteca-Puebla style, like their painted codices, was compact, angular, and bright (see pl. 10). The decorative nature of Mixteca-Puebla designs resulted from abstracting animal forms to the point that they were often unrecognizable by the uninitiated. The Spanish tradition of majolica pottery encouraged the substitution of vegetative forms for the animal ones which had religious associations, thereby neutralizing the importance of the pottery and converting it from a major expressive art to a minor decorative one, which it remains today. Perhaps only the fantasy world created in some of the best folk traditions such as Tonalá ware of Mexico transcend the purely decorative limitations imposed during the colonial era.

6) In the Andes, weaving in Pre-Columbian times was a high art, and cloth was a major element of exchange, ritual, and social status. The indigenous highland communities of Ecuador, Peru, and Bolivia conserve many aspects of the earlier significance of textiles in their lives (see fig. 5.36). Decorative motifs have changed from Pre-Columbian emphasis on geometric patterns, many with definite meaning, and animal motifs, often symbolic of deities, to plant motifs and decorative patterns borrowed from European folk traditions.

7) In the Central Andes, other crafts practiced by skilled native specialists were converted into minor decorative arts in the service of the Catholic Church and the Spanish oligarchy. Metalworking, a skill at which the Andean kingdoms excelled (see, for example, pl. 13, fig. 4.27), was channeled into silversmithing in Peru, using the abundant raw material mined in Alto Perú, now Bolivia. The pre-Hispanic skill in woodcarving evident from many coastal sites and burials (see figs. 4.29, 4.31) was put to the service of the Church in the form of pulpits, choir stalls, *retablos*, and grill screens.

8) Pre-Hispanic architecture and urban planning demonstrate skills later adapted to colonial needs. Urban settlements of the Inca empire had large square plazas in the center, where political authority was manifested in spectacle and redistribution of goods. Streets separated into walled blocks enclosed rooms on courtyards, as in the Spanish tradition. Sometimes the overall plan of Inca cities took the form of a symbolic animal (see fig. 4.34); other times it was a regular grid, especially when the city was created at one time, such as the garrison towns of the Inca or the imperial compounds of the Chimú at Chan Chan (see

fig. 4.32). Architectural construction was executed in its most permanent form using stone in the highlands, whereas the coast traditionally
built of mud-brick or puddled earth. Inca stonework, although best
known for its large, biomorphically irregular blocks fitted together
without mortar with incredible precision, was most often constructed
of rectangular, smaller blocks (pl. 14). This latter technique was put to
immediate service by the Spaniards for its correspondence in appearance to European construction. On the coast, adobe walls were covered
with busy plaster reliefs of two-level animal designs, providing the
precursors of the teeming carved surfaces of colonial stucco façades.

IBERIAN TRADITIONS

Mention has been made of imported Spanish traditions of art and architecture where they correspond with indigenous features. Four specific
components of the Hispanic artistic tradition need to be highlighted.
These are (1) the Moorish survivals, (2) Reconquest architecture, (3)
northern European book illustration, and (4) the design principles of the
Italian Renaissance:

  1) The Moorish conquest of Spain in the eighth century A.D. inaugurated more than seven centuries of Islamic presence in Spanish culture.
Some of the Islamic traditions are common Mediterranean forms
which had been found in Spain during Roman times. One such feature
is the house built around an interior court. The Arabs had taken that
basic Mediterranean plan and exaggerated the contrast between the
exterior of the house, which presented a blank wall to the outside, and
the sheltered garden in the courtyard (*patio* in Spanish), which created
an oasis paradise (fig. 5.3). Private Hispanic patios even today preserve
the sense of a lush garden away from the world. The severe high walls
on the exterior contrasted in later Moorish architecture with the rich
decoration around the doorway and sometimes around windows or
balconies on the second story. Among the treatments used to create
this ornament, one stands out as important in the transfer to the colonies in the New World: the *alfiz,* a rectangle which surrounds the
arched upper part of the door opening. Within this rectangular field,
dense two-dimensional ornament plays off against the smooth, planar
surface of the rest of the exterior wall. Within the Moorish style building, woodwork is often decorated with complex geometric motifs, often incorporating star shapes. Doors bear this decoration in low relief,
and ceilings show it in the rich three-dimensional interplay of their
cross-beams and rafters. Geometric and floral patterns worked into
brilliantly colored tile designs cover floors and the lower section of the

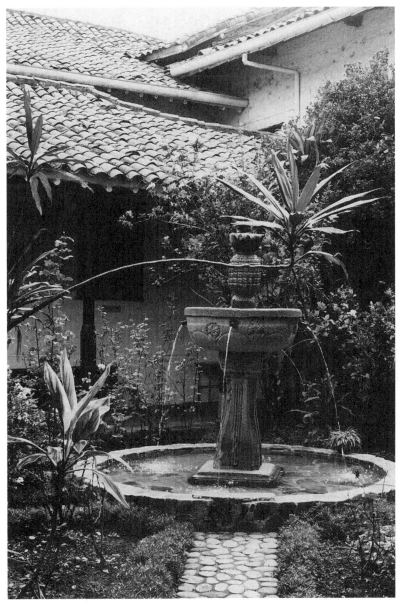

FIG. 5.3. Anonymous. Patio of convent with surrounding wooden colonnades. 17th century; central fountain, 1820. Cali, Colombia: Museo Colonial La Merced. Photo by John F. Scott.

walls. Many of these Moorish features had been quite thoroughly assimilated into Spanish art of the Reconquest period; they were called *mudéjar*, like the tributary Moorish subjects of Christian kings.

2) The Reconquest of Spain from the Moors during the later Middle Ages brought to the Spanish architectural tradition certain features which were considered appropriate to newly conquered areas and which demonstrated a military aesthetic. Major buildings assumed a

fortified appearance from the outside, with crenelations on the upper profile of the walls. In many cases these were not actually functional but bespoke a siege mentality. Urban settlements created in the newly conquered territories took the form of Roman military camps, laid out in a rectangular grid with the major streets intersecting at right angles in a central plaza. This grid was then introduced to the newly conquered colonies in America as the image of Spanish civilization. Ultimately it became required as part of the Laws of the Indies for the establishment of new towns.

3) The accession of the Hapsburg emperor Charles V to the Spanish throne in 1516 brought increased influence from beyond the Pyrenees, especially from Flanders (now in Belgium), which was also part of the Hapsburg realm. The Flemings, as the most brilliant practitioners of the new art of oil painting, had already provided fifteenth-century Spain with paintings often framed into *retablos,* large paneled structures behind church altars. The *retablo* format derived from movable triptychs, but by the fifteenth century they had grown to elaborate architectural extravaganzas, often filling the entire end of the sanctuary to the height of the vaulting. On a more humble scale, Flemish and German artists who never trod on Spanish soil had perhaps a deeper influence on Spanish-American art through their mastery of the new techniques of engraving and other graphic arts, including woodcuts. Publishers in northern European cities flooded the European market with cheaply made prints illustrating religious texts and, later, reproducing important oil paintings. European prints had a profound influence on the paintings executed in the far-off territories of the Spanish Empire. Through the prints the new styles of art were spread: first the intense realism of fifteenth-century northern painters, then the more idealized naturalism coming from the Italian Renaissance in the sixteenth century, and finally the non-naturalistic exaggerations now termed Mannerism. Book decorations, especially those on title pages, brought Mannerist architectural decoration into the hands of any literate man and were adapted in America on a monumental scale to architecture in a degree that would astonish the original designers of the humble woodcuts.

4) The principles of the Italian Renaissance in the sixteenth century, when it finally reached Spain, were often misunderstood. Logical organization of parts and a careful attention to proportions were often lost on the provincial copyists, who freely used designs from the various editions of architectural pattern books published first in Italy and then elsewhere in translation. In the representational arts, the greatest influ-

ence of the Italian Renaissance is in its last stylistic stage, Mannerism, which was picked up by other Western European countries during the sixteenth century and made into their own styles. It was in this tradition that the first professional painters worked who came to the Spanish colonies in the second half of the sixteenth century.

EARLY RENAISSANCE WITH GOTHIC SURVIVALS:
ABOUT 1500–1540

When Columbus set sail, the Renaissance spirit was in men's minds but the waning Gothic style provided the architectural backdrop for human activities everywhere but in Italy. The first European settlement that provided more than mere shelter, Santo Domingo, was established at its present location in 1502. The plan of the city, a grid modified by the irregularity of the sloped site, derived from the precedents of military camps like Santa Fé de Granada, established at the location of the final attack on the Moors prior to their expulsion from Spain in 1492. The individual buildings in downtown Santo Domingo, many of which are preserved and carefully restored, reveal aspects of the fast-disappearing Gothic style in flame-shaped tracery; richly sculpted portals such as the north entrance to the Santo Domingo Cathedral, which has slender colonnettes supporting ribbed archivolts (fig. 5.4); and the interior ribbed vaulting, forming a network of closely spaced lines over the interior surface. Vaulting in Latin America retained the Gothic-style ribbing well into the seventeenth century, although it had disappeared in Spain during the sixteenth.

In the secular center of Santo Domingo, the Palace of Diego Columbus (fig. 5.5), son of Christopher, was in part the fortified stronghold implied by its mudéjar name *alcázar,* Arabic for "the fortified place." Like medieval castles, it has heavy walls and crenelated cornices; wall openings in the two end blocks are small. In the middle, however, it opens on both stories and both sides to graceful arcades which shelter porches overlooking the river and the new city. The building combines the medieval military style of Reconquest headquarters with the grace of the Italian Renaissance, although some detailing is still Late Gothic. A nearly identical building was erected in Cuernavaca, Mexico, for Hernán Cortés as the manor house for his newly bestowed marquisate. Undoubtedly the builders in Mexico had already seen the Santo Domingo construction for Columbus's son and wished to emulate it.

The earliest monastic structures in Mexico were built by natives under the direction of mendicant friars, members of Roman Catholic religious orders (Franciscans, Augustinians, and Dominicans) who had

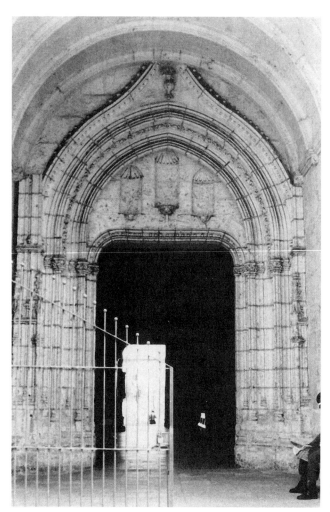

FIG. 5.4. Bishop Alejandro Geraldini and assistants, designers. Santa María la Menor Cathedral north portal, Santo Domingo, Dominican Republic, Gothic style, ca. 1521. Photo by John F. Scott.

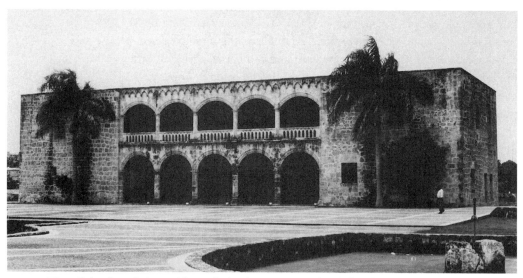

FIG. 5.5. Diego Columbus, designer. Alcázar (Palace), reconstructed west façade, Santo Domingo, Dominican Republic, 1509–1523. Photo by John F. Scott.

vowed poverty and were committed to living among the people they were charged with converting. Their buildings also displayed certain features which reflect the continued presence of the Gothic style. Stone vaulting, as in Santo Domingo, was uniformly in the Late Gothic tradition of complex rib-vaults. The first cloister patio inside the friars' residence compound at Acolmán in Mexico, built around 1539, displays other Gothic features such as narrow high openings between heavy buttressed piers. The second cloister patio of Acolmán, built in the 1560s, reveals a dramatic change from the design of the first. Its patio proportions were expanded to a gracious, open space. The massive, closely spaced buttresses of the first gave way to the lighter arcades of the second. The flattened arches of the earlier first-floor cloister are replaced by the Classical semicircular arches on both levels of the second. In other words, the designers have moved from the medieval concept of form to the Renaissance one. The high, crenelated profile of the walls of the church at Acolmán recalls the image of fortress churches established during the Reconquest to subjugate the Moors. Once inside the second court, though, the proportions are harmonious, creating the balance sought by the Renaissance. The designers believed they were resurrecting a universally valid language based on the classical orders of columns, themselves reflecting what human minds would perceive as the right amount of structure to support the apparent load, as if a human body were weighted down with it. The style reflects the Humanist principles found in other creative enterprises of the age.

Beautiful Plateresque decoration is carved around the main entrance to the church (fig. 5.6). While the term Plateresque was later applied to suggest the resemblance of the forms to ornate silverwork, its architectural vocabulary is that of the Corinthian order of Antiquity as revived by the Italian Renaissance. The structural logic of the columns, however, has been compromised by the wrapping of garlands and sashes around their shafts and by the dissolution of the base into a number of acanthus-ridged drums curving in at the bottoms, so that what is the lower half of the column appears to be a series of stacked pots.

The necessity of handling great masses of potential converts stimulated an original solution in Mexico: the creation of a large enclosed forecourt, called an atrium after those courts in front of the early Christian churches of the fourth and fifth centuries in the Mediterranean. The large single-nave interiors of the churches created enclosed spaces unknown to Pre-Columbian builders, who were restricted to narrow, corbel-vaulted chambers or to a forest of stubby stone columns. The

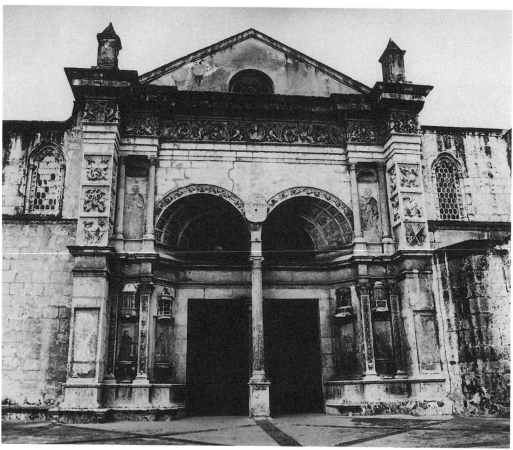

FIG. 5.6. Alonso Rodríguez, designer. Santa María la Menor Cathedral main portal, Santo Domingo, Dominican Republic, Plateresque style, before 1540. Photo by Roy C. Craven, Jr., courtesy of Center for Latin American Studies, University of Florida.

richness of the exterior decoration, however, corresponded to Pre-Columbian traditions of dense low-relief designs used by both Mixtec and Maya architects. And the large enclosed atrium, rectangular in plan and bounded on all sides by walls and shrines but focusing on the soaring façade of the church, recalled pre-Conquest ceremonial spaces created by four-sided plazas, where the people stood to observe the ritual which generally took place at the top of a steep pyramid. Like the placement of some churches directly on the site of native temples, the form chosen by the early friars attempted to relate the kind of religious experience the natives had known to the new Christian one by means of creating the same kind of ceremonial space.

Crucial to this substitution was the inclusion of open-air chapels within the atrium spaces. Although their location varied considerably, ideally they were raised above the heads of the throngs of worshippers and were framed by architecture, much as the Pre-Columbian temples had provided a backdrop for the ritual performed on top of a platform. Acolmán has such a chapel to the right of the church (fig. 5.7). Instead of the low altar placed in the center of the Pre-Columbian plazas, the Christian atriums had a massive cross on a heavy square base. The crosses placed in atriums were an ingenious mix of representation and symbol; they merged the image of the crucified Christ with that of the Pre-Columbian world tree (see fig. 3.34), often with leaves sprouting from the crossbar. Christ is only represented by the face at the center of the cross, but by implication the rest of the cross becomes his outstretched arms and hanging trunk (fig. 5.8). Other symbols of the Passion story are applied in a flat, raised relief common in Pre-Columbian carvings (see fig. 4.2). The sculptor thereby chose to communicate via the symbolic language to which the natives were accustomed rather than in a naturalistic language then being accepted in western Europe. Finally, in each corner of the enclosure, small rest-stops called *posas* open onto the atrium; in these, processions around the atrium paused briefly for instruction.

The friars in Mexico undertook with enthusiasm and sincerity their charge to convert the natives. Their defense of the natives' rights was

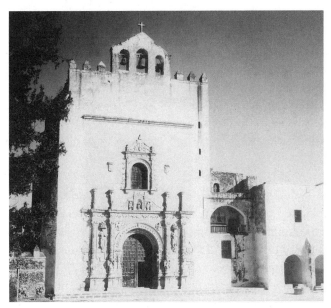 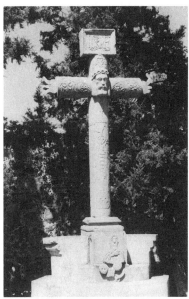

Left: FIG. 5.7. Maestro Palomira (and others?), architects. San Agustín, cut stone and plastered façade and open chapel, Acolmán, State of México, Mexico. 1539–1571. Photo by Judith Hancock Sandoval, courtesy of Condumex, Mexico City.

Right: FIG. 5.8. Anonymous native sculptor. Raised relief cross from atrium, San Agustín, Acolmán, State of México, Mexico, stone, ca. 88½" high, mid-16th century. Photo by John F. Scott.

not appreciated by the secular authorities, who were trying to fulfill a different charge to exploit the riches of these new territories for Spain. This conflict in aims and an increasing emphasis within the Church on doctrinal purity in religious practices (which the friars had relaxed to appeal more to native traditions) resulted in a decrease in the friars' influence in the late sixteenth century.

In contrast to the quantity of rich monastic establishments in Mexico during the 1560s, Colombia preserves only some simple open chapels in the formerly Chibcha highlands. Peru, the other main area of indigenous civilization and dense population, was converted later and has only a few remains of atriums and open chapels, such as the one at Copacabana on the shores of Lake Titicaca. Significantly, Copacabana had been an important Inca shrine.

Painting within the cloisters was primarily executed in black on the white plaster ground of the walls. The resulting *grisaille* (tones of grey) murals seem to be enlarged versions of European prints, very popular in the sixteenth century. Some may have been painted by friars, although the sometimes illiterate lettering and geometric conventions suggest native hands (Toussaint 1967: 41). Pre-Columbian mural painting had often been monochrome, as at Mitla and Tulum, so the native artists undoubtedly felt no compunction about retaining the black-and-white scheme. In Malinalco, formerly a center of an Aztec warrior cult (see fig. 4.14), murals inside a new Christian cloister created a garden filled with both Spanish and Mexican plants and animals, inspired in part by the herbal books created in Mexico City to inform Spaniards of the living resources of their empire (Peterson 1993). Most of the images, however, were familiar to the Europeans and closely copy Renaissance precedents.

MANNERISM: ABOUT 1540–1640

Paradoxically, the late phase of the Renaissance in Italy was often the first style transferred to the many areas of the New World. For this reason, Latin American designers might not understand the rational structural and naturalistic basis of early and high Renaissance art and architecture. They copied instead the fantastic and highly idealized designs executed in the "beautiful manner"—hence Mannerism— which transcends realistic limitations.

In the structures built for the friars, the decorative bands painted in such profusion as frames or architectural friezes are in the *grotesque* tradition derived from first-century A.D. Roman fresco decoration newly unearthed in the later fifteenth century. The buried rooms re-

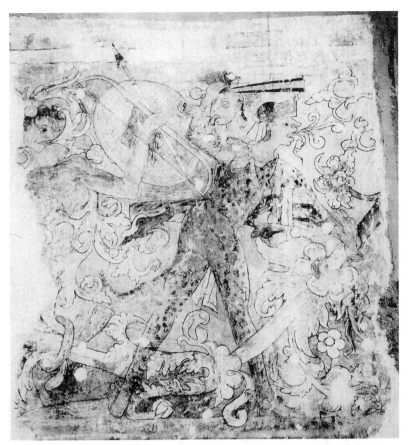

FIG. 5.9. Anonymous native Otomí painter. *Battle Between Indians and Centaurs,* polychromed fresco, Ixmiquilpan, Hidalgo, Mexico, ca. 72" high, ca. 1569–1572. Photo by Judith Hancock Sandoval, courtesy of Condumex, Mexico City.

minded contemporary observers of grottoes, hence our name *grotesque* from the French. Such designs, which can defy natural and structural logic, became popular during the Mannerist phase of the later Renaissance, particularly when reproduced by Flemish wood engravers as space fillers or border decoration in their books. From here they were adapted and transferred to the walls of structures in New Spain.

A cycle of paintings uncovered in a small church in Ixmiquilpan, northeast of Mexico City, depicts a series of battle scenes showing men with obviously native battle dress and weapons fighting monsters enlarged from *grotesque* woodcut ornament (fig. 5.9). These are clearly original compositions by Indian painters, directed toward their own people, who were by then converted Christians but who would understand the battle between Christians and pagans better if presented in their own vernacular (Pierce 1981: 7). This mural, unlike most of those on cloister walls, was rendered in full color. The figural style is European, with warriors of natural proportions rendered in three-quarter

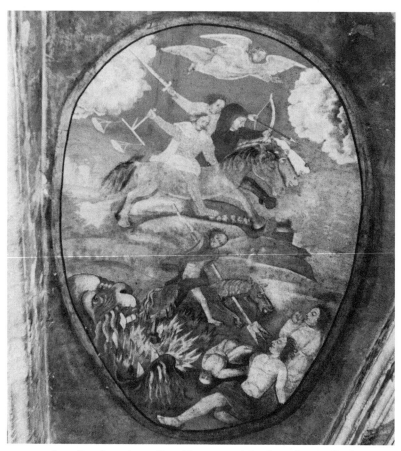

FIG. 5.10. Juan Gersón, painter, *Four Horsemen of the Apocalypse*, oil painting on fabric under rear choir, Tecamachalco, Puebla, Mexico, ca. 42" high x 28" wide, 1562. Photo by John F. Scott.

view, a difficult posture for Pre-Columbian artists to draw in torsos and never done for faces.

The complete assimilation of a known native artist is revealed in the Franciscan church at Tecamachalco, southeast of the European-style city of Puebla. Full color oil paintings on cloth are glued to the masonry of the vaults under the choir loft (fig. 5.10). Although the date of the paintings (1562) and the name of the artist (Juan Gersón) have long been known, he was assumed to be a European because of his Flemish name and his relatively skilled northern Renaissance style. Archival research, however, revealed that Gersón, who adopted this name in honor of a then-famous cleric, was, in fact, a native (Camelo et al. 1964: 28). That a native could have assimilated so completely the European style so that he was able to convert black-and-white compositions of woodcuts from a sixteenth-century German Bible into fully modeled and colored oil paintings highlights how much some native artists had absorbed the lessons of their friar teachers and surpassed all but the professional painters.

By the latter sixteenth century, professional artists were arriving from Europe to meet the needs of the new commissions and the stricter requirements regarding qualifications for painters executing religious subjects. These requirements were imposed by an ecclesiastical council in 1555 and reinforced in Mexico by the establishment of an artists' guild in 1557. The Fleming Simón Pereyns, who arrived in Mexico in 1556, assembled around him an impressive group of European artists, who by their skill—and because of the increasing prejudice of the authorities against natives—began to supplant native artists in the important civil and ecclesiastical commissions. Pereyns's paintings were incorporated in *retablos* which filled the walls behind altars. The assembling of these enormous *retablos* demanded considerable cooperation among painters, sculptors, carpenters, and gilders. In the *retablo* in the monastery church at Huejotzingo of 1586 (fig. 5.11), constructed by

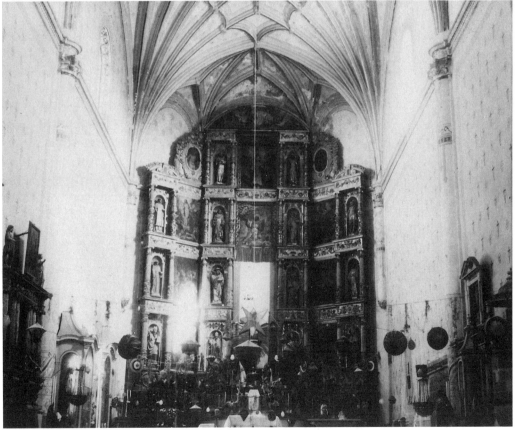

FIG. 5.11. Pedro de Requeña, assembler; Simón Pereyns, painter; Luis de Arciniega, sculptor; and others. Retablo, painted and gilded wood, San Francisco, Huejotzingo, Puebla, Mexico, 1586. Photo by Judith Hancock Sandoval, courtesy of Condumex, Mexico City.

Pedro de Requeña as assembler, eight paintings by Pereyns are placed in the frames created by the rectangular wooden architectural grid, much like Roman stage designs. Fourteen wood figures were carved, possibly by Luis de Arciniega, in a style that is still High Renaissance in its balance, strength, and stability; the heavily robed figures emerge from niches with conch-shell arches which appear to be sunburst halos behind their heads. Finally, a gilder took charge not only of applying the gold leaf but also the many enameled layers of skin tones (*encarnación*—"putting on the flesh") and painting the draperies. The creation of the great *retablos* was a major undertaking of colonial Latin America, important both for the high quality of artistic skill and for the quantity of such works executed. Many of the significant advances in colonial arts first appear in *retablos*, then later spread to more independent forms of art. The very integration of the arts traditional in the *retablos* may have stimulated each artist to try to outshine his colleagues and produce finer works.

Mexico was not alone in attracting European artists of high quality to work on artistic commissions. The South American viceroyalty centered in Lima attracted notable Italian artists: Angelino Medoro, Mateo Pérez de Alesio, and Bernardo Bitti. Bitti was an Italian Jesuit who came to Lima in 1574, where he worked on the decorations for San Pedro. He then went to the highlands, where his works are found in Arequipa, Juli, and La Paz. By 1587 he was in Ecuador. The formats seen in surviving paintings by Bitti suggest most were designed for *retablos* (pl. 15). His works are the most recognizably Mannerist of all this group: His faces have a linear elegance, his bodies sway in graceful curves and have characteristically elongated proportions. His icy pastel colors have the shimmering reflections associated with Tintoretto in Italy and carried to Spain by El Greco. Native viewers would not have expected realistic naturalism anyway, and so they could appreciate Mannerism's decorative qualities.

The last of the great Mannerist painters, Baltasar de Echave Orio, founded a virtual dynasty of painters which dominated official commissions in Mexico for more than a century. This first Echave married the daughter of an important associate of Pereyns, Francisco Ibía, called Zumaya after the same small town of that name in Spain from which Echave also came. Although Echave Orio is an early seventeenth-century painter, like El Greco he continued a shimmering Mannerist style well after it had died out in many parts of Europe. His major commission was to make fourteen paintings for the *retablo* of Santiago Tlatelolco, of which three dated to 1609 have survived. In *Porziuncola*, the

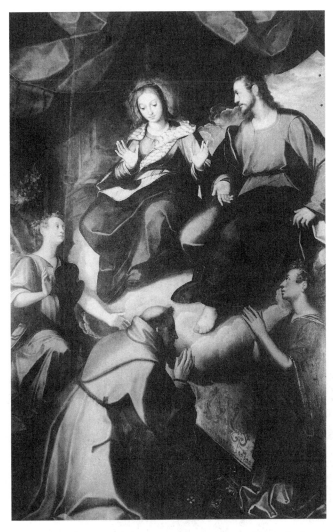

FIG. 5.12. Baltasar de Echave Orio, painter, *Porziuncola*, oil on canvas, formerly in retablo of Santiago Tlatelolco, Federal District, Mexico, 99¼" x 63" wide, 1609. Mexico City: Pinacoteca Virreinal de San Diego. Photo courtesy of Instituto de Investigaciones Estéticas archive, Universidad Nacional Autónoma de México.

figures of Christ and the Virgin levitate on clouds in front of the kneeling Saint Francis (fig. 5.12). Although this suggests the believable reality of the miracle, an illusion which Baroque painters loved to depict, the elongated bodies of the holy figures, the mannered finger postures, and the crackling highlights of their drapery clearly make this work more in the spirit of late Mannerism, as does the paradoxical perspective of the scene. Two of this painter's sons (the Echave Ibía) were also painters, and his grandson, Baltasar de Echave Rioja, had a firm command of the Baroque style (see fig. 5.18).

The major architectural undertaking by the mendicant friars in South America during the sixteenth century, the church of San Francisco in Quito, Ecuador (fig. 5.13), displays the clearest presence of Mannerist architecture in Latin America. Constructed by Jodoco Ricke, a Flemish friar, beginning around 1564, in the rusticated style of the Late Renaissance popular in his homeland, it displays a willful

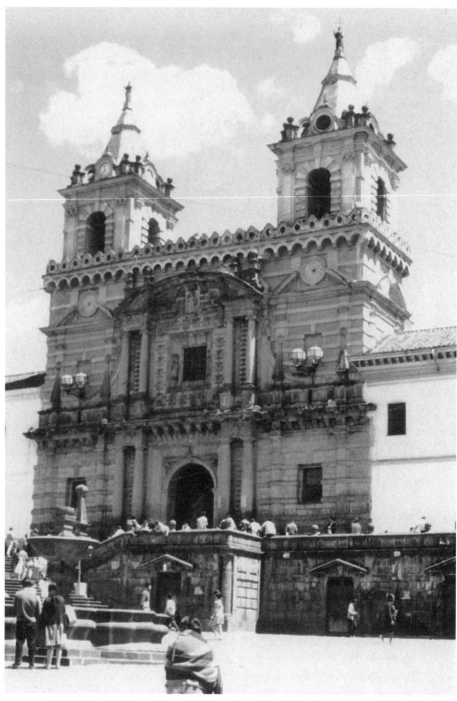

FIG. 5.13. Fray Jodoco Ricke, architect, San Francisco church façade, cut stone, Quito, Ecuador, 1564–1581. Photo by Roy C. Craven, Jr., courtesy of Visual Resources Center, University of Florida.

confusion of architectural statement which characterizes a mannered variation on the classical orders. While the columns surrounding the main portal and its upper story are correct Roman orders, with plain shafts and full entablatures, the similar arrangements of orders on each side are eaten away by the horizontal rusticated bands expressing the massive stone walls needed to support the twin towers. The verticality of the columns becomes obscured by the busier, more visually arresting horizontality of alternately projecting and recessed bands of stone blocks. Rusticated designs like this were found not only on actual buildings in Flanders but also as framing devices on title pages of European books. Whatever its source, the façade of San Francisco stands as one of the clearest expressions of Flemish design in Latin American architecture. The influence of the Quito church on other architectural designs built in South America is so pronounced that George Kubler has written, "If it were not standing now, we should have to reconstruct it from texts and images" (Kubler and Soria 1959: 87).

PURISM: ABOUT 1580–1650

The century from the 1560s to the 1650s was dominated by the building of the cathedrals, massive establishments which, although spacious inside, austerely look down on the visitor standing outside. In the Spanish American cities no open chapels reach out to the multitudes. The cathedrals mark the dominance of the secular clergy, ruled by the bishops as an extension of the Spanish national church, over the mendicant friars, ruled by their own international hierarchy answerable only to the Vatican.

Plans for the first great cathedrals beginning in the latter sixteenth century show the insistence on bilateral symmetry established by Juan de Herrera, whose works in Spain, notably the Escorial Palace (1563–1582) and Valladolid Cathedral (around 1585), are ultimately based on Italian design books. His style, called Herreresque or Purist, reveals a Mannerist priority given to formal qualities above structure through its very abstract, unornamented designs of rigid bilateral symmetry and strictly regular proportions that give only secondary consideration to function. The perfect geometry forces the choir of the cathedral to be of equal length as the nave, in spite of the functional need of the nave to accommodate the larger congregation. The four equal towers placed on each corner in Valladolid Cathedral were never realized in Latin American cathedrals. Central domes mark the crossing of the transept and the main axis of the nave-choir. These plans were most completely achieved in the twin cathedrals of Mexico City and Puebla, the former by Claudio de Arciniega after 1584 and the latter attributed to him, although at least the plan is also credited to Francisco Becerra. A number of buildings in South America are also credited to Becerra: the churches for the Dominicans and the Augustinians in Quito in 1581 and the cathedrals of Lima and of Cuzco in 1582 have similar plans. The Lima and Cuzco cathedrals do not have the rigid symmetry of those in Mexico City and Puebla, and their squared piers, ribbed vaults, and high side aisles retain more medieval aspects than do the round columns and saucer domes built in the seventeenth century when Mexico City and Puebla cathedrals were vaulted. The exteriors of all these cathedrals show a ponderous repetition of long walls broken by buttresses designed like pilasters. Massive corner towers frame the low, broad façades in the front, creating an image of ponderous stability sometimes nicknamed "Earthquake Baroque" (fig. 5.14).

After 1590, rustic churches in the highlands of Peru exhibit portals of austere simplicity set in severely plain walls (fig. 5.15) and lacking the exuberant explosion of form around the arched opening manifested by the Plateresque style. In their striving for correctness above all, the builders of Purist architecture bring Catholic civilization of the orthodox, austere version of King Philip II not only to the European-founded towns of Latin America but also to the indigenous communities in the Peruvian highlands.

The severe Renaissance style of Herrera found a strong echo in Brazil, which was more tightly wedded to Portugal than were the Spanish colonies to Spain. From 1580 until 1640, Portugal and Brazil had been a viceroyalty under the Hapsburgs who ruled Spain, yet this political link was not reflected in Portuguese art. In Brazil the constructions of the first century of colonization, from 1549 to 1650, had been so unpretentious as to be almost styleless, although their clear geometry ties them to the Plain style in Portugal, related to Herreresque Purism. The subsequent century, 1650–1750, saw the northeastern coastal settlement of Salvador (originally known as Bahia) become the center of metropolitan building. The former Jesuit collegiate church, now the Cathedral of São Salvador, was rebuilt in 1657–1672 in a fine expression of Portuguese Mannerism, characterized by an emphasis on verticality and a flat, linear treatment of the surfaces, notably the flat-surfaced scrolls which support the central pediment. Most interesting is the continuous spatial flow of the interior which allows the interior divisions to float free of the spatial envelope created by the exterior box. This feature prefigures the more active treatment of space in Luso-

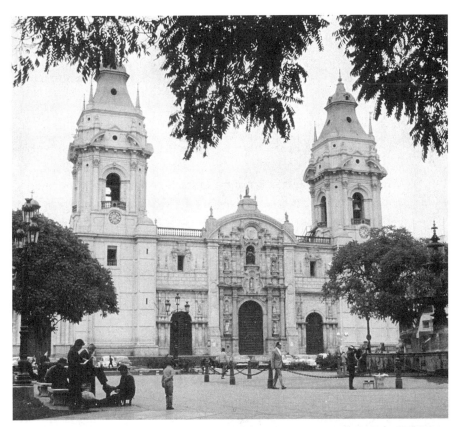

Above: FIG. 5.14. Francisco Becerra, original designer. Lima Cathedral, Lima, Peru, 1598–1604, rebuilt after 1746. Photo by Roy C. Craven, Jr., courtesy of Visual Resources Center, University of Florida.

Right: FIG. 5.15. Juan Gómez and Juan López, carpenters, and Juan Jiménez, mason. San Miguel façade, Ilave, Puno Department, Peru, 1590–1601. Photo by John F. Scott.

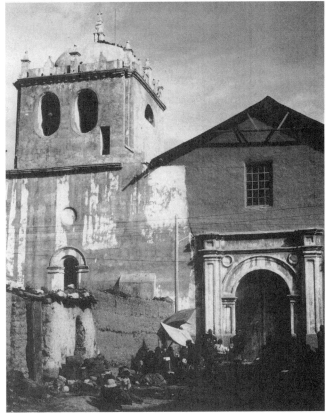

Brazilian architecture as contrasting with the more active surfaces of Spanish America.

BAROQUE: ABOUT 1640–1750

The Baroque style of painting reached the Americas in the middle of the seventeenth century, about fifty years after it had begun in Italy. Artists working in this style rejected the fantastic colors, impossible proportions, and illogical and extreme spatial and structural relationships preferred by Mannerist artists of the sixteenth and early seventeenth century. They preferred the realistic directness and clarity, following the Counter-Reformation recommendations of the Council of Trent (1545–1563) made to combat Protestantism. They desired to make the religious events depicted in their paintings as believable as possible, so that the viewers could relate directly to the event and feel emotionally as if they were participants. Most popular in the earlier part of the style was the dramatically spotlit scene which showed unidealized large-scale figures pushed close to the picture plane. This style, created by Caravaggio in Italy, became immensely popular with Spanish artists such as José de Ribera (actually working in the Hapsburg Viceroyalty of the Two Sicilies) and Francisco Zurbarán, active in Seville, the city from which most American settlers departed. The style appears suddenly in Mexico with the monumental canvas of Sebastián López de Arteaga, *Doubting Thomas*, painted in 1643 (fig. 5.16). The subject is beautifully attuned to the aims of the Baroque: the need to feel the presence of Christ and experience His suffering, as the Apostle Thomas does by inserting his finger in the wound in Christ's side. The protagonists, whose life-sized torsos fill the canvas, are believable in their ordinariness—disheveled old men with wrinkled brows, except for Thomas and a figure in the upper left which may be the artist's self-portrait (Toussaint 1967: 150). The single source of light comes shining brightly from the left, eliminating nonessential elements in the background by the deep shadows and spotlighting the wound, emphasizing Christ's fleshiness. Here the Word is made flesh, and dwells among us (paraphrasing John 1:14), exactly the goal of Catholic Baroque art.

Introduction of the Baroque style in South America is not so emphatic as it is in Mexico with López de Arteaga. Most South American painters preferred not to be in the forefront of change, but rather executed attractive images following expected patterns, usually derived from prints. Lack of signed pictures and proper attribution for many paintings prevents sure dating, and earthquakes, such as the disastrous one which hit Cuzco in 1650, destroyed much evidence of early Ba-

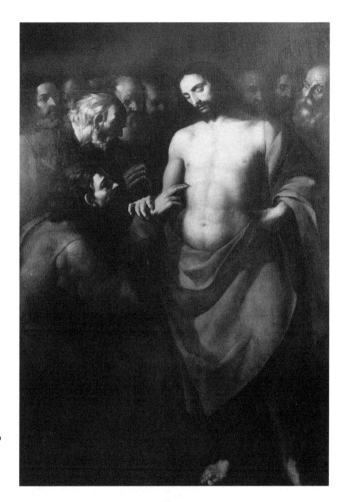

FIG. 5.16. Sebastián López de Arteaga, painter. *Doubting Thomas*, oil on canvas, 60⅝" high x 38½" wide, 1643. Mexico City: Pinacoteca Virreinal de San Diego. Photo courtesy of Instituto de Investigaciones Estéticas photo archive, Universidad Nacional Autónoma de México.

roque masters. One anonymous painter, whom I call the St. Jerome Master on the basis of the common theme of his identified works (Scott 1984), may well have been influential in bringing the Caravaggesque style to Peru (fig. 5.17). His works elude firm dating but certainly are seventeenth century. His half-length study of St. Jerome, based on an Italian engraving of St. Paul the Hermit dated 1613, shows a realistically aged man with furrowed brow lit by a strong spotlight coming from the edge of the frame. Once again, the artist intended to make the image jump out at the viewers, so that we can identify with Jerome, a fourth-century Father of the Church, as if an old man were physically present. The St. Jerome Master must be an important early painter in the Cuzco School of painting, the flowering of which we shall see in the eighteenth century.

Even more important than Caravaggio as an inspiration to Latin American painters was the Fleming Peter Paul Rubens, the knowledge of whose works was spread through engravings and mezzotints. Rubens's work reappears in innumerable copies, from small painted mar-

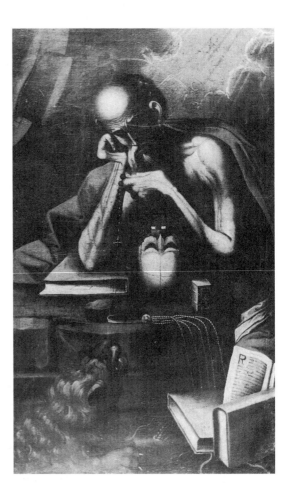

FIG. 5.17. St. Jerome Master, painter. *Penitent St. Jerome,* oil on canvas, 57" high x 37¾" wide, ca. 1650. Arequipa, Peru: Museum of the ex-Convent of Santa Catarina. Photo courtesy of museum.

ble slabs to huge canvases. The handsome canvas of *The Adoration of the Magi* (see fig. 5.18) by Baltasar de Echave Rioja is ultimately derived from Rubens's various engraved versions of that subject, interpreted both by Zurbarán and José Juárez (Burke and Bantel 1979: 25–26, 33–35, 89–90); all these sources were put together creatively by Echave Rioja in a work of great power and lush texture. Rubens's popularity in Latin America lies in his combination of the immediacy of Caravaggio with his Venetian-derived sumptuous colors and pictorial effects. His paintings soften the shocking realism of Caravaggio while retaining his compelling physical presence through large scale (seen in the way in which the figures fill the frame) and sensuous naturalism (seen in the fleshy skin tones and illusionistic tactile textures). Rubens established the grand manner so popular in the international Baroque style, where it served the propaganda needs of the noble courts and the Church.

In Latin America, Baroque painting was primarily placed in the service of the Church, since the king's personal representatives in the hemisphere, the viceroys, were transient appointments. In the Rubensian tradition, painting expanded from its previous position within architectural frames of *retablos* to colossal canvases independent of them. The best example of this new scale are works of Cristóbal de Villalpando in two great cathedrals of Mexico. Between 1684 and 1686 he covered all the walls of the sacristy of Mexico City Cathedral with archetypical Counter-Reformation themes attached to the wall by arched frames which echo the vaults of the ceiling, thereby becoming part of the architecture. In the sixteenth century, fresco painting occupied the same position, but rarely was it so large in scale. One visionary scene, *The Triumph of the Eucharist*, derived from cartoons by Rubens (De la Maza 1964: 66), has a sweep unmatched in any Renaissance-style work in America, which had preferred more compartmentalized compositions. The colossal figures have a physical reality in their simulated textures which marks them as Baroque, and a fluid brush stroke that communicates the dashing urgency of the event. Even the light coming in the window is incorporated into the scene as a sunburst from which archangels emerge. By their grand manner, Latin American painters

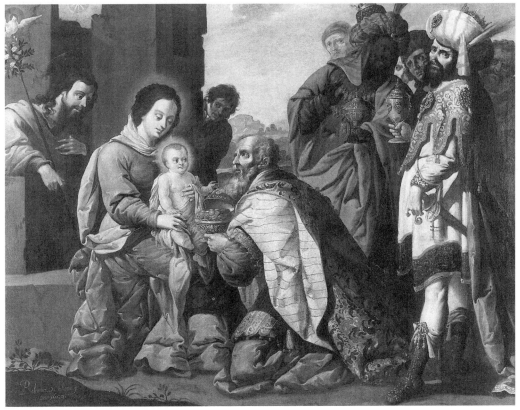

FIG. 5.18. Baltasar de Echave Rioja, painter, *Adoration of the Magi*, oil on canvas, 60⅝" high x 78" wide, 1659. Davenport, Iowa: Davenport Museum of Art, 25.84, gift of C. A. Ficke. Photo courtesy of museum.

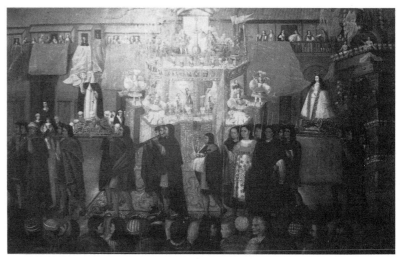

FIG. 5.19. Santa Ana Master, painter. *Corpus Christi Procession with the Parish-ioners of Saint Cristopher*, oil on cloth, 46½" high x 73¼" wide, ca. 1640. Cuzco, Peru: Museum of Art. Photo by John F. Scott.

were trying to capture the emotions and hearts of their viewers, to catch them up in the thrill of the Church's mission.

The most totally Baroque program, illusionistic ceiling painting, was undertaken by Villalpando in 1688. He represented a celestial Glory in the dome of Puebla Cathedral, in which he treated the entire surface as one billowing composition of clouds filled with angels and saints cul-minating in the Dove of the Holy Spirit descending directly next to the intense light of the cupola, which thus becomes the real light of God's grace.

In Cuzco, Peru, an anonymous artist domesticated these Rubensian spectacles to commemorate the more earthly Corpus Christi proces-sions (fig. 5.19). He used the large scale and scintillating color of Europe yet depicted what may be the first contemporary scenes of a Latin American event. Included are all segments of colonial society, from the aristocratic Spaniards observing from their balconies to the *mestizo* lower classes standing on curbside, but the painting focuses on the leaders of the procession, one apparently a descendant of the noble Inca and still wearing the distinctive Inca tunic. Another of the series takes place in front of the Cathedral of Cuzco as it appeared before the earth-quake of 1650 (Cossío del Pomar 1928: 175).

In wooden sculpture, the fine, balanced Renaissance carving of the sixteenth century was replaced by more compelling, actively spatial carvings of the seventeenth. Some actual works attributed to Spanish masters such as Juan Martínez Montañés were shipped to the Ameri-cas. Their Baroque qualities reside in their life size, their stunningly realistic skin tones achieved by *encarnación*, and the simulation of rich, gold-threaded tapestry garments achieved by *estofado*, the application of colored paint over gold leaf. An early work of the Quito school, by a Father Carlos, shows these techniques in a fine sculpture of an apostle which assumes a characteristic Baroque twist (pl. 16). Sculptors chose to depict emotionally charged moments, such as the bleeding Christ on his way to his crucifixion, in order to appeal to the lower classes, who could then identify with Jesus' suffering. The reality of the life-sized image, in other works dressed in actual garments, is thus forced on every viewer. During religious feasts, these figures would be carried on the shoulders of church fraternity members. The masterful sculpture of the Virgin of the Apocalypse carved by Bernardo Legarda in 1734 reveals even more spatial expansion in late Baroque sculpture, which can no longer be confined to a small niche in a *retablo* but demands more space in which to twist (fig. 5.20). The deeply carved, large folds of the drapery emphasize the dynamism of the figure's motion as

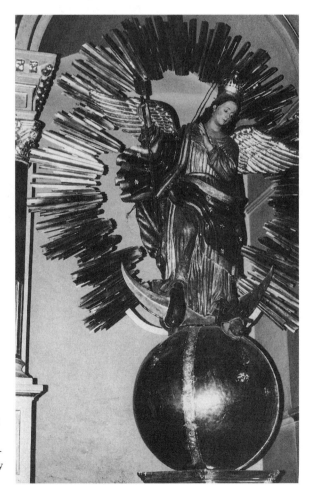

FIG. 5.20. Bernardo Legarda, sculptor. *Virgin of the Apocalypse*, polychromed wood with silver sheets, nearly life size, ca. 1734. Popoyán, Colombia: Cathedral camarín. Photo by John F. Scott.

the crowned Virgin plunges her lightning bolt into the writhing serpent symbolizing Satan below. Legarda stands at the pinnacle of the Quito School of sculpture, the most esteemed in the Spanish American world.

The reality of sculpture is dramatized by the new kind of architectural setting provided for it. In many churches in Spanish America the statues of the Virgin are not only dressed in real clothing but may be provided a small room called a *camarín* behind the altar. In Portuguese America the sculptor known as Aleijadinho (the "little cripple") in 1797–1799 housed a whole series of life-size wooden figures representing scenes in the Passion of Christ in independent structures lining a zig-zag pathway up a hill to the church of Bom Jesús de Matozinhos in Congonhas do Campo, Brazil (fig. 5.21).

The spatial assertiveness found in Baroque sculpture is also characteristic of Baroque architecture. The calm stability and structural clarity of the Renaissance style is supplanted by active, moving surfaces and visual complexity. The hallmark of this new style is the Solomonic column, characterized by its spiral twist. Legend had the form originating in Solomon's temple in Jerusalem, although these forms can actually be documented in the fourth century around the high altar of old

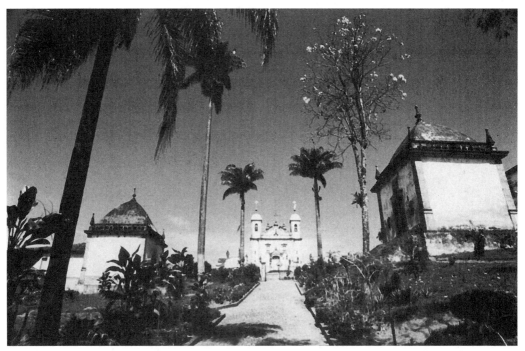

FIG. 5.21. Bom Jesús de Matozinhos church, zig-zag path with stations of the cross inside small structures, Congonhas do Campo, Minas Gerais, Brazil, late 18th century. Photo by Roy C. Craven, Jr., courtesy of Visual Resources Center, University of Florida.

St. Peter's church in Rome. These inspired the Italian sculptor-architect Gianlorenzo Bernini in 1627–1633 to create the column's more immediate precedent in the great bronze canopy over the high altar in new St. Peter's in Rome. The Solomonic columns are intended to recall the mother church in the Vatican, housing the Pope whose power extends to all the Roman Catholic world. In Latin America the form first appears around the mid-century in *retablos* in church interiors. The gilded altar of San José in Panama City, hidden under tar to save it from looting and burning by the British pirate Henry Morgan in 1671 (pl. 17), has Solomonic columns supporting broken entablatures to allow the upward flow of the curved arches and niches. The central section of the *retablo* is higher than the side sections, thereby breaking the horizontal continuity which had been characteristic of Renaissance *retablos*. The movement of the columns and the projection of the entablatures supported by them creates great energy in these altars and moves the eye quickly over the surface. The end result is a visual integration of the altar wall in which the parts are merged by overall surface ornament and the penetration of one level into the other. This visual unity is the ultimate aim of the Baroque, in contrast to the Renaissance aim of clarity and balance.

Retablo designs, first executed by carpenters, soon inspired architects to apply similar multitiered compositions to the façades of their churches. For example, the façade of La Compañía de Jesús, which faces the main plaza of Cuzco, Peru (fig. 5.22), has a slightly recessed portal with projecting side sections framed by sculptural columns and flanked by two strong bell towers. Its continuous central section explodes upward through broken segmental pediments. A heavy cornice barely cushions the central portal's upward thrust of this design, in the way that interior vaulting limits the height of the wooden *retablos* which served as prototypes for façade designs. Such aggressive buildings intentionally express the power of the Roman Catholic Church and were typically placed directly on the main plaza of the city where they would be seen by the entire populace.

During the Baroque era, provincial areas in both New Spain and the Viceroyalty of Peru produced church façades and interiors which shared overall richness of color and relief texture with the metropolitan centers, but which have a characteristic planar quality which have led many to call their style "mestizo" (e.g., Wethey 1949). Especially characteristic is a two-level relief which does not depend on sculptural modeling but rather on drilling into the surface to create a screenlike effect. Pre-Columbian stone- and woodcarving techniques, such as

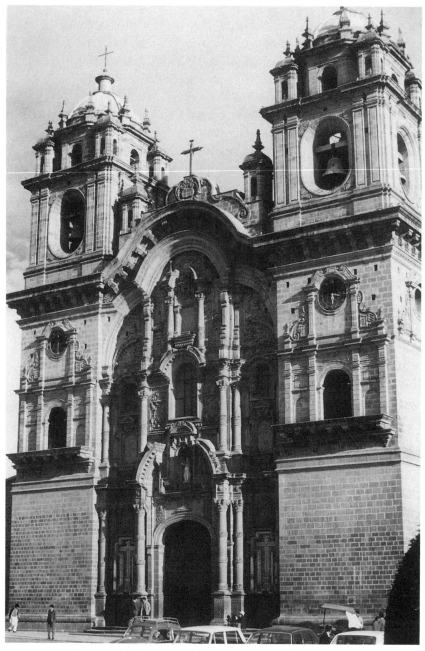

FIG. 5.22. Diego Martínez de Oviedo, architect. La Compañía de Jesús, Cuzco, Peru, exterior façade, 1651–1668. Photo by John F. Scott.

those of the Mixteca-Puebla style of Mexico and the Tiwanaku style of Bolivia (see fig. 4.24), created similar dense, bilevel relief designs. In fact, most of the areas producing such churches—the southern Peruvian highlands and Alto Perú (now Bolivia), southern and western Mexico, and Guatemala—were centers of high indigenous civilizations and still contain a large percentage of native or mixed (mestizo) Spanish-Amerindian blood. Certainly many of the craftsmen who carved these seventeenth- and eighteenth-century church reliefs had indigenous forebears, but how much of the old, pre-Spanish and even pre-Inca styles could they possibly retain? Artistic style is not located in a gene which can be inherited; it is a cultural phenomenon that must be learned.

The "mestizo" style first appeared in Arequipa, in the southern mountains of Peru, an area between strong Pre-Columbian centers. The Jesuit church of La Compañía manifests this tradition, first on the side portal of 1654, where it is primarily seen in the relief representation of Santiago Matamoros above the door, and then, more extensively, on the front façade of 1698 (fig. 5.23), where all the surfaces except the columns are densely decorated with very flat floral designs and half-figure atlantean supports primarily derived from Mannerist prints and woodblock book decorations. The transference of two-dimensional graphic designs into three-dimensional relief accounts for the flat modeling, not the recurrence of some Pre-Columbian manner of carving. Characteristic is an uncomfortable jump in scale from one part to another, such as the grotesquely oversized Santiago Matamoros above the side portal which clearly was enlarged from a tiny print. The image intentionally reminded the natives of their conquest by the Spaniards. The dramatic light-dark contrast between the powdery white surface of the native stone used everywhere in Arequipa and the dark shadows cast in the usually sunny climate also must have encouraged the overuse of the drill to achieve these rich, screenlike effects.

A similar mestizo origin has been attributed to the painted and gilt stucco work in southern Mexico, especially the states of Puebla and Oaxaca, where dramatic sculptural and coloristic effects are achieved. The Rosary Chapel of Santo Domingo in Puebla and the church of Santo Domingo in Oaxaca both show such stucco used as skillfully as their southern Spanish counterparts to achieve sculptural movement and curves. The little parish church of Santa María Tonantzintla, Puebla (fig. 5.24), used the same techniques in a folk idiom, filling the surface of the vaults, domes, and vertical walls with charming angels. The teeming little floral and figural motifs overload the eye and make dis-

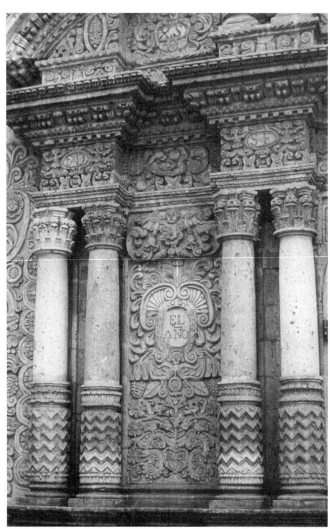

Left: FIG. 5.23. Anonymous. La Compañía, Arequipa, Peru, detail of front façade, inscribed and dated, "el año de 1698," (the year 1698). Photo by John F. Scott.

Below: FIG. 5.24. Anonymous native plasterer. Stuccoed dome, interior, Santa María Tonantzintla, Puebla, Mexico, 1714–1724 or 1750s. Photo by John F. Scott.

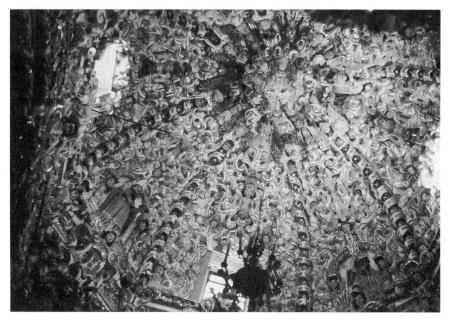

passionate analysis impossible. The stuccoed surface vibrates with a riot of color and high-relief modeling. Church surfaces in Puebla are enriched by dazzlingly intricate glazed tiles, part of the *mudéjar* tradition. Domes especially herald the church's presence by their bright yellow and blue oval forms easily seen from a distance.

ROCOCO: ABOUT 1750–1800

The riotous forms of dazzling polychromy characterize the most exuberant phase of the Baroque style, often called Ultrabaroque or Churrigueresque, after the Churriguera family, important *retablo* designers in Spain. But neither as sculptors nor architects do the Churrigueras deserve the honor—or, as classicists would say, the insult—to be innovators of the exuberant, anticlassical style which sometimes bears their name. More deserving, especially for Mexico where the style had its greatest flowering, is Jerónimo de Balbás of Seville, who designed the *retablo* for the high altar of the Seville Sagrario in 1706. He then went to Mexico in 1717 to repeat his success on the high altar known as the Retablo de los Reyes in the Mexico City Cathedral. Here the use of columns is completely abandoned, replaced by flattened decorative devices known as *estípites,* which are primarily composed of upward-flaring pedestals supporting a teetering pile of horizontal blocks linked by scallops and scrolls which cut in and out, destroying any illusion of a continuous channeling of weight that would increase from top to bottom. The sources of this design may well be the long-lived Mannerist woodcuts which framed the title pages of so many books preserved in Mexico. The geometric forms parallel the elaborate nonstructural floral designs of contemporary French Rococo wall surfaces without actually copying them. It should be recalled that imperial succession placed a French Bourbon king on the Spanish throne in 1700; French influence begins to be felt in Spanish artistic styles after that, although it is never pronounced, especially in the Americas.

The deep curve of the half-dome and the soaring verticality of the *estípites* manipulate the space of the Retablo de los Reyes in a manner seldom found in native Mexican descendants of Balbás's design. Instead, the numerous gilded wooden *retablos* and carved stone façades of churches throughout Mexico are usually flattened and do not encourage much Baroque interpenetration of space. The wealth of New Spain in the eighteenth century unleashed a frenzy of building, especially notable in the mining districts in north-central Mexico. In that area, an early, heavy version of the *estípite* façade appears on La Compañía of Guanajuato, designed by Fray José de la Cruz and Felipe Ureña in 1747 (fig. 5.25). Later *retablos* become more delicate, and some lose their columns altogether, such as *retablos* by Balbás's son Isidoro in Santa Prisca, Taxco, of 1758, and on the 1768 portal attributed to Pedro Huizar of the San José mission church in San Antonio, Texas (fig. 5.26). Such compositions are called "astyle" because they lack columns, *stylos* in Greek. Serving in theory as frames for oil paintings or illusionistic low-relief panels and as supports for statuary, Rococo *retablo* designs overwhelm these representational arts. The church interiors become an orgiastic feast for the senses: sight, primarily; touch, by inference; smell of the incense; and hearing, when one considers the sound of the great wooden organs which are an important part of most churches (Kelemen 1967: ch. 13).

Throughout Spanish America in the eighteenth century, the wealthy aristocracy built palaces taking up much of a square block in the urban

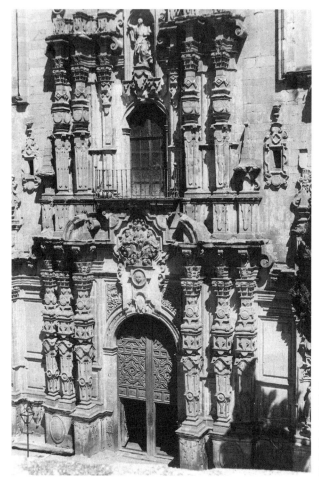

FIG. 5.25. Fray José de la Cruz and Felipe Ureña, architects. Façade, La Compañía (now La Trinidad), Guanajuato, Mexico, 1747–1765. Photo courtesy of Instituto de Investigaciones Estéticas photo archive, Universidad Nacional Autónoma de México.

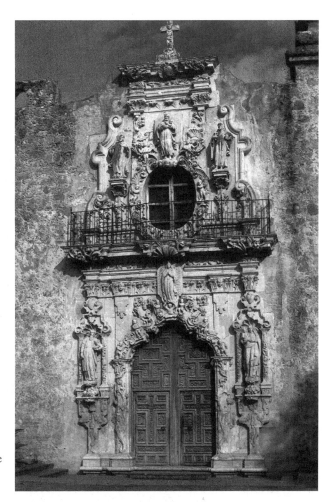

FIG. 5.26. Pedro Huizar, sculptor. Portal façade, cut stone, San José y San Miguel de Aguayo, San Antonio, Tex., United States of America, 1768. Photo by John F. Scott.

centers, with grandiose Baroque entrances and projecting wooden balconies to allow the women to observe the street, as seen in the Torre-Tagle Palace in Lima (fig. 5.27), and two- and three-story interior courtyards often with dramatic arches.

The European Rococo style is more typically one of intimacy and delicacy and is reflected in the delightful interior of Santa Rosa in Querétaro, Mexico (fig. 5.28), begun by Mariano de las Casas and finished in 1752. Oval frames executed in gilded wood contain painted busts of the saints on the great choir screen, which is topped by delicate filigree wood and ironwork. Simulated drapery held back by baby angels provides a canopy over angled glass cases containing statues of saints. In spite of the considerable size of the vaulted space, its scale is small and its effect charming, not overwhelming as in the Ultrabaroque *retablos* that stress their towering (even uncomfortably teetering) vertical height.

Rococo spirit can be found in another, rarer type of eighteenth-century structure, the curvilinear churches such as the small oval chapel

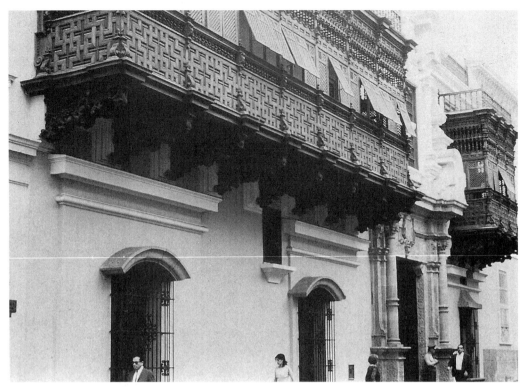

FIG. 5.27. Anonymous architect. Palace of the Marquis of Torre-Tagle, stuccoed masonry with wooden overhanging balconies, Lima, Peru, 1735. Photo by John F. Scott.

next to the Basilica of Guadalupe, called the Pocito (pl. 18) and built between 1777 and 1791 by the architect Francisco Guerrero y Torres. On the exterior he downplayed the size of this delightful building by providing a half-oval entrance structure with a low, multilobed door, reminiscent of Islamic design. Six-pointed star windows in the upper story seem to express the exploding interior space. Inside, the bulging space bites into the mass of the walls to create niches, much like those in the south German Rococo churches of the same century.

Brazilian architecture of the last half of the eighteenth century approximated this Rococo type of southern Germany more fully than did Spanish America. Although very close to northern Portuguese designs, these colonial buildings display a variety and quantity which reflect the financial prosperity also brought about by mining activity centered in the interior state of Minas Gerais. In the picturesque town of Ouro Preto in that state, with its many extant churches, the Rosário Chapel designed by Manuel Francisco de Araújo in 1784 carries this Rococo approach furthest. Paired ovals in plan link the sanctuary to the altar space, although the latter is both smaller and lower. A characteristic Portuguese double-envelope plan separates the interior from the exterior walls. The three-dimensional nature of the façade, so different from the contemporary Spanish planar façades, prepares the viewer for the embracing experience inside. The small scale and thinness of the components, especially the little oval windows, create a delicacy unknown in most Spanish American exteriors. The curving portico, crowned by an undulating gable, presses out between two recessed cylindrical towers, themselves oriented diagonally to the main axis of the building. In the Americas, only Brazilian designs consistently incorporate space actively in the façade and in the interior of the structures.

Embracing space is similarly expressed in the culminating monumental staircase and accompanying sculptures of prophets by the mulatto Aleijadinho (António Francisco Lisboa), son of a Portuguese architect and a black woman, for the church of Bom Jesús de Mato-

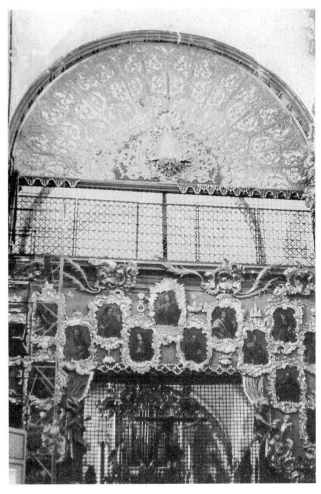

FIG. 5.28. Mariano de las Casas or Francisco Martínez Gudiño. Santa Rosa, Querétaro, Mexico, interior of nave with gilded wooden screen and oils on canvas, 1752. Photo by John F. Scott.

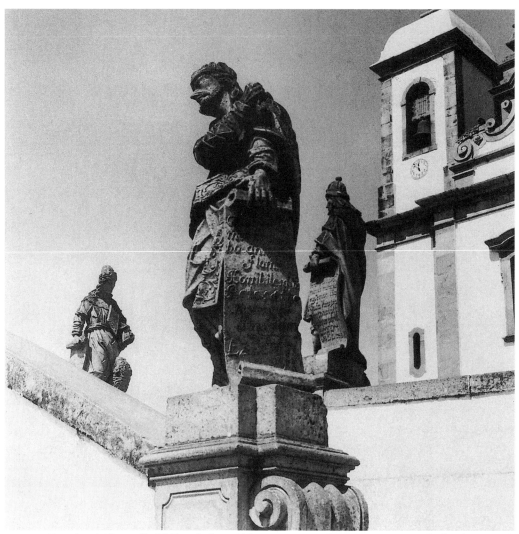

FIG. 5.29. Francisco Lisboa, called "Aleijadinho." Old Testament prophets on staircase: Ezekiel in foreground, Hosea to right, Daniel to left, soapstone, over life size, 1800–1805, Bom Jesús de Matozinhos, Congonhas do Campo, Minas Gerais, Brazil. Photo by Roy C. Craven, Jr., courtesy of Center for Latin American Studies, University of Florida.

zinhos in Congonhas do Campo (fig. 5.29), in which the small structures below with scenes of the Passion have already been mentioned (see fig. 5.21). The sweeping, double-armed staircase changes direction as it climbs to the scalloped platform on top of the hill which supports the church, each pivot point marked by a soapstone carving of an Old Testament prophet whose torsion keeps the space moving up and around. Unlike the usual rounded, soft, dainty figures of the Rococo age, these powerful, massive-headed figures model the light and deflect the space in faceted planes, recalling the African woodcarving tradition, which Aleijadinho could have known.

The standard Rococo doll-like sculpture of the eighteenth century was best executed in the School of Quito, of which Father Carlos and Legarda had been more monumental predecessors (see pl. 16, fig. 5.20). The soft, pink-toned *encarnación* of the infant Christ child (fig. 5.30) seems the very epitome of the Rococo world, like a three-dimensional version of a François Boucher painting. Unless we look at the signed and dated inscription on a tenon of the hand, the figure betrays no hint that the carving was produced by an Amerindian, Manuel Chil, whose pock-marked face suggested his nickname "Caspicara." Quito served as the sculptural center of northwestern South America, which in 1717 became the independent Viceroyalty of New Granada. The kingdom of Guatemala served a similar role as a sculptural center in the southern part of the Viceroyalty of New Spain. The indigenous and mestizo origins of its sculptors are equally imperceptible.

The Cuzco School of painting, established in the seventeenth century, was also composed of indigenous and mestizo artists. Some believe that in the flat, ornamental painting of the woven cotton and wood surfaces can be found a continuation of the Pre-Columbian textiles and pottery design tradition. The living presence of the Inca culture could still be found reflected in eighteenth-century Cuzco in painted wooden beakers, folk weavings, and portraits of indigenous dignitaries; the Tupac Amaru rebellion of 1780 reveals the continuing presence of Inca royalty around whom the rebels coalesced. By the eighteenth century, Cuzco painting embodied many of the stylistic features of the Rococo: soft colors, often powdery versions of reds,

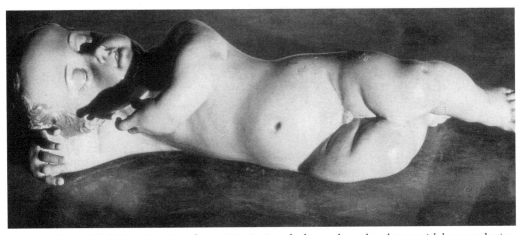

FIG. 5.30. Manuel Chil "Caspicara," sculptor. *Niño Jesús*, polychromed wood sculpture with lacquered paint, ca. 18" long, ca. 1792. Cuenca, Ecuador: Museo Municipal. Photo by John F. Scott.

blues, and ochres, with a surface application of gold leaf which, because it is stenciled on the painted drapery, does not follow the drapery's contour; small scale; doll-like features; and a tender, intimate expression (fig. 5.31). The Virgin Mary is often dressed in a Spanish peasant costume, adding an informal touch typical of the Rococo. The tropical landscape in which they are often placed seems primarily imaginary, based on prints showing European conceptions of Egypt rather than on direct Peruvian observation of the not-too-distant Amazonian rain forest.

The intimate atmosphere sought by Rococo designers appears in works by the creole (native-born white) painters of Quito and Mexico. Manuel Samaniego of Quito executed a charming depiction of Joseph's workshop which features domestic tasks being carried out by the Holy Family: Joseph engaged in carpentry, the young Jesus spinning while Mary rolls the yarn (fig. 5.32). These activities would be instantly recognized by the indigenous peasants. The small scale of the figures is achieved not only by their slightly childlike proportions but also by their small size in relation to the frame.

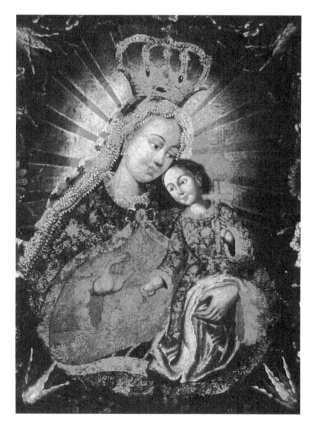

FIG. 5.31. Anonymous Cuzco Indian painter. *Virgin Mary with the Christ Child*, oil on cloth, 24" high x 20" wide, ca. 1730. Private collection. Photo courtesy of Mint Museum of Art, Charlotte, N.C.

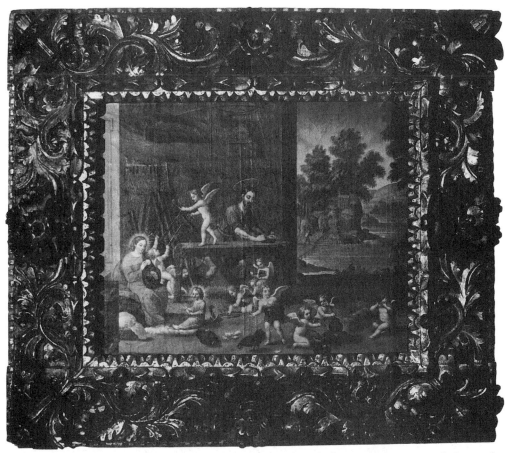

FIG. 5.32. Manuel Samaniego, painter. *Joseph's Workshop*, oil on cloth, 18½" high x 24½" wide, late 18th century. Quito: Galería de Arte del Banco Central. Photo by John F. Scott.

Although commissioned portraits of the aristocracy are stiff and haughty, self-portraits of painters in Mexico reveal their more informal humanity. The best of this tradition is a pastel by José Luis Rodríguez de Alconedo in 1811, which reveals him as a Mexican mestizo with tousled hair and an open-necked shirt, wrapping a garland of flowers around the head of a classical bust. The informality comes not only through the disheveled dress but also by the choice of a half-length image, whose body goes in one direction but whose head turns to look spontaneously out of the canvas in another direction, and in the very informal, quickly executed pastel medium much favored by Rococo artists. He created a completely captivating glimpse of a man who soon would be executed for his participation in the War of Independence.

Some actual visions of life in New Spain on the eve of Independence come in several new subjects which colonial painters treat, revealing a willingness to go beyond the commissions of church and state. An anonymous landscape of a wooded glen and rushing stream probably was done from nature, although its specific location has not been determined. No pretext is here necessary to justify the landscape by having religious characters inhabit it, as had been the case in the seventeenth century. The fruit of the land is revealed in kitchen still lifes (*bodegones*) such as those by Antonio Pérez de Aguilar. In Quito, Vicente Albán combined such still lifes in landscapes with idealized portraits of indigenous and European people in their typical costume. An anonymous artist of Alto Perú (now Bolivia) rendered pairs of people of different ethnic groups, including representatives from what is now Argentina, in their distinctive costumes around 1790–1800 (Ramsey 1954: 166).

The different strata of colonial society are best shown in several series of sixteen small paintings called *castas* which represent intermarriage of different races and assign often humorous terms to refer to each "caste" or mixture. Often, the further removed from purebreds the couples are, the more humble their surroundings and the more poorly behaved they act. One expects Spaniards to be presented elegantly, but even the pureblood blacks and the Amerindians are beautifully dressed and dignified in the series of sixteen unusually large paintings by Miguel Cabrera, New Spain's most distinguished artist of mid-century. In our example in plate 19, he depicts an Indian woman in beautifully embroidered *huipil* married to a fine-looking gentleman whose ancestry is African and Indian, here called *chino cambujo*, a mixture more typically referred to as sambo (*zambo*). Their child is waggishly called a she-wolf (*loba*). Local crafts and fruits are shown and even labeled, emphasizing the exoticism of the scene. While the households depicted in these paintings are more allegorical than factual, the backdrops, clothing, and life-styles seem very true to their eighteenth-century existence.

NEOCLASSICISM: 1783–ABOUT 1830

The mother country made its first attempt in 1783 to exert control on the colonial American arts by establishing the Royal Academy of San Carlos in Mexico City. Spaniards were dispatched to Mexico to head each artistic section. The most impressive was Manuel Tolsá, who taught sculpture and then served as director of the Academy. His major surviving sculpture is the noble equestrian bronze statue of King Carlos IV (fig. 5.33). In the tradition of the equestrian ruler portrait of the Roman emperor Marcus Aurelius, this monumental work, cast in 1803 on a scale never before attempted in the colonies, conveys the pride and power of the king transformed into a Roman emperor dressed in a toga.

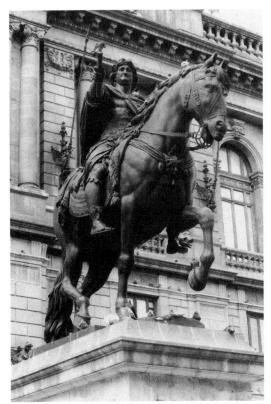

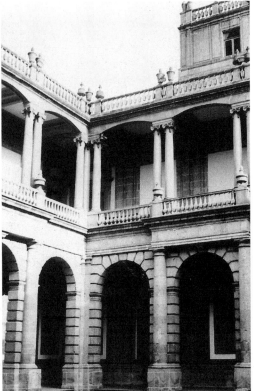

FIG. 5.33. Manuel Tolsá, sculptor. *Carlos IV*, cast bronze equestrian statue, twice life size, 1803. Mexico City: Museo Nacional de Arte. Photo by John F. Scott.

FIG. 5.34. Manuel Tolsá, architect. School of Mines, Mexico City, interior courtyard, 1797–1813. Photo by John F. Scott.

The term Neoclassic is applied to this style in part because of the conscious Roman references but also because it marks a return to calmer, more stable, rational, and simplified forms. Such qualities can best be seen in the architecture designed by Tolsá, which returns to sober right angles. Graceful touches of curves add a quality of elegance to his work, such as the low arches in the galleries overlooking the courtyard of the College of Mines in the Mexican capital (fig. 5.34).

Architecture in the mining state of Guanajuato at the turn of the nineteenth century shows the talented stamp of Francisco Eduardo Tresguerras, native-born and self-taught from classical treatises. His Neoclassic style is best seen in the handsome urban House of the Count of Casa Rul in Guanajuato, finished by 1803 when the scientific traveler Baron von Humboldt visited and described it. A severely rusticated ground floor supports a projecting, gabled central block flanked by a horizontal entablature with carved Greek keys supported by paired pilasters. Tresguerras was also a painter of considerable talents, his self-portrait recalling his Spanish contemporary Francisco Goya in its unflattering realism and severe coloration with neutral grey background. He contributed his own fresco decoration to a chapel in his church of El Carmen in his birthplace, Celaya (pl. 20). The airy figures and pale colors recall the now destroyed frescoes in the dome of Mexico City Cathedral executed by the Spanish instructor of painting in the Academy, Rafael Ximeno y Planes.

Most building activity stopped in Spanish America when the wars of independence broke out against Spain in 1810, although the Franciscan mission churches far to the northwest in present-day California seemed unaffected by the conflict in the population centers. The mission of Santa Bárbara, then part of Alta California, an enormous complex built between 1815 and 1820 for the resettlement and technical training of the previously nomadic Chumash Indians, has a handsome church with geometrically powerful towers and an applied Ionic temple façade recalling ancient Greek temples. After Mexico gained its independence from Spain in 1821, California became part of the new republic.

During this period, Brazil became the seat of the Portuguese kingdom in exile while the homeland was menaced by Napoleonic troops. In 1816 the monarchy imported a group of French Academicians for an artistic mission. Subsequently this cadre became the faculty of the newly founded Imperial Academy of Fine Arts, which provided proper training in the rules and practice of art in Rio de Janeiro. The design of the Academy building itself, by Grandjean de Montigny, is a clear statement of Neoclassic architecture. The Taunay brothers were responsible for sculpture (Auguste) and painting (Nicolas): Nicolas Taunay's oil-painted view of Rio is a realistic depiction of a local scene with emphasis on the great expanse of space of the New World. Brazil would declare its independence from Portugal in 1822 with the king's son as its emperor.

Haiti, after proclaiming its independence from France in 1804, also imported French architects to build for the self-proclaimed Emperor Henry I Christophe (reigned 1806–1820): his Sans Souci Palace was intended as an elegant retreat in the hills overlooking the north coast, while the massive Citadel in the nearby mountains would be used in more threatened times (fig. 5.35) and reflects the brutality of that revolutionary era. The Citadel's stripped-down geometry is a clear expression of the most advanced, radical French Neoclassic aesthetics, while its mountaintop location foreshadows the emotional impact of the newer Romanticism (to be discussed in chap. 6).

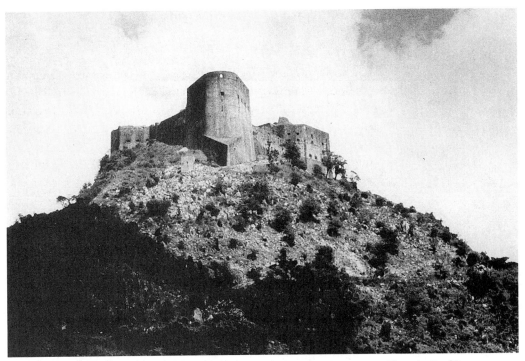

FIG. 5.35. Citadel of Henry I Cristophe, south of Cap Haïtien, Haiti, 1806–1820. Photo by Fred Rex, courtesy of Visual Resources Center, University of Florida.

NON-HISPANIC ARTISTIC SURVIVALS

The powerful presence of African descendants in Haiti, submerged by the slave system and imperfectly assimilated into the dominant French culture, was relieved from further absorption by the winning of Haiti's independence in 1804. As a result, Haiti remains the most African of any American nation. Although all examples of the visual arts come from more recent times, African survivals clearly must be descended from the colonial era when slaves were still being imported directly from Africa. Haitian voodoo religion preserves much of its Dahomean origins, but associated art is restricted to bilaterally symmetrical abstract designs drawn on the ground which summon the deities, then are erased in the ritual activity which follows. Their African origins are obscure, but they seem to blend ritual ground designs of Dahomey with Congolese cruciform cosmograms (Thompson 1983: 188). In neighboring Cuba, however, the cult of *santería*, which integrates voodoo and Catholicism, has produced more permanent objects recalling the West African religion of the Yoruba people. Forged metal staffs of the god of herbs, Osanyin, are re-created in Cuba with similar designs in scrap metal. Images of the *orisha*, or Yoruba deities, take the form of Catholic saints who share some of their attributes. The comparable religion in eastern South America, especially around Bahia, Brazil, is called *candomblé*. There, wood carvings like those in Africa re-create images of female worshippers of Changó, as the Yoruba god of thunder Shango is locally known.

A more uniquely American syncretism has been identified in the rain forest camps populated by the descendants of runaway slaves in the Guianas of northeastern South America, especially formerly Dutch Surinam, independent only since 1975. There groups from many African ethnicities, sometimes already blended in the slave camps, established new tribal conglomerates along the interior rivers of the rain forest. Many designs on their textiles and woodwork recall parallel African designs from the former Gold Coast (now Ghana), but similar shapes can be found around the Niger Delta and east to Cameroon, so that it is no longer possible to identify one specific ethnic source. Although these Afro-American groups surely escaped and began making such objects during the colonial era beginning in the seventeenth century, most of what has been preserved to study comes from collections made in this century.

After the conquest of the native groups, certain artistic media adapted in technique and subject matter to reflect new materials and represent new realities of Indian life. Pottery lost its religious imagery and either remained abstract in design, such as the burnished black-ware of Oaxaca, or picked up floral motifs acceptable in Western folk ceramic production. New domesticated animals from the Old World became an intimate part of the Amerindian economy and were often reflected in the ceramics, such as the bisque pottery bulls of Pucará in the Lake Titicaca basin. From Quinua, in the Ayacucho area of Peru, and Guerrero state in Mexico come very similar ceramic church models in the Baroque style even after such churches had ceased being built in actual architecture. The abstract Inca style of stone carving, which had rendered alpacas and their long shaggy hair in highly stylized geometric simplification, engendered a technique in highland Peru and Bolivia of rendering llamas in alabaster and even including them in corrals within miniature villages.

Masks were carved for village festival masquerades, no doubt as they had been before the Conquest, but they no longer represented the faces of the indigenous deities. Papier-mâché masks may continue some types produced for Maya Pre-Columbian dancers. Often masks burlesqued the conquerors and the slaves they imported. A favorite masquerade is Moors and Christians, where black-face masks represent

Africans and pink-face masks with blond mustaches represent Spaniards. Fine eighteenth-century examples of such masks come from the Mexican states of Michoacán and Guerrero and from the highland Maya of Guatemala.

Also very close to Pre-Columbian traditions are the clothing woven by the Amerindians of Mexico, Guatemala, Peru, and Bolivia (fig. 5.36). Women weaving the untailored ponchos of South America and serapes of Mesoamerica adapted their designs to the Spanish wide looms and the wools available from sheep and goats imported to the New World. Aniline dyes made brighter colors possible; metallic thread and glass beads were incorporated in place of the metal danglers and shell beads used in Pre-Columbian textiles. In metalwork, although traditional media like copper and silver continued in use, the greater commercial availability of tin sheets and tin cans provide material for cut-out and crimped items like lamps and sculpture. The black inhabitants of the

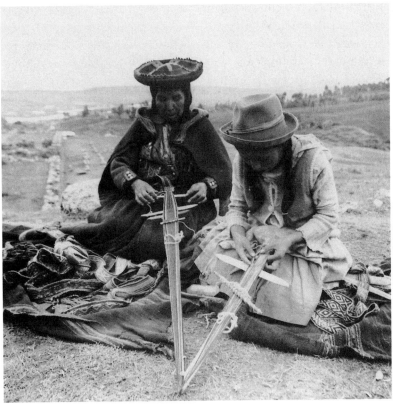

FIG. 5.36. A Quechua woman and her daughter weaving, Chincheros, Apurímac, Peru, 1975. Photo by Roy C. Craven, Jr., courtesy of Center for Latin American Studies, University of Florida.

Lesser Antilles have converted cast-off petroleum barrels into musical instruments for their steel-drum bands.

Perhaps the most unacculturated craft in South America to survive the Conquest was featherwork. We know the Central Andean natives traded with their tropical forest neighbors to the east, where they acquired the brightly colored feathers used on their clothing; however, no feather ornaments have been preserved which were crafted in the Amazonian region before the European arrival. With the beginning of European scientific expeditions at the end of the eighteenth century, however, headdresses were collected and preserved by Europeans, at first in princely cabinets of marvels and then in national museums of natural history. Only in the twentieth century have the artistic qualities of these works been recognized.

Indigenous groups in Latin America continued artistic production for their own purposes into this century, when those crafts became appreciated for their artistry. At that point they can be considered ethnic art: an art which is recognizably distinct from that of the dominant culture and prized for this distinctiveness. Traders developed markets for these products, and outstanding craftspersons were identified and promoted by name, their uniqueness and quality stressed. In this way, a more Western marketing strategy was applied to traditional crafts, causing them to respond to market pressures.

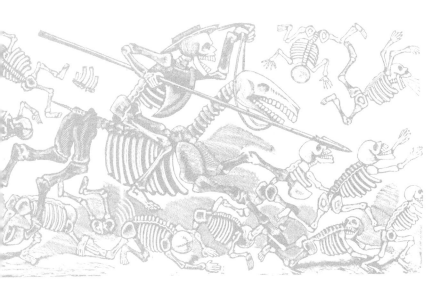

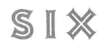

ART AFTER INDEPENDENCE

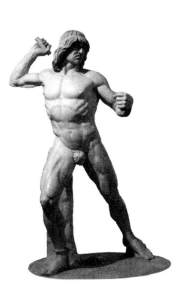

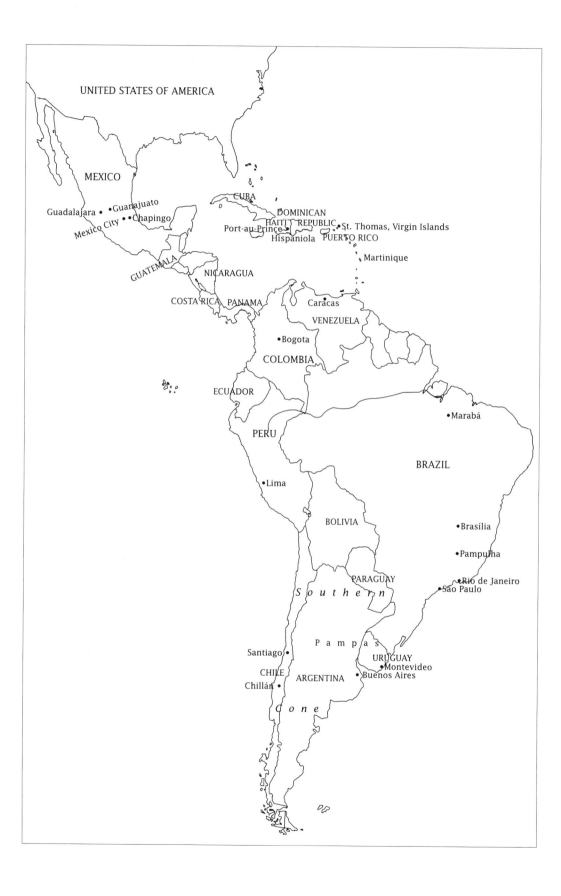

BETWEEN 1810 AND 1824 the Latin American nations on the American mainland achieved independence from the two mother countries, Spain and Portugal, already weakened by the Napoleonic Wars. In spite of the vain attempts by the Spanish American liberators to maintain unity, however, the four former colonial viceroyalties had broken up into sixteen independent republics by 1839. Economically and culturally these new states were oriented toward Europe during the remainder of that century and increasingly toward the United States in the twentieth century.

In the new nations, self-taught artists commemorated their heroes and the great events of their recent history in a straightforward Neoclassic idiom: clear delineation of figures in intense local colors against a plain grey background. Historical scenes such as battles were rendered from a normal human vantage point, with little rhetorical emphasis either by size or by lighting: figures in such scenes are small, subordinate to the dominant horizontals of the land and the architecture. Neoclassic lighting is usually even, almost flat. Depiction of details is realistic, often with clearly recognizable local character.

The architecture throughout the first century of independence retained the classical vocabulary imposed on it by the academies during the Neoclassic era. Continuing links to the French Academy, better known as the École des Beaux-Arts in the nineteenth century, resulted in the popularity of a French Renaissance version of Classicism in the mid-nineteenth century and a Baroque revival around the turn of the twentieth century. Unlike the Victorian taste in the English-speaking world, Latin American architects had little interest in Romantic revivals of the medieval European styles such as the Romanesque and Gothic. The representational arts did, however, reflect Romantic stylistic tendencies toward the exotic, the landscape, and the heroic.

ROMANTICISM: ABOUT 1830–1860

After the wars of independence, a number of European travelers came to see the Americas for themselves in their Romantic search for the unusual and the dramatic. Jean Baptiste Debret, a member of the French artistic mission of 1816, drew sketches of the varied inhabitants of Brazil, which he published as lithographs in Paris from 1834 to 1839. Also in Brazil, the Bavarian artist Johann Moritz Rugendas began his South American journey. He subsequently went to Mexico in 1831–1834, then to Chile between 1833 and 1845, during which time he also documented Argentina from 1837–1838 and Peru from 1842–1844. Although unusual in his constant movement from country to country,

Rugendas is no different from others in his search for the unusual, the dramatic, and the picturesque (pl. 23). In *Landscape with Cowboys on Horseback*, the energetic Chilean cowboy in his colorful poncho moves away from us, leading our eye down the dangerously twisting road to the port in the distance. The quick brush stroke and sketchy execution plus the vibrant colors strongly recall the Romantic style then in vogue in Europe. These qualities embody the true spirit of the Romantic movement, although they are best seen in the small oils by Rugendas, which can be considered preparatory sketches for never-realized major canvases. These foreign artists brought the beauty, excitement, and distinctiveness of the newly independent countries to the attention of their own native-born citizens.

Directly descended from the French who came to Brazil in 1816 was the grandson of Grandjean de Montigny, João Leon Pallière, born in Rio de Janeiro. Typical of the educated native-born artists of the nineteenth century, he studied in Paris, but returned to South America to paint scenes of the distinctive life of Brazil, Argentina, and Chile. Like many other painters we call *costumbristas*, he focused primarily on local traditions (*costumbres*) that set each region apart from the others. This group of artists are more than painters of native costumes; they depict actions within a naturalistic setting. Pallière examined the jungle of the Argentine missions and the life of the gauchos on the pampas. This interest was shared by Prilidiano Pueyrredón, son of one of the first presidents of the Argentine Republic, who with his family went to Paris in political exile. He may have learned painting in the Academy in Rio de Janeiro, then made architecture his career after studying at the École des Beaux-Arts in Paris. Successful in both arts, he helped implant the classicizing taste which gave Buenos Aires its characteristic Beaux-Arts appearance, then after 1860 turned to painting portraits and genre scenes taken from ordinary life in Argentina. These two men are archetypes of artists in the new republics of Latin America: well-born; usually educated in Europe, especially Paris; continuously cosmopolitan, with frequent changes of residence sometimes caused by political instability; and intensely interested in the quaint and picturesque sights of Latin America, which they still viewed from a cultural distance, more European than Latin American.

Self-taught artists, especially in provincial areas, produced portraits of the local bourgeoisie and ex-votos dedicated to the Virgin or a saint in gratitude for prayers answered. An example of this type of artist, José María Estrada from Guadalajara—then a small city in western Mexico—was much beloved by early twentieth-century critics for his directness and lack of Academic skills (Scott 1968: 76–80). His works have an iconic flatness and static permanence, but their intensely realistic subjects are easily recognizable. These popular artists viewed their Latin American society from within and peopled it with believable individuals, unlike the foreign travelers who viewed it from without and peopled it with more idealized physical types engaged in picturesque activities.

ACADEMIC REALISM: ABOUT 1850–1900

Presidents of the new Latin American republics often disdained native artists, preferring instead to award commissions to Europeans and hire them as teachers. Although somewhat second-rate in their own European countries, these artists could give the veneer of elegant Old World civilization to the new national capitals which, until recently, had been only provincial outposts of great colonial empires. This movement toward Europe was reflected by the eagerness of these leaders to acquire the newest technology of the industrial age, even though they thus became more dependent on the industrialized Northern Hemisphere. General López de Santa Anna, the sometimes-president and longtime-dictator of Mexico, clearly favored Europeans when he reestablished the National Academy of San Carlos in 1847. Instead of hiring capable Mexicans like Juan Cordero, then studying in Rome, he acquired a distinguished but conservative faculty in Spain and Italy: Pelegrín Clavé, a Catalán painter resident in Rome under the influence of the German Nazarenes, headed the new Academy; the only works of local interest he painted were sparklingly naturalistic, recognizably realistic portraits of the intelligentsia. His fellow Catalán, Manuel Vilar, inaugurated the indigenist interest in native themes in his sculptures of native leaders such as Tlahuicol (fig. 6.1), executed in plaster in 1851 using an overly muscular style reminiscent of the Hellenistic Greek Laocoön group. Even when the subject is Pre-Columbian, the technique remained classicizing.

A later Mexican dictator, General Porfirio Díaz, whose great architectural projects such as the National Theater (now Mexico City's Palace of Fine Arts) were designed by Europeans, nevertheless commissioned an important sculptural monument to Pre-Columbian kings which was erected in 1887. A handsome bronze statue of the last Aztec emperor, Cuauhtémoc, by the Mexican sculptor Miguel Noreña, stands on top of a base which mixes rusticated Roman with Pre-Columbian pyramidal design (fig. 6.2).

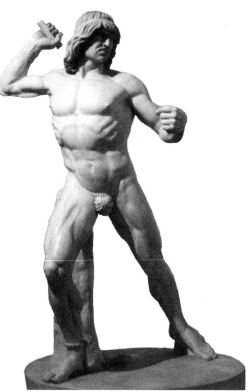

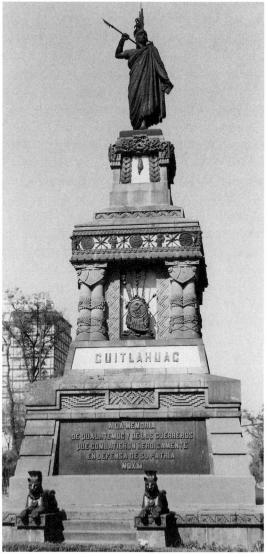

Above: FIG. 6.1. Manuel Vilar, sculptor. *Tlahuicol*, plaster master model, 84¼" high, 1851. México: Museo Nacional de Arte. Photo by John F. Scott.

Left: FIG. 6.2. Miguel Noreña, sculptor. *Monument to Cuauhtémoc*, bronze statue, well over life size, 1887. Base by engineer Francisco Jiménez. Mexico City: Paseo de la Reforma. Photo courtesy of Instituto de Investigaciones Estéticas photo archive, Universidad Nacional Autónoma de México.

Academic painters seeking to achieve a re-creation of Aztec times through realistic illusionism portrayed totally believable settings populated with natives who were clearly based on poses by live indigenous models in the studio; their costumes followed the depictions illustrated by natives in painted manuscripts made around the time of the Conquest. Lord Kingsborough had published these as lithographs between 1831 and 1848. The architecture represented in *The Discovery of Pulque* (fig. 6.3), a painting by José Obregón, is adapted from Pre-Columbian Mixtec codices (see pl. 11) by reading their cross-sectioned conceptualization of temples as a very naturalistic design for a throne. Obregón and his Academic colleagues who were trying to re-create ancient events were unable to comprehend that the Pre-Columbian artist had not intended to represent the external appearance of his architecture, but rather wanted to convey its essence.

In South America artists of the latter nineteenth century also attempted to render subjects which incorporated their national traditions in realistic Academic style. These artists were more concerned with representing essential aspects of their own countries than were the earlier artists of the independent period, who had been more cosmopolitan and European in their attitudes and style. In the mid-century painting *Indian Potter* (fig. 6.4) by Francisco Laso of Peru, an early

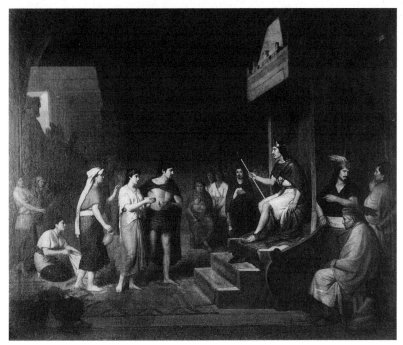

FIG. 6.3. José Obregón, painter. *Discovery of Pulque*, oil on canvas, 74½" high x 90½" wide, 1869. México: Museo Nacional de Arte. Photo courtesy of Instituto de Investigaciones Estéticas photo archive, Universidad Nacional Autónoma de México.

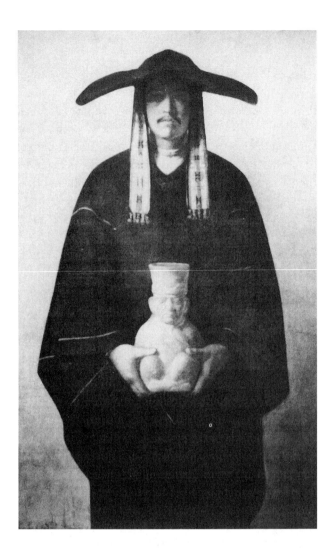

FIG. 6.4. Francisco Laso, painter, *Indian Potter*, oil on canvas, 53⅛" high x 33⅞" wide, 1855. Lima: Pinacoteca Municipal Ignacio Merino de la Municipalidad de Lima Metropolitano. Photo courtesy of museum.

exponent of indigenist themes, a native model in stark black costume wears a multicolor Pre-Columbian textile sash hanging from his hat and carries a Moche human effigy vessel, obviously painted from an archaeological piece in the style of plate 5. Rodolfo Amoêdo of Brazil was not well-born but learned his craft first in the Rio Academy, only later winning a scholarship in Paris and then returning in 1890 to execute major paintings in public halls. He used a female nude allegorical figure lounging in a tropical rain forest to abstract the essence of *Marabá*, a town in the Amazonian basin. The painting is as sensuous as its subject.

Two excellent artists of the latter nineteenth century surpass the *costumbrista* and *indigenista* traditions of the early National era by making the subjects no longer exotic but part of universal human experience. Although Juan Manuel Blanes of Uruguay studied in Florence, Italy, with a government stipend, he returned to document historical events and typical genre scenes, especially depictions of gauchos in the rolling grasslands of the Southern Cone. His realism, however, transcends earlier Romantic treatment of such themes and allows us to identify with the humans portrayed in the atmospheric scenes. Realism, as a nineteenth-century artistic movement which sweeps aside sentimentality and emphasizes the physical nature of both the object represented and the materials which create those illusions, also characterizes the works of José María Velasco of Mexico. Although he did paint indigenist themes such as *Aztec Hunters* and *The Pyramid of Teotihuacán*, these oils focus on the tangible feeling of atmosphere and place rather than on emotional responses to past times and ruined monuments. His great series of panoramic vistas of the Valley of Mexico (such as fig. 6.5) analyze the structure of nature as profoundly as his French contemporary Cézanne did with Mount Sainte-Victoire, although in different styles. He does not choose to heighten the magnificence of Mexico's sere landscape by the golden light effects or reference to Arcadian antiquity which Velasco's Italian teacher Eugenio

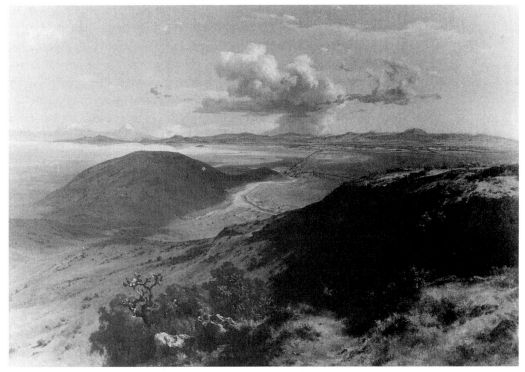

FIG. 6.5. José María Velasco, painter. *View of the Valley of Mexico from Hill of Santa Isabel*, oil on canvas, 63" high x 90½" wide, 1877. Mexico City: Museum of Modern Art. Photo courtesy of Instituto de Investigaciones Estéticas photo archive, Universidad Nacional Autónoma de México.

Landesio had used to render the Valley of Mexico while the instructor of landscape painting at the Academy in mid-century. The presence of an eagle grasping a serpent makes reference to the legendary founding of the Aztec capital.

Modernismo: ABOUT 1890–1920

The move away from visual realism in Latin American art parallels *modernismo*, an Hispanic literary movement away from long realist novels and towards poetic, sonorous words and rich images. In this highly self-conscious art, subject matter was less important than the aesthetic way it was presented. The Mexican graphic artist Julio Ruelas created etched images of agonized human heads tormented by serpents and pecking birds. His use of tortured and twisted lines recalls the even more abstract paintings of his Norwegian contemporary Edvard Munch. In drawings and paintings, Saturnino Herrán portrayed indigenous Mexican life with visible outlines around bright colors, traits of Post-Impressionism in France. The elongated lines and sinuous curves of his works are typical of the Art Nouveau movement in Europe. Retail stores in Latin American cities were built in the Art Nouveau style. New materials such as cast iron and reinforced concrete were used to make continuously flowing lines inspired by vegetative forms.

In contrast to the meticulous style of the classicists in the Academies, a looser, more spontaneous style developed to express greater emotion. Originally employed by the Romantic painters such as Rugendas for on-the-spot oil sketches (see pl. 23), this painting style began to be consciously sought by well-trained painters toward the end of the century in Latin America in order to express scintillating animation both of people and of nature. The Impressionists, who used this technique, had originally intended to capture the optical sensation of light on the retina. Camille Pissarro, one of the original creators of Impressionism in Paris, had been born and spent his early maturity in the Caribbean: a native of St. Thomas in the then-Danish West Indies, he made his first important landscape painting studies in Caracas, Venezuela, in 1852–1855 before going to Paris. He was still a Realist then, as was another Caribbean painter, Francisco Oller of Puerto Rico, who studied with Gustave Courbet, converted to Impressionism, and became friendly with Pissarro. Also a convert to Impressionism while in Europe in the 1890s was the Mexican lawyer Joaquín Clausell, whose colorful works are composed of separate splotches of very intense pigment which, when seen next to each other on the canvas, are more vibrant than if they were mixed on the palette (pl. 21). In the early years of the twentieth century, the Impressionist technique had become so accepted that it was used by stylish society painters, among the best of whom are two Peruvians, Carlos Baca-Flor and Teófilo Castillo. Castillo's subject matter recreates the Colonial legacy of Peru, but with an emphasis on people of European descent such as St. Rose of Lima.

Typically in the early decades of the twentieth century, this broad-brushed style of painting replaced the more meticulous realism of the nineteenth-century Academies. While the style has many sources, including Impressionism and Post-Impressionism, it remains more illusionistic than those two movements. In all three, the viewer is certainly aware of the surface of the painting and the process of its creation. This bravura painterly style has academic roots in the work of Baroque masters, notably Velázquez, whose influence on the Spanish-American world had been minimal in his own time (1599–1660). Spanish painters such as Joaquín Sorolla and Ignacio Zuloaga used it to create scenes celebrating the regional diversity of Spain, and Spanish-American artists who studied in Europe, such as the Cuban painter Leopoldo Romañach, returned to apply this technique to subjects in their own homelands. The latter's colorful and apparently quickly executed painting of an older bourgeois lady going to mass (pl. 22) emphasizes the culture Cuba shared with Spain, not its American uniqueness, even though Cuba had won its independence from Spain in 1898. The rich and variegated browns in the background are almost as captivating as the sparkling personality of the lady who engagingly confronts us.

Reaction against Academic realism took more political overtones in Mexico, where on the eve of the great political Revolution of 1910, the anarchist who called himself Dr. Atl organized a dissident exhibition in the Centro Artístico of Mexico City to show purely Mexican artists and compete with the European exhibit sponsored by the government. Dr. Atl's given name was Gerardo Murillo, but he despised its association with Bartolomé Murillo, the Baroque painter of saccharine Immaculate Conceptions. Instead, he adopted the Aztec word for water, *atl*, and granted himself the title of Doctor. In his own work of volcanic landscapes he used Expressionistic colors and nontraditional waxy pigments, following Post-Impressionist tendencies he had learned in Europe. Many artists during this time desired to communicate more directly with the uneducated Mexican masses. They admired the directness of the graphic images by José Guadalupe Posada, quickly produced in his workshop near the Academy to illustrate popular broadsides such as those eulogizing public figures on the Day of the Dead

(November 2) using mocking satirical couplets. Posada's illustrations, engraved in type metal, etched on zinc, or carved for woodcuts, show very lively skeletons, such as those being knocked about by the galloping Don Quixote, bizarre hero of Spain's most important novel, behaving like a bullfight *picador* (fig. 6.6). While clearly recognizable, Posada's images use simplified but expressive graphic marks, such as these bold diagonals, which could not be ignored even by unsophisticated readers.

Diego Rivera, a precocious youth who was awarded a scholarship by the Mexican government to study in Europe, incorporated even more avant-garde artistic styles in his work. In Paris he learned the technique of Cubism, in which the artist flattened and twisted forms so they could be seen simultaneously from different angles. Although Rivera's subject matter included café scenes such as those painted by Cubism's originators Georges Braque and Pablo Picasso, he maintained an interest in his homeland, which by 1915 was in the throes of a great social revolution. The followers of Emiliano Zapata, mainly peasants of native extraction, were fighting to gain ownership of the land on which they labored. In *Zapatista Landscape* of 1915 (fig. 6.7), the essential elements of one such follower—straw hat, rifle, and serape—are ar-

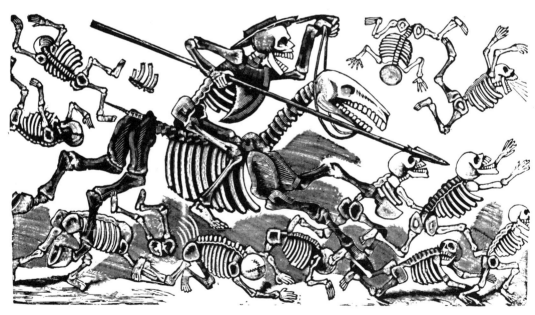

FIG. 6.6. José Guadalupe Posada, draftsman. *Skeleton of Don Quixote*, type-metal engraving, 5¾" high x 10¾" wide, printed on newsprint broadside of *Ilustrador*, ca. 1900. Colorado Springs: Taylor Museum, 5541. Photo: University Gallery, University of Florida.

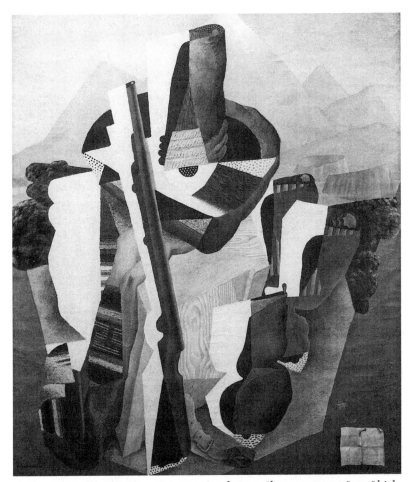

FIG. 6.7. Diego Rivera, painter. *Zapatista Landscape,* oil on canvas, 49¼" x 57" high, 1915. Mexico City: Museo Nacional de Arte. Photo courtesy of Instituto de Investigaciones Estéticas photo archive, Universidad Nacional Autónoma de México. Reproduction authorized by the Instituto Nacional de Bellas Artes y Literatura.

ranged in a flattened collage against a simplified, snow-capped volcano in the compressed background. In this work, Rivera has merged a nonnaturalistic European style with a sympathetic rendering of a current Mexican Revolutionary subject. In the lower right-hand corner, however, he has painted a small piece of paper apparently nailed to the canvas in academic *trompe l'oeil* ("fool the eye") technique to demonstrate his ability to create an optical illusion which jarringly contrasts with his dominant avant-garde modernity.

MEXICAN MURAL RENAISSANCE: 1921—ABOUT 1950

After the tumult of the Revolution had died down in 1921 and a more stable government controlled the country, the new Mexican Secretary of Education, José Vasconcelos, invited many Mexican artists, some of whom were still working or on scholarship in Europe, to participate in government-sponsored projects to turn the walls of public buildings into didactic inspiration for the populace. The first major project was the National Preparatory School for boys in Mexico City, housed in a colonial Jesuit building with three floors of arcades and monumental stairs with vaulted ceilings. Diego Rivera leapt at the chance to put into practice theories, which he and fellow Mexican student David Alfaro Siqueiros had discussed, to have art express the life of the people. He had greatly admired the ability of Italian Renaissance muralists to communicate the important elements of their faith to illiterate parishioners via fresco painting directly on freshly plastered walls of public buildings. In his first project, for the theater of the Preparatory School, Rivera used colored wax to paint an allegorical scene much in the style of Renaissance religious frescoes except that its angels had mestizo features. Already he had abandoned Cubism in the belief that it could not be understood by the masses but soon decided that such European-based allegories were equally irrelevant. In his next project, for the Ministry of Public Education headquarters in downtown Mexico City, he employed the true fresco technique by painting directly on wet plaster (pl. 24). His subjects illustrate indigenous and mestizo culture while retaining the geometrically simplified, expressive contours which he admired in the works of Giotto and other early Renaissance artists.

Rivera's greatest artistic success is the fresco decoration for the National Agricultural School in Chapingo, executed between 1924 and 1927, which presents an integrated vision which relates brilliantly to the architectural shapes on which he painted (fig. 6.8). The organization especially recalls that of the Sistine Chapel, painted by Michelangelo and other Renaissance artists, with its geometric framing devices painted on the cross-vaulted ceiling. The major subjects are primarily allegorical but are conveyed in images recognizable to the populace. The side panels are a generalized history of the revolution: the abuses before, the suffering during, and the populist reforms after. Most importantly the shapes are smoothly stylized to enhance their legibility and symbolic content, as when human figures buried in the earth become seeds from which new life springs. Integration-period Mixtec codices depicted similar images of heart-sacrificed humans from whose chest cavity a world tree springs (see fig. 3.34 for a similar composition of the dead king sinking into the earth with the world tree which he will ascend at his resurrection soaring behind him). In Rivera's compositions here, forms are neither crowded nor bear too much rhetorical content, both of which later become excesses in his work, such as in the frescoes in the National Palace.

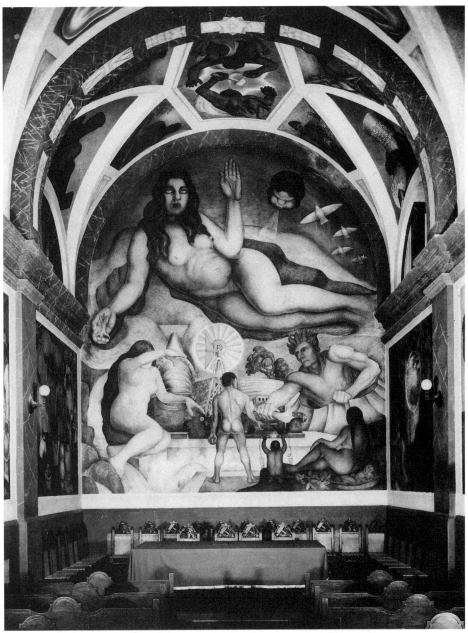

FIG. 6.8. Diego Rivera, painter, *The Fertilized Earth Served by All the Elements* (end), *The Harvest* (vault), frescoes in the former colonial chapel of the National School of Agriculture, Chapingo, State of México, Mexico, 1928. Photo courtesy of Instituto de Investigaciones Estéticas photo archive, Universidad Nacional Autónoma de México. Reproduction authorized by the Instituto Nacional de Bellas Artes y Literatura.

The career of José Clemente Orozco, the second major figure of the Mexican Mural Renaissance, takes an opposite path to that of Diego Rivera: after an initial failed attempt at Italianate allegory, Orozco's work in the Preparatory School is far angrier than Rivera's, expressed in drab colors, bristling diagonals, and a pessimistic vision of human cruelty and brutality. Only the beautiful stairway mural of a Franciscan friar succoring an emaciated native (fig. 6.9) reveals underlying human compassion, interestingly demonstrated here by a European, the traditional target of the muralists' hate for having caused the destruction of the genuinely Mexican Pre-Columbian civilizations. This subject provides early evidence of Orozco's ability to rise above politically correct propaganda, a talent then nurtured doing commissions in the United States during the years 1927–1934 when most mural commissions had dried up in his homeland.

On his return to his home city of Guadalajara, Orozco produced his finest murals, which transcend their Mexican subjects to achieve

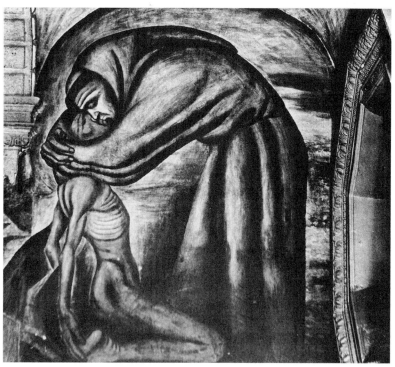

FIG. 6.9. José Clemente Orozco, painter. *Franciscan Friar Succoring Indian*, over-life-size fresco in staircase, west patio, National Preparatory School, Mexico City, 1926. Photo courtesy of Instituto de Investigaciones Estéticas photo archive, Universidad Nacional Autónoma de México. Reproduction authorized by the Instituto Nacional de Bellas Artes y Literatura.

universal communication of man's struggles and achievement. Of the three state-owned buildings in Guadalajara on which he worked concurrently, his frescoes for the Hospicio Cabañas must be considered his and the whole movement's masterpiece. The beautiful clean lines and curves of the interior, designed by Manuel Tolsá a century earlier, provide a triumphal setting to the allegorized story of the conquest of Mexico, in which the Spaniards and their horses are represented as machines, thus suggesting a link to contemporary life. The culmination of the cycle appears in the dome fresco (pl. 25), the composition of which seems inspired by a circular Dutch Mannerist print by Goltzius owned by the Mexican Academy, where Orozco studied; if so, this would be a surprising echo of the colonial tradition of compositional borrowing from prints. The falling figure of Ixion in the print—the man who was burned for attempting to possess the divine—appears transformed into the man on fire, consumed while he strides upward in foreshortened perspective. Recumbent allegorical figures of the elements symbolically underlie man's transformation in his future. The expressive lines, vibrating colors, and broad brush strokes which help communicate the emotional content of the murals relate Orozco's work to the Expressionist movement in twentieth-century art. At the time, though, his recognizable imagery was seen as a reaction against the more abstract currents of Modernism.

The last of the triumvirate of great Mexican muralists, David Alfaro Siqueiros, was the most radical of the group. A more doctrinaire Communist than Rivera, he expended much of his energy in writing polemics and organizing labor unions. His paintings of crowds of workers show the interchangeability of proletarian massed figures. He energetically produced art with inventive use of commercial materials such as pyroxylin paint applied with air guns, a technique appropriate to large scale and rapid execution. His work often transcends the traditional boundaries of media, integrating sculpture and painting to architecture in a more total conception than seen in the work of other muralists (pl. 26). He transformed the architectural space by the addition of panels and even plastered lath and linked the composition over the entire surface. Some early works of his mature style were commissioned in the Southern Cone: In the Escuela México in Chillán, Chile, of 1941, the histories of Mexico and Chile are united by means of similar iconographies of indigenous rulers, conquistadors, and liberators on opposite walls linked by a rocket-like sweep of colors across the ceiling. Siqueiros dramatically emphasized movement by means of extreme foreshortening and lines of force he derived from Italian Futurist style,

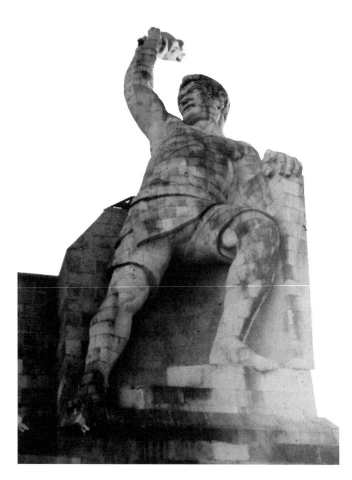

FIG. 6.10. Juan Olaguíbel, sculptor. *Pípila,* colossal pink stone monument, on hilltop overlooking Guanajuato, Mexico, 1939. Photo by John F. Scott.

but he realized it in monumental scale as a more all-encompassing visual and spatial experience.

Via numerous public commissions throughout Mexico, bulky figure sculpture exhorted the proletariat to continue the struggle. An example is the colossal sculpture of Pípila (1939), a worker-hero of the War of Independence, which stands on a hilltop overlooking Guanajuato (fig. 6.10). Grossly heavy and obviously rhetorical, it reflects the Socialist Realist style popular among the leaders of Fascist dictatorships in Europe at the time. Large proportioned, mantle-cloaked indigenous women convey an eternal earth-mother expression in the nearly life-size stone and bronze sculptures and the drawings of Francisco Zúñiga, a transplanted Costa Rican active in Mexico.

The Mural Renaissance in the 1920s and 1930s profoundly affected the history of Western art—the first time that Latin American art can be said to have done so. The headlong rush toward nonrepresentational abstraction was stopped and deflected after World War I by, among other factors, the exciting example that Mexico provided of an art deeply involved in redirecting society by its spirit and its images. Naturally the enthusiasm spread to other nations of the hemisphere, both north and south. The United States not only contains important commissions by the Mexican muralists and had several of its own artists painting walls in Mexico, but its important Regionalist movement and the public works murals of the Depression were directly inspired by the Mexican example. Carlos Mérida, an essential participant in early Mexican commissions, returned to his native Guatemala and referred to indigenous topics in his mural reliefs and prints reflecting the *Popol Vuh*, the legend of the Quiché Maya.

South American countries with strong Pre-Columbian traditions also glorified the still-extant indigenous cultures through art, although

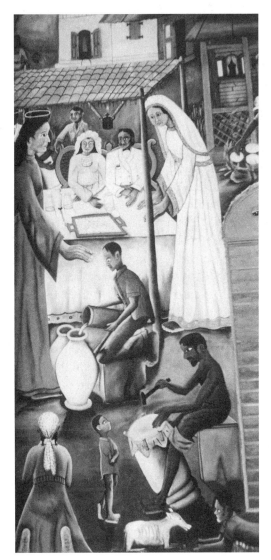

FIG. 6.11. Wilson Bigaud, painter. *Feast at the Wedding of Cana*, detail of wall fresco, Sainte Trinité Episcopal Cathedral, Port-au-Prince, Haiti, 1947. Photo by John F. Scott.

surprisingly they did not use Pre-Columbian motifs: José Sabogal led the indigenist movement in Peru; Oswaldo Guayasamín heads it still in Ecuador; Ignacio Gómez Jaramillo received important government mural commissions in Colombia. The encouragement by expatriate Americans of Haitian painters engendered a lively primitivist school of art by self-taught painters focusing on typical Haitian scenes and subjects. Although most were easel paintings or sculptures to be sold to tourists, some mural paintings were commissioned, notably to Wilson Bigaud for the Episcopal Cathedral in Port-au-Prince (fig. 6.11). Scenes of daily life in Haiti surround a re-creation of the banquet at Cana, during which Jesus performed his first miracle. All participants including Christ are black or mulatto and are surrounded by brilliant flat colors. And in Brazil, Cândido Portinari integrated his murals into the modern architecture there; on the outside wall of the church of São Francisco in Pampulha, he executed paintings in glazed tiles, recalling a Portuguese colonial decorative technique and also providing a durable exterior (pl. 27).

ABSTRACTION: 1922–ABOUT 1970

Meanwhile, non-Indian South America, east of the Andes and in the Southern Cone, had been far more receptive to avant-garde European modernism. Whereas Diego Rivera had quickly abandoned Cubism upon returning to Mexico, Emilio Pettoruti of Argentina remained firmly wedded to that style which he had learned from the Spaniard Juan Gris, an early member of the movement in Paris. When Pettoruti returned to Buenos Aires in 1924, his first exhibition of Cubist paintings received a cold reception. In *Quintet* (fig. 6.12), a work of that era, the forms of five musicians are flattened into boldly colored geometric planes, jostling against each other in jazzy counterpoint. In spite of rejections, Pettoruti persisted long enough to see Argentina become a major center in the international abstract art movement in the 1960s.

Before returning to Montevideo in 1934, Joaquín Torres-García of Uruguay had been firmly entrenched in the modern art scene in Europe, first in Barcelona, then in Paris, where he perfected his Constructivist style—deriving from the collages of Synthetic Cubism—by flattening three-dimensional objects into even-colored geometric shapes separated by thick black lines (fig. 6.13). While not as abstract as the paintings of Theo van Doesburg, his Dutch contemporary and inspiration, Torres-García's work reveals the same underlying unity in the structure of visible forms. Such a philosophy does not encourage regionalism, nationalism, or stylistic uniqueness. Nevertheless, while still in

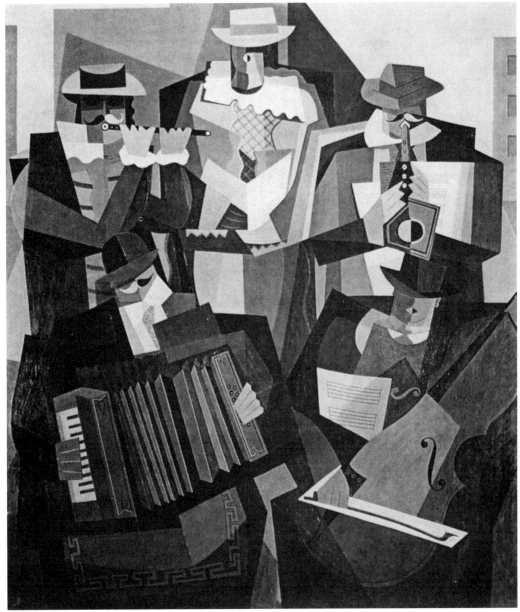

FIG. 6.12. Emilio Pettoruti, painter. *Quintet,* oil on plyboard, 23½" high x 20¼" wide, 1927. Formerly San Francisco Art Museum. Photo used with permission of Sotheby's New York.

Paris, Torres-García visited natural history museums in search of Pre-Columbian motifs from South America to incorporate in his art (Braun 1993: 259–274). In particular, the geometric designs of Tiwanaku, such as the sun image and the shape of the large vessel on the upper right of figure 6.13 (see fig. 4.25), lent themselves to his Constructivist aesthetic and even encouraged him to hammer together totemic divinities from found pieces of lumber (Day and Sturgis 1987: 78).

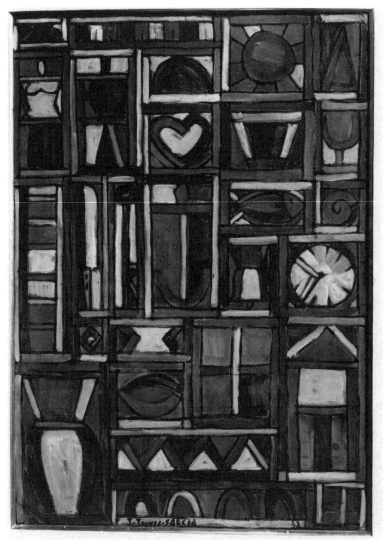

FIG. 6.13. Joaquín Torres-García, painter. *Composition #548*, oil on cardboard, 41½ high x 30½" wide, 1932. Providence: Museum of Art, Rhode Island School of Design, 65.070, Nancy Sayles Day Fund. Photo courtesy of museum.

The Brazilian organizers of Modern Art Week in São Paulo in 1922, although interested in the modern movements in European art such as Cubism and Expressionism, were also very concerned with "the use of Brazilian themes for a national art" (Chase 1970: 184). In fact the leading Cubist painter of the group, Tarsila do Amaral, returned to Brazil from Paris in 1924 to discover her native country, as she put it, and incorporate it into her art. She soon was painting abstracted images of tropical landscapes (pl. 28) and geometrically rounded black and indigenous women. However avant-garde Brazilian art might be, it always reflected an awareness that it was Brazilian and not a homogenized international style.

The same approach is found in Brazilian modern architecture, definitely the strongest and most creative national building style in Latin America. Although the few modern buildings during the 1920s were in the International modern style, which denied regional variations, the visit of Le Corbusier, the French-Swiss architect, to Rio de Janeiro in 1936 served to coalesce a truly national style, founded on functional modernism but expressing emotion through curved forms already visible in Brazilian Rococo churches (see fig. 5.21). Anathema to International-style architects because of its irrationality, the sensuous curve became the hallmark of the distinctive Brazilian adaptation. The thin linearity of the International style was enriched by Le Corbusier via the addition of sun screens on the north façade of the Education Ministry building, which added a plastic depth to its otherwise flat geometry. Oscar Niemeyer became the hero of the movement; his church of São Francisco in Pampulha, already mentioned for its colorful tile decoration by Portinari, has a façade composed of catenary curves, the inverse of hanging chains, formed of reinforced concrete shells (pl. 27). North American architects and local building inspectors had been wary of thin-shelled reinforced concrete vaulting because it defied secure engineering analysis. Latin Americans, less restricted by building codes, loved reinforced concrete because it could be manipulated into any shape. Félix Candela, a Spanish engineer who emigrated to Mexico in 1939 to escape retaliation from the Franco dictatorship in Spain, designed astonishingly thin and beautifully soaring forms out of concrete even without reinforcing steel. The world was amazed by Latin American thin-shell concrete design, so like the Baroque spirit of an earlier age of greatness.

City planning, virtually ignored in Latin America since the sixteenth-century Laws of the Indies, received a new burst of creativity with impressive urban projects. A new capital city named Brasília was constructed for Brazil in the sparsely settled central plateau, fulfilling an old dream from the time of independence to place a capital in the center of the country. Lúcio Costa won the competition for the design in 1956 with a project (fig. 6.14) amazingly incomplete compared to the foreign entries, but with a gestural sweep and bold conception reminiscent of the contemporary Action Painting of the New York School, visible in São Paulo since the inauguration of its important biennial international art exhibition in 1951. The axis of the monumental gov-

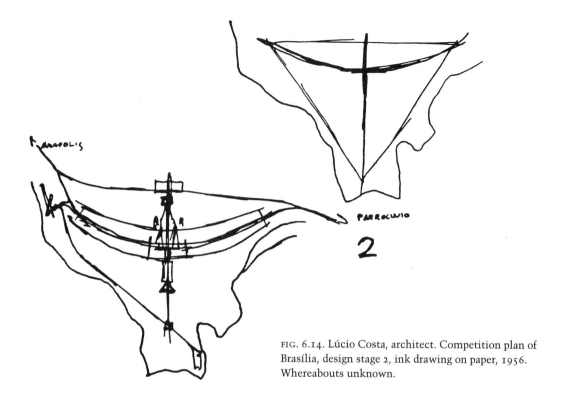

FIG. 6.14. Lúcio Costa, architect. Competition plan of Brasília, design stage 2, ink drawing on paper, 1956. Whereabouts unknown.

ernment buildings crosses the swept-back wings composed of the residential blocks to form the image of a jet plane, so necessary to cover Brazil's vast distances. The importance of the main buildings, all designed by Niemeyer, is stressed through dramatic curves made of reinforced concrete. The two chambers holding the national legislature, the smaller senate domed and the larger chamber of deputies bowl-shaped, contrast with the twin office towers for support staff behind and between them (fig. 6.15).

New campuses for national universities in Mexico and Venezuela are like small-scale cities. The buildings of the National Autonomous University of Mexico, constructed between 1949 and 1954, favor nonutilitarian curves, right and some sharp angles, primary colors, and textures of local materials. Their subjects often refer to the Pre-Columbian past. The focal point of the largest space is the Library building, by architect Juan O'Gorman (see pl. 26 right). The public rooms extend out by means of rough-textured walls covered with feathered serpent designs in relief; the upper stack area, a sealed treasure box enclosed with brilliant mosaics with dense motifs in a geometric, vaguely Pre-Columbian style, is visible from all corners of the campus. The same O'Gorman surprisingly had been the most severe exponent of functionalist Modernism in the 1930s when he returned from Europe, making no reference to the Mexican culture nor accommodating the tropical sun in his designs. But later, shortly after the library was built, his design for his own home was completely irrational: a free-form structure which did not follow efficient construction techniques, thereby rejecting Le Corbusier's dictum that architecture should be "a machine for living." O'Gorman can thus stand for Latin America's architectural conversion from International abstraction to regional Expressionism as its architects attempted to translate international movements into their own vocabulary.

A Cuban artist, Amelia Peláez, after studying in Cuba with Leopoldo Romañach, went to Paris and adopted the later Cubist style, more ornamental by this time in the work of Braque, Rouault, and Matisse. When she returned to Cuba in 1934, a decade after Tarsila returned to Brazil, she transformed the bourgeois world of sunlit patios, wrought-iron screens, and fruit-laden dining tables into wonderful canvases of bright but carefully balanced colors separated by strong black lines, almost like stained glass (fig. 6.16). As Carol Damian has written (1991:

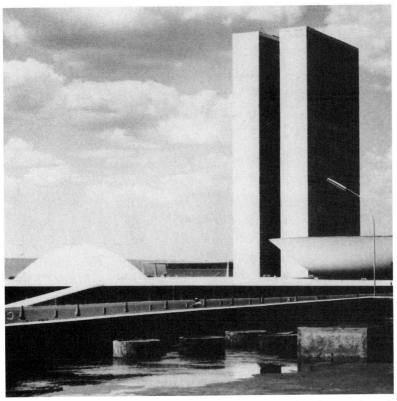

FIG. 6.15. Oscar Niemeyer, architect. The National Congress, Brasília, Brazil, steel, reinforced concrete, glass, marble, 1958. Photo by Roy C. Craven, Jr., courtesy of Center for Latin American Studies, University of Florida.

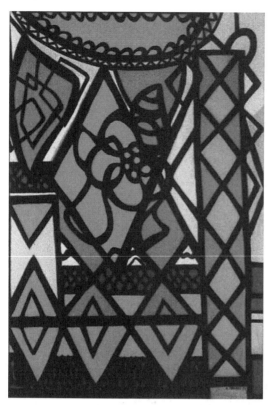

FIG. 6.16. Amelia Peláez, painter. *Still Life*, oil on canvas, 24" wide x 35" high, 1955. Daytona Beach, Fla.: Cuban Foundation Collection of the Museum of Arts and Sciences. Photo courtesy of museum.

29), "Peláez introduced a modern European stylistic vocabulary to the island of Cuba and encouraged an entire generation of artists to aspire to a new level of creativity and independence. Her art was very much of the international mainstream, but it was especially a celebration of Cuba."

SURREALISM: 1938–1970S

The European modern style with the most specific affinity to Hispanic America is Surrealism. Its name signifies "beyond or above the real," and searches beneath what is visible on the surface to explore the subconscious, personal or collective. The emphasis this style places on the irrational, the emotional, the personal, seems to be very congenial to the Latin temperament. The visits of the French poet-philosopher André Breton, the founder of Surrealism, to Mexico in 1938 and 1940 proved to be the catalyst for the flowering of this style in America. He considered Frida Kahlo, then the wife of the more famous Diego Rivera, to be an instinctive Surrealist because she painted intense portrayals of herself in various transformations, as if her imagination were superimposed on visual reality. Her double self-portrait, *The Two Fridas* (fig. 6.17), reveals her dual inheritance—the proper nineteenth-century Western lady on the viewer's left, the swarthy indigenous woman from

Tehuantepec on the right, linked by the same blood system, which she has cut to suggest her own infirmity and mortality. More recently she has become "St. Frida, the holy patroness of ethnofeminists," according to the witty Mexican performance artist Guillermo Gómez Peña (1993 brochure). She has recently received critical adulation because more personalized and individualized art has recently supplanted the universal and abstract concerns of earlier Modernism. Lucy Lippard, a feminist art critic, notes that, "It's very courageous work. This sort of pain and vulnerability that a lot of women have not had the guts to express, she had the guts to do so" (Tully 1994: 127). Kahlo's work often

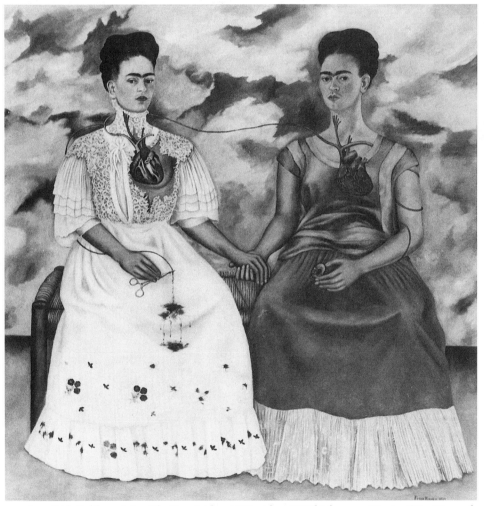

FIG. 6.17. Frida Kahlo, painter. *The Two Fridas*, 68⅜" wide x 68⅛" high, 1939. Mexico City: Museo de Arte Moderno. Photo: Instituto de Investigaciones Estéticas photo archive, Universidad Nacional Autónoma de México. Reproduction authorized by the Instituto Nacional de Bellas Artes y Literatura.

includes references to Mexican folk art and the Pre-Columbian village arts of West Mexico. In general, Surrealist artists examined early art and folk art to reveal the instinctive spirit of the people.

Fascination with personal transformation of received culture, such as the great paintings of Europe, is characteristic of Alberto Gironella and José Luis Cuevas in Mexico and of Fernando Botero from Colombia. Cuevas—one of Latin America's outstanding draftsmen—often includes his self-portrait in scenes, personalizing his art almost as much as Frida Kahlo did. He depicts characters visually quoted from Velázquez, Goya, and Picasso—the great artists of the Spanish motherland. Botero also transforms icons of European painting by inflating them to super-Rubensian proportions, filling the canvas and their world with their presence. In the mid-1990s his heroic sculptures of childhood images cast in bronze have been installed along some of the great boulevards of the world, where they hold their own magnificently against surrounding skyscrapers. He denies that he is mocking the conventionalized world he depicts, as Pop Art also was doing in the U.S. in the 1960s. This artistic interest in quoting art history first appeared before 1960 in Latin America, and so prefigures an important aspect of Post-Modern art popular elsewhere in the West after 1970. As with the muralists, here Latin American art seems precocious in relationship to general Western art trends, although it has not been shown to be the model for developments in the northern hemisphere.

The late Rufino Tamayo, an indigenous Zapotec painter, although sometimes working as a muralist, made his most potent statements since 1940 by combining ancestral references to Mexican identity with surrealistic abstraction and expressionistic colors. His work thus combines all three major European art movements into his singular vision. His preference for easel painting is characteristic of the more private vision which Surrealist works communicate.

Other Latin Americans have made important contributions after coming in contact with Breton and his Surrealist circle: Roberto Matta left Chile permanently in 1934 for Paris, where he abandoned his training in architecture for Surrealist painting under the inspiration of Breton and others; his renderings of abstracted biomorphic forms have made him the best known Latin American Surrealist. Wifredo Lam joined the Breton group in Marseilles in 1940 just before they fled the Vichy puppet government for exile in Martinique, after which Lam continued on to his native Cuba. Tropical fantasies abound in Lam's paintings (fig. 6.18), in which some forms reflect African sculpture, which the Surrealists saw as part of humankind's common heritage.

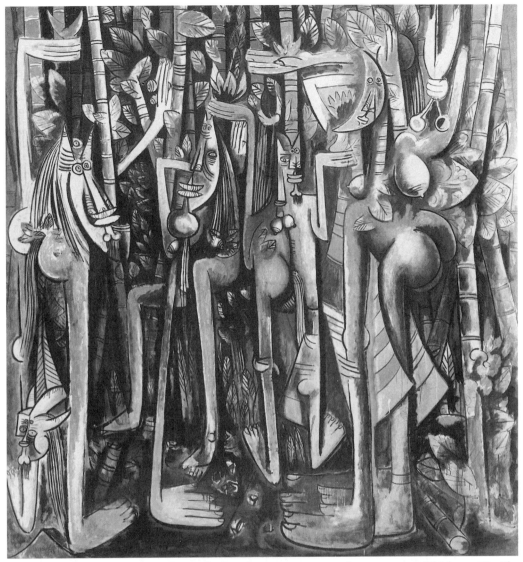

FIG. 6.18. Wifredo Lam, painter. *The Jungle,* gouache on paper mounted on canvas, 94¼" high x 90½" wide, 1943. New York: Museum of Modern Art, Inter-American Fund. Photo © The Museum of Modern Art, New York.

Lam had a more direct African heritage, though, since his mother was Afro-Cuban and his godmother a priestess in the *santería* cult, which combines Catholic images with Yoruba African religion. The African impact in Latin America, well documented in the musical traditions of the Atlantic seaboard countries, has already been discussed for the arts at the end of chapter 5. One must remember, however, that Lam's first Paris contact had been Picasso, who at the beginning of the century had used African sculpture as an important source of Cubism. To the Surrealists, all such native artistic expression taps the common subconscious forms of human experience.

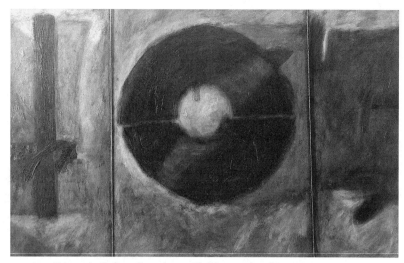

FIG. 6.19. Fernando de Szyszlo, painter. *The Execution of Tupac Amaru, XII*, encaustic on wood, triptych, 59" high x 94¼" wide open, 1965. Providence: Museum of Art, Rhode Island School of Design, 76.040, Nancy Sayles Day collection of Modern Latin American art. Photo courtesy of museum.

The Japanese-Peruvian artist Tilsa Tsuchiya examined numerous myths, especially of birdwomen, in her paintings; significantly, one is titled *The Myth of the Dreams* (1976), spelling out a continuing Surrealist concern. Another of her paintings (1974) transforms the vertical, biomorphically cut sun stone at Machu Picchu, the fabulous lost city of the Incas, into a figure rising on an altar.

The modern Abstract Expressionist movement centered in New York has grown out of Surrealism and has many adherents, some originally from and some still working in Latin America. There and in Europe it is called Informalism, contrasting its intuitive application of paint to the more geometric and carefully constructed works of the "Formalists" such as Torres-García. Many of these Latin American Informalist artists have references to the primordial natural forces of their homelands. Fernando de Szyszlo of Peru seems to capture turbulent forces of creation; his titles refer to Inca proper names, such as the martyred revolutionary Tupac Amaru, but his painted massive shapes communicate the turbulent nature and events not literally but emotionally (fig. 6.19). In the case of the illustrated triptych, the darkly brooding sphere painted on the closed panels becomes fractured with a red line in the smoldering fire of the fully opened, three-part interior. Perhaps Alejandro Obregón of Colombia best exemplifies the abstract Surrealist trend in Latin America by his lushly colored, painterly canvases, at times abstract, then, through suggestions of the titles or naturalistic fragments, icons of nature: the condor, the cock, the tropical flora (fig. 6.20). They erupt like the fantastic images in the novels of his

LATIN AMERICAN ART

Colombian contemporary, Gabriel García Márquez, also set in the steamy Caribbean jungle; naturalistic images come in and out of focus in favor of totally imaginary ones. The best of Latin American art often refers to inner emotional reality: religious visions in colonial times, then the spiritual soul of a nation in the period after independence.

RECENT ART: AFTER 1970

Some artists who began painting in an Informalist style have recently returned to realistic representation. Armando Morales of Nicaragua, honored in the early 1960s for his bold painterly geometric abstractions, has more recently created classic images in the Surrealist style

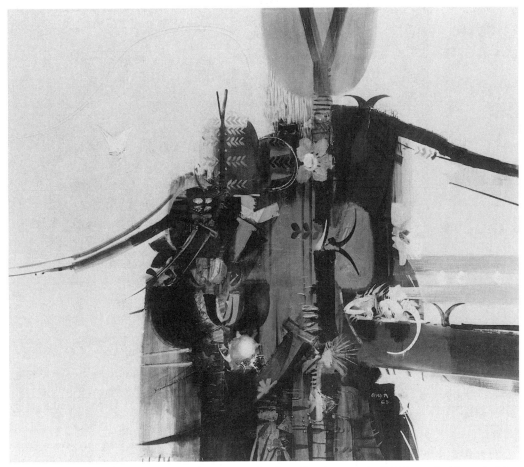

FIG. 6.20. Alejandro Obregón, painter. *The Baroque Garden*, oil on canvas, 67⅝" high x 79" wide, 1965. New York: The Solomon R. Guggenheim Museum, FN 67.1843, purchased with funds contributed by Fundación Neumann, Caracas, Venezuela, 1967. Photo by David Heald, © The Solomon R. Guggenheim Foundation, New York.

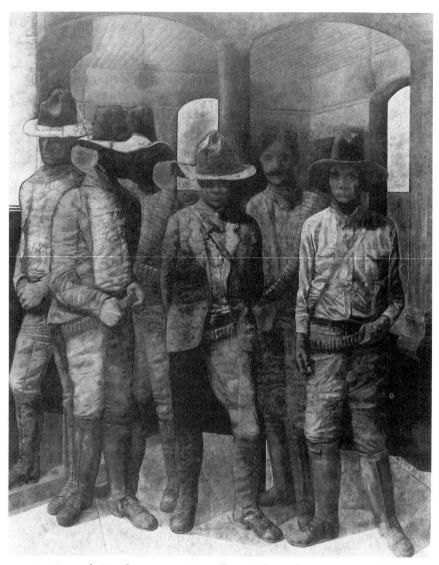

FIG. 6.21. Armando Morales, painter. *Farewell to Sandino,* oil on canvas, 79⅛" high x 65" wide, 1985. Private collection. Photo courtesy of Galérie Claude Bernard, Paris.

of De Chirico. After the political revolution in Morales's homeland brought the Sandinistas to power in 1979, he commemorated the 1930s precursors of the revolution in a 1985 painting, *Farewell to Sandino* (fig. 6.21), which composes them like a sacred conversation of saints in a Renaissance altarpiece, deemphasizing their faces by shadows and blurring. They fade into history like old photographs, becoming icons to modern martyrs. He also paints luxuriant tropical forests reminiscent of paintings by the slightly younger Uruguayan, José Gamarra, who populates his forests with figures which seem to go back to the time of the Conquest and yet bring us across the five centuries to include, in his *Links* of 1983, what may be Sandino appearing like a vision to the bow-wielding Indian. Such images have been linked to the "magic realism" of modern Latin American literature. In both Gamarra's and Morales's paintings, the forest dominates and presses in upon the viewer. Neither artist has lived in Latin America for decades, yet their subject matter reflects archetypical images of the region: jungles, exotic animals, and bandolier-draped revolutionaries.

Economic necessity as well as the search for artistic stimulus has led many Latin American artists into expatriation in Paris, New York, or elsewhere. While these reasons have dwindled, politics can still make self-exile prudent, as attested by the dispersal of the vibrant Argentine School following the establishment of the military dictatorship in Buenos Aires in 1966. Recently, with the return of pluralist democracy there and in Brazil, the creative environment and even the economic opportunities have significantly increased. Buenos Aires has more than sixty galleries dedicated to contemporary art and is home to Latin America's major auction house (Cembalest 1990: 146).

In its images and its materials, recent Latin American art has closely reflected popular culture. The artists often incorporate the junk of industrial society, debris cast off when worn out, much as Latin American people see themselves cast off by the Western industrialized world after being exploited either for their cheap labor or for the raw materials they extract. European art had already established the validity of mixed media in Modernism, beginning with collages created by the Cubists out of old newspapers. Rather than merely providing neutral abstract texture, the subjects in the newspapers had personal significance to Cubist artists. Similarly in Latin America, the material used in collages can express the garbage-filled environment in which the poor eke out a living. By the 1970s the Argentinian painter Antonio Berni was focusing on the lives of two fictional characters, Juanito Laguna (fig. 6.22) and Ramona Montiel, the first a street urchin and the second a prostitute. Although they "are embodiments of urban poverty, the worlds they inhabit are described with humour and compassion rather than social proselytizing. Berni's large canvases combine a simple figurative style with more knowingly modernist collage technique" (Baddeley and Fraser 1989: 134). Large sculptures by the young working-class artist Francisca Núñez of Chile are constructed from materials she found in the streets around her home (Shaw 1990: 140). The dizzying devaluation of South American currencies has led the Brazilian assemblage artist Jac[queline] Leirner to string her worthless cruzeiro notes into long strands (1986, 1991) which then are rearranged into beautiful

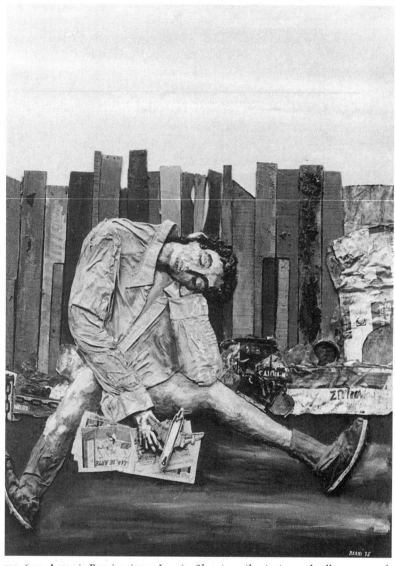

FIG. 6.22. Antonio Berni, painter. *Juanito Sleeping*, oil painting and collage on wood, 61½" high x 43⅞" wide, 1978. Private collection. Photo courtesy of Ruth Benzacar Gallery, Buenos Aires.

curves by curators in whatever exhibition space they are placed. The Latin American adaptability in accommodating such financial instability is thus transferred to art. Money and art, closely connected in modern capitalism, becomes fused and their relationship even reversed: money has become the beginning raw material of art rather than the final reward for the artist's work.

Folk arts which have survived since the Conquest are often chosen as their media by trained artists. In the Andes, textiles had a long and noble history. Oswaldo Viteri of Ecuador gathers brightly colored little fabric dolls made by highland indigenous villagers and incorporates them into his dense collages by gluing them to monumental square wooden boards. After the military crackdown under Gen. Pinochet following the toppling of the Communist Allende government in Chile (1970–1973), women commemorated the lives of beaten, missing, or incarcerated family members in *arpilleras*, compositions of fabric remnants stitched on burlap. The scene shown in plate 29, while colorfully taking place in front of the beautiful Andean mountains, alludes to the poverty of the people who must steal their electricity from overhead wires to participate fully in modern society. These works strongly echo the traditional crafts created by indigenous women, such as Andean textiles made for sale to tourists or even Panamanian Cuna Indian *molas*, dress panels made by elaborate negative cutouts from trade cloth but which express images of their own world.

Another folk art, the "ex-voto," a small painting created by or for a person who believed that a saint has answered prayers, can be documented as early as the eighteenth century and continued as a folk tradition into modern times. Typically formed out of tin or other scrap material, this technique was echoed in Frida Kahlo's primitivist style of painting. These works were considered the most authentic expression of Latin American art by artists like Kahlo and critics following Surrealist philosophy, an attitude buttressed by political revolutionaries' rejection of European high culture. Many more recent painters and assemblage-sculptors reflect the personal subject and naive style of ex-votos. Their strong expressions of personal belief transcend the stylish abstractions seen as typical of Western gallery-generated high art.

In current terminology, this folk art would, among other styles, be called "outsider art" in the U.S. because it was produced by untrained folk artists. Latin America, however, is even further outside the loop from the accepted artistic centers. Bárbaro Rivas of Venezuela appropriates cheap reproductions of religious images such as the Mexican Virgin of Guadalupe or the Sacred Heart of Jesus. This latter was incorporated by Juan Camilo Uribe of Colombia with another print of a turn-of-the century Venezuelan doctor to create his own valentine for Venezuela. Note that these artists are not the same nationality as the images, making us aware that such cults and symbols do not observe political borders but imply a unity in Latin American culture.

Latin American artists are searching for their own identity, sometimes in their past, sometimes in the dynamism of popular culture, sometimes within their own souls, with its personal imagination and contradictions. Much as their politics rejects the harmonious balances of two-party democracy (with its loyal opposition) and prefers the personality of a strong leader or the intense emotion in religion, nationalism, or revolution, so their art has often adapted imposed styles from Europe and the United States to reflect images authenticated by the uneducated masses who bring their idols—from Pre-Columbian and African survivals and misunderstood Roman Catholicism, embodied in local heroes and charismatic leaders—with them as they move from the rural countryside to the squatter settlements of the great urban centers of the hemisphere.

BIBLIOGRAPHY

Adams, Richard E. W. 1991. *Prehistoric Mesoamerica,* rev. ed. Norman: University of Oklahoma Press.

Ades, Dawn, with contributions by Guy Brett, Stanton Loomis Catlin, and Rosemary O'Neill. 1989. *Art in Latin America: The Modern Era, 1820–1980.* New Haven: Yale University Press.

Alva, Walter, and Christopher Donnan. 1993. *Royal Tombs of Sipán.* Los Angeles: Fowler Museum of Cultural History, University of California.

Angulo Iñiguez, Diego. 1945–56. *Historia del arte hispanoamericano* (History of Latin American art), 3 vols. Barcelona, Spain: Ediciones Calpe.

Baddeley, Oriana, and Valerie Fraser. 1989. *Drawing the Line: Art and Cultural Identity in Contemporary Latin America.* London and New York: Verso.

Bayón, Damián. 1981. *Artistas contemporáneos de América Latina* (Contemporary artists in Latin America). Barcelona, Spain: Serbal/UNESCO.

Bayón, Damián, and Murillo Marx, with contributions by Myriam Ribeiro de Oliveira, Aurea Pereira da Silva, and Hugo Segawa. 1989. *History of South American Colonial Art and Architecture: Spanish South America and Brazil.* New York: Rizzoli.

Benson, Elizabeth P. 1972. *The Mochica: A Culture of Peru.* New York: Praeger.

Braun, Barbara. 1993. *Pre-Columbian Art and the Post-Columbian World: Ancient American Sources of Modern Art.* New York: Harry Abrams.

Burger, Richard L. 1985. "Concluding Remarks: Early Peruvian Civilization and Its Relation to the Chavín Horizon," in *Early Ceremonial Architecture in the Andes,* ed. C. B. Donnan, pp. 269–89. Washington, D.C.: Dumbarton Oaks.

Burke, Marcus, and Linda Bantel. 1979. *Spain and New Spain.* Corpus Christi: Art Museum of South Texas.

Camelo Arredondo, Rosa, J. Gurría Lacroix, and Constantino Reyes Valerio. 1964. *Juan Gersón: Tlacuilo de Tecamachalco* (Juan Gersón, native painter of Tecamachalco). México: Instituto Nacional de Antropología e Historia, Departmento de Monumentos Coloniales 16.

Carcedo Muro, Paloma, and Izumi Shimada. 1985. "Behind the Golden Mask: Sicán Gold Artifacts from Batán Grande, Peru," in *The Art of Precolumbian Gold,* ed. J. Jones, pp. 60–75. New York: Metropolitan Museum of Art.

Castedo, Leopoldo. 1969. *A History of Latin American Art and Architecture.* New York: Praeger.

———. 1988. *Historia del arte iberoamericano,* vol. 1: *Precolombino. El arte colonial;* VOL. 2: *Siglo XIX. Siglo XX* (History of Latin American art, vol. 1: Pre-Columbian. Colonial art; vol. 2: 19th and 20th centuries). Madrid: Alianza Editorial.

Catlin, Stanton Loomis, and Terence Grieder. 1966. *Art of Latin America Since Independence.* New Haven: Yale University Art Gallery and the University of Texas Art Museum.

Cembalest, Robin. 1990. "Triumph Amid Tumult," *ArtNews,* 89, no. 8 (October): 144–49.

Chase, Gilbert. 1970. *Contemporary Art in Latin America.* New York: The Free Press.

Ciudad Ruiz, Andrés. 1989. *Las culturas del antiguo México* (The cultures of ancient Mexico). Madrid: Alhambra.

Coe, Michael D., and Richard A. Diehl. 1980. *In the Land of the Olmec,* vol. 1: *The Archaeology of San Lorenzo Tenochtitlán.* Austin: University of Texas Press.

Coggins, Clemency Chase. 1984. "The Cenote of Sacrifice: Catalogue," in *Cenote of Sacrifice: Maya Treasures from the Sacred Well at Chichén Itzá,* pp. 23–166. Austin: University of Texas Press.

Cossío del Pomar, Felipe. 1928. *Pintura colonial (escuela cuzqueña)* (Colonial painting [Cuzco School]). Cuzco, Peru: H. G. Rozas.

Cowgill, George L. 1983. "Rulership and the Ciudadela: Political Inferences from Teotihuacán Architecture," in *Civilization in the Ancient Americas: Essays in Honor of Gordon R. Willey,* ed. R. M. Leventhal and A. L. Kolata, pp. 313–43. Albuquerque: University of New Mexico Press.

Damian, Carol. 1991. "Amelia Peláez," *Latin American Art,* 3, no. 2 (spring): 27–29.

Day, Holliday T., and Hollister Sturges. 1987. *Art of the Fantastic: Latin America, 1920–1987.* Indianapolis: Indianapolis Museum of Art.

Day, Kent C. 1982. "Ciudadelas: Their Form and Function," in *Chan Chan: Andean Desert City,* ed. M. E. Mosely and K. C. Day, pp. 55–66. Albuquerque: School of American Research, University of New Mexico Press.

Diehl, Richard A. 1983. *Tula: The Toltec Capital of Ancient Mexico.* London: Thames and Hudson.

Donnan, Christopher B., and Carol J. Mackey. 1978. *Ancient Burial Patterns of the Moche Valley, Peru.* Austin: University of Texas Press.

Fernández, Justino. 1969. *A Guide to Mexican Art,* trans. Joshua C. Taylor with additions by the author. Chicago: University of Chicago Press.

Fiedel, Stuart J. 1987. *Prehistory of the Americas.* Cambridge, England: Cambridge University Press.

Flannery, Kent V. 1976. "Contextual Analysis of Ritual Paraphernalia from Formative Oaxaca," in *The Early Mesoamerican Village,* ed. K. V. Flannery, pp. 333–45. New York: Academic Press.

Gómez-Peña, Guillermo. 1993. "The New World Border—prophesies for the end of the century." Pamphlet for performance at the Harn Museum of Art, Gainesville, Florida.

González Lauck, Rebecca. 1996. "La Venta: An Olmec Capital," in *Olmec Art of Ancient Mexico*, ed. E. Benson and B. de la Fuente, pp. 73–81. Washington, D.C.: National Gallery of Art.

Greene Robertson, Merle. 1983. *The Sculpture of Palenque*, vol. 1: *The Temple of the Inscriptions*. Princeton, N.J.: Princeton University Press.

Grizzard, Mary. 1986. *Spanish Colonial Art and Architecture of Mexico and the U.S. Southwest*. Lanham, Md.: University Press of America.

Herkenhoff, Paulo, and Geri Smith. 1991. "Latin American Art: Global Outreach," *ArtNews* 90, no. 8 (October): 88–93.

Herrera, Leonor, Marianne Cardale de Schrimpff, and Warwick Bray. 1984. "El hombre y su medio ambiente en Calima (altos río Calima y río Grande, Cordillera Occidental)" (Man and his environment in Calima [upper Calima and Grande Rivers, Western mountain chain]), *Revista colombiana de antropología*, 24 (años 1982–83): 381–424. Bogotá, Colombia: Instituto Colombiano de Cultura.

Heyden, Doris. 1975. "An Interpretation of the Cave Underneath the Pyramid of the Sun in Teotihuacán, Mexico," *American Antiquity*, 40, no. 2: 131–47.

Heyden, Doris, and Paul Gendrop. 1988. *Pre-Columbian Architecture of Mesoamerica*. New York: Rizzoli.

Horcasitas, Fernando. 1978. "Mexican Folk Art," *National Geographic Magazine*, 153, no. 5 (May): 648–69.

Jennings, Jesse D., ed., 1983. *Ancient South Americans*. San Francisco: W. H. Freeman.

Joralemon, Peter David. 1996. "In Search of the Olmec Cosmos: Reconstructing the World View of Mexico's First Civilization," in *Olmec Art of Ancient Mexico*, ed. E. Benson and B. de la Fuente, pp. 51–59. Washington, D.C.: National Gallery of Art.

Kelemen, Pál. 1967. *Baroque and Rococo in Latin America*, 2 vols., 2nd ed. New York: Dover Publications.

Kolata, Alan. 1993. *The Tiwanaku: Portrait of an Andean Civilization*. Cambridge, Mass.: Blackwell.

Kowalski, Jeff Karl. 1987. *House of the Governor: A Maya Palace at Uxmal, Yucatan, Mexico*. Norman: University of Oklahoma Press.

Kubler, George. 1973. "Iconographic Aspects of Architectural Profiles at Teotihuacán and in Mesoamerica," in *Iconography of Middle American Sculpture*, pp. 24–39. New York: Metropolitan Museum of Art.

Kubler, George, and Martín Soria. 1959. *Art and Architecture in Spain and Portugal and Their American Dominions, 1500–1800*. Baltimore: Penguin Books.

Lange, Frederick W., Ronald L. Bishop, and Lambertus van Zelst. 1981. "Technical Appendix: Perspectives on Costa Rican Jade: Compositional Analyses and Cultural Implications," in *Between Continents, Between Seas: Precolumbian Art of Costa Rica*, pp. 167–75. New York: Harry Abrams.

Lathrap, Donald W. 1971. "The Tropical Forest and the Cultural Context of Chavín," in *Dumbarton Oaks Conference on Chavín*, ed. Elizabeth P. Benson, pp. 73–100. Washington, D.C.: Dumbarton Oaks.

——. 1975. *Ancient Ecuador: Culture, Clay and Creativity, 3000–300 B.C.* Chicago: Field Museum of Natural History.

Lathrap, Donald W., Jorge G. Marcos, and James A. Zeidler. 1977. "Real Alto: An Ancient Ceremonial Center," *Archaeology*, 30, no. 1: 2–13.

Lowie, Robert H. 1937. *The History of Ethnological Theory.* New York: Farrar and Rinehart.

Lucie-Smith, Edward. 1993. *Latin American Art of the 20th Century.* London and New York: Thames and Hudson.

Lumbreras, Luis G. 1974. *The Peoples and Cultures of Ancient Peru,* tr. Betty J. Meggers. Washington, D.C.: Smithsonian Institution Press.

Marcus, Joyce. 1976. *Emblem and State in the Classic Maya Lowlands.* Washington, D.C.: Dumbarton Oaks.

Marcus, Joyce, and Kent V. Flannery. 1996. *Zapotec Civilization.* New York: Thames and Hudson.

Maza, Francisco de la. 1964. *El pintor Cristóbal de Villalpando* (The painter Christopher Villalpando). Mexico City: Instituto Nacional de Antropología e Historia, Memorias IX.

McAndrew, John. 1965. *The Open-Air Churches of Sixteenth-Century Mexico.* Cambridge: Harvard University Press.

Means, Philip Ainsworth. 1931. *Ancient Civilizations of the Andes.* New York: Charles Scribner's Sons.

Meggers, Betty J. 1966. *Ecuador.* New York: Praeger.

Meighan, Clement W. 1978. "Analysis of Rock Art in Baja California," in *Seven Rock Art Sites in Baja California*, pp. 1–18. Socorro, N.M.: Ballena Press.

Meltzer, David. 1993. *Search for the First Americans.* Washington, D.C.: Smithsonian Books.

Mesa, José de, and Teresa Gisbert. 1966. "La capilla abierta de Copacabana" (The open chapel at Copacabana), in *Contribuciones al estudio de la arquitectura andina*, pp. 15–23. La Paz: Academia Nacional de Ciencias de Bolivia.

Messer, Thomas M., and Cornell Capa. 1966. *The Emergent Decade: Latin American Painters and Painting in the 1960s.* Ithaca, N.Y.: Cornell University Press.

Miller, Mary Ellen. 1985. "A Re-Examination of the Mesoamerican Chacmool," *Art Bulletin* 47, no. 1 (March): 7–17.

——. 1996. *The Art of Mesoamerica from Olmec to Aztec,* rev. ed. London and New York: Thames and Hudson.

Millon, Clara. 1988. "A Reexamination of the Teotihuacán Tassel Headdress Insignia," in *Feathered Serpents and Flowering Trees: Reconstructing the Murals of Teotihuacán*, ed. Kathleen Berrin, pp. 114–34. San Francisco: Fine Arts Museums.

Moseley, Michael Edward. 1975. *The Maritime Foundations of Andean Civilization.* Menlo Park, Calif.: Cummings.

———. 1992. *The Inca and Their Ancestors: The Archaeology of Peru.* New York: Thames and Hudson.

Pasztory, Esther. 1976. *The Murals of Tepantitla, Teotihuacán.* New York: Garland Press.

Peterson, Jeanette Favrot. 1993. *The Paradise Garden Murals of Malinalco: Utopia and Empire in Sixteenth-Century Mexico.* Austin: University of Texas Press.

Pierce, Donna L. 1981. "Identification of the Warriors in the Frescoes of Ixmiquilpan," *Review of the Research Center for the Arts,* 4, no. 4: 1–8.

Ramírez, Mari Carmen. 1992. "Beyond 'the Fantastic': Framing Identity in U. S. Exhibitions of Latin American Art," *Art Journal,* 51, no. 4 (winter): 60–68.

Ramsey, L. G. G. 1954. "Dress and Customs of Colonial Latin America in a Series of Unique Paintings," *Connoisseur,* 133, no. 537 (April): 162–67.

Rasmussen, Waldo, ed. 1993. *Latin American Artists of the Twentieth Century.* New York: Museum of Modern Art.

Reents-Budet, Dorie. 1994. *Painting the Maya Universe: Royal Ceramics of the Classic Period.* Durham, N.C.: Duke University Press.

Reichel-Dolmatoff, Gerardo. 1985. *Monsú: un sitio arqueólogico* (Monzu, an Archaeological Site). Bogotá, Colombia: Biblioteca Banco Popular.

Ricard, Robert. 1966. *The Spiritual Conquest of Mexico: Essay on the Apostolate and the Evangelizing Methods of the Mendicant Orders in New Spain, 1523–1572,* trans. of 1933 French edition by Leslie Byrd Simpson. Berkeley: University of California Press.

Rick, John W. 1988. "The Character and Context of Highland Preceramic Society," in *Peruvian Prehistory,* ed. Richard W. Keatinge, pp. 3–40. Cambridge, England: Cambridge University Press.

Robertson, Donald. 1959. *Mexican Manuscript Painting of the Early Colonial Period: The Metropolitan Schools.* New Haven: Yale University Press.

Roosevelt, Anna. 1989. "Lost Civilization of the Lower Amazon," *Natural History Magazine* (February): 74–83.

Rowe, John H. 1967. "Form and Meaning in Chavín Art," in *Peruvian Archaeology: Selected Readings,* pp. 72–103. Palo Alto, Calif.: Peek Publications.

Sawyer, Alan R. 1963. *Tiahuanaco Tapestry Designs.* New York: Museum of Primitive Art Studies, no. 3.

Schele, Linda, and David Freidel. 1990. *A Forest of Kings: The Untold Story of the Ancient Maya.* New York: William Morrow.

Scott, John F. 1968. "La evolución de la teoría de la historia del arte por escritores del siglo XX sobre el arte mexicano del siglo XIX" (Development in the theory of art history by 20th-century writers on 19th-century Mexican art), *Anales del Instituto de Investigaciones Estéticas,* 37: 71–104.

———.1978. *The Danzantes of Monte Albán,* 2 vols. Washington, D.C.: Dumbarton Oaks Studies in Pre-Columbian Art and Archaeology, no. 19.

———. 1980. "Post-Olmec Art in Veracruz," in *La Antropología americanista en la actualidad: Homenaje a Raphael Girard,* vol. 1, pp. 235–51. Mexico City: Editores Mexicanos Unidos.

———. 1984. "El maestro cuzqueño de San Jerónimo" (The Cuzco Master of St. Jerome), *Historia y cultura,* 17: 17–30.

———. 1987. "The Role of Mesoamerican Funerary Figurines," in *Arte Funerario: Coloquio International de Historia del Arte,* vol. 2, pp. 7–16. Mexico City: Universidad Nacional Autónoma de México.

———. 1988. "Potbellies and Fat Gods," *Journal of New World Archaeology,* 7, nos. 2,3: 25–36.

———. 1995. "El dragón mítico en el arte prehispánico andino," in *Cultura y medio ambiente en el área andina septentrional,* ed. Mercedes Guinea, Jean-François Bouchard, and Jorge Marcos, pp. 319–342. Quito: Abya-Yala.

Sebastián López, Santiago, José de Mesa Figueroa, and Teresa Gisbert de Mesa. 1989. *Arte iberoamericano desde la colonización a la independencia* (Latin American art from colonization to independence), 3d ed. Summa Artis, vols. 28, 29. Madrid: Espasa-Calpe.

Shaw, Edward. 1990. "The End of Solitude: Young Artists on the Rise," *ArtNews,* 89, no. 8 (October): 138–43.

Silverman, Helaine. 1988. "Cahuachi: Non-Urban Cultural Complexity on the South Coast of Peru," *Journal of Field Archaeology,* 15, no. 4 (winter): 403–30.

Stirling, Matthew W. 1950. "Exploring Ancient Panama by Helicopter," *National Geographic Magazine,* 97, no. 2 (February): 227–46.

Stuiver, Minze, and Renee Kra, eds. 1986. "Calibration Issue, Proceedings of the 12th International Radiocarbon Conference, 1985, Trondheim, Norway," *Radiocarbon,* 28, special ed. 2B: 805–1030.

Thompson, Robert Farris. 1983. *Flash of the Spirit: African and Afro-American Art and Philosophy.* New York: Random House.

Toussaint, Manuel. 1967. *Colonial Art in Mexico,* trans. and ed. Elizabeth Wilder Weismann. Austin: University of Texas Press.

Townsend, Richard Fraser. 1979. *State and Cosmos in the Art of Tenochtitlán.* Washington, D.C.: Dumbarton Oaks, Studies in Pre-Columbian Art and Archaeology, no. 20.

Tully, Judd. 1994. "The Kahlo Cult," *ArtNews,* 93, no. 4 (April): 126–33.

Weismann, Elizabeth Wilder; photographs by Judith Hancock Sandoval. 1985. *Art and Time in Mexico from the Conquest to the Revolution.* New York: Harper and Row.

Wethey, Harold. 1949. *Colonial Architecture and Sculpture in Peru.* Cambridge: Harvard University Press.

Whittington, E. Michael. 1990. "Moche Ceramic Portraiture: Theme and Variation in Ancient Peruvian Art." M.A. thesis, Department of Art, University of Florida.

INDEX